H. L. MENCKEN

PREJUDICES

A SELECTION

The Maryland Paperback Bookshelf

Publisher's Note

Works published as part of the Maryland Paperback Bookshelf are, we like to think, books that are classics of a kind. While some social attitudes have changed and knowledge of our surroundings has increased, we believe that the value of these books as literature, as history, and as timeless perspectives on our region remains undiminished.

H. L. MENCKEN

PREJUDICES

A SELECTION

MADE BY

JAMES T. FARRELL

AND WITH AN INTRODUCTION BY HIM

The Johns Hopkins University Press
Baltimore and London

Originally published by Vintage Books, a division of Random House,
New York. Published by arrangement with Alfred A. Knopf, Inc.
Johns Hopkins Paperbacks edition, 1996
05 04 03 02 01 00 99 98 97 96   5 4 3 2 1

The Johns Hopkins University Press
2715 North Charles Street
Baltimore, MD 21218-4319
The Johns Hopkins Press Ltd., London

Library of Congress Cataloging-in-Publication Data will be found at
the end of this book.

A catalog record for this book is available from the British Library.

ISBN 0-8018-5341-9 (pbk.)

Frontispiece: Photograph by Carlo Leonetti, New York, 1925.
Courtesy of the Enoch Pratt Free Library.

CONTENTS

go to 91-92

CONTENTS

INTRODUCTION *by James T. Farrell*

During the last year or so, there have been signs of a Mencken revival. His books are selling well, and his name once again appears frequently in the press. I keep meeting intelligent younger people interested in his work and personality. The Mencken legend is being restored.

The time seems ripe for a Mencken revival. There are at least superficial resemblances between the present decade and the 1920's, when Mencken reached the peak of his influence. We are never without buncombe in the world, and today we have more than our share of it. Mencken was more than expert and witty in letting the air out of the buncombe artists. And, further, plutocracy is back both in the saddle and in the forefront of the national consciousness. With the aid of many hired publicity hands, plutocracy is seeking to restore some of the prestige and self-acknowledged honor which it enjoyed in the 1920's. And, while Mencken was conservative in his economic views, he only laughed at many of the pretensions of businessmen who turned money-making into a farcical pseudo religion of service, and sometimes into a ludicrous cult of Inspiration. Mencken would never have advocated that the wealth of the late Judge Elbert H. Gary be expropriated. All he did was to describe the big industrialist as though he were a nonentity. His respect for the Rockefellers was no greater. In Mencken's eyes, Gary, the Rockefellers, and Sam Gompers were all inferior men. Of the politician, Mencken had little good to say. With very, very few exceptions, he considered politicians a low order whom the citizen, at best, must bear in fortitude. Until 1936 he usually voted the Democratic ticket, except in 1924, when he cast his ballot for Senator Robert M. La Follette, Sr. He did not agree with La Follette's program or ideas, but he regarded the Wisconsin Senator as a rare bird in politics, an honest man who bravely refused to water down his convictions. Toward Harding, Coolidge, and "Lord Hoover" he was merciless. However, as late as 1934 he regarded President Franklin D. Roosevelt as a gentleman, "honest, gallant and mellowed." Soon after this his view of "Dr. Roosevelt" changed and he wrote of the man with bitterness, rather than with the contempt which he had for some of Roosevelt's predecessors. "Roosevelt Minor" became for him "a milch cow with 125,000,000 teats." Once when I was visiting Mencken during his long years of affliction, he spoke quite differently of President Eisenhower. He remarked: "That fellow has dignity. He's all right." As is known, some of Mencken's most demolishing work dealt with politicians.

Washington is as rich a field for a man of Mencken's talents today as it was in the 1920's. However, it is doubtful that a younger Mencken could now write with the directness and the fearless bluntness of H.L.M. and be published regularly. The conformity and the complacency which he scorned are more noticeable in our publications than at any other period in my own lifetime. There is now perhaps more relevance in Mencken's writing than during the 1930's or the war period. However, his work was always tonic and stimulating. We only reduce its buoyant force and the value and pleasure we can gain from it, if we think of Mencken as relevant merely to one or another selected era. Many of his essays, journalistic reports, sundry and miscellaneous writings have risen above and beyond their own time. Is his marvelous satire "Star-Spangled Men" pertinent only to the 1920's? If we interpret Mencken merely as a man of the gaudy, crazy twenties, we will see him only in part. Mencken has always been a stimulating and valuable writer.

II

Mencken shocked and delighted a generation of college students who read *The American Mercury*. But there were and there are values for the mature in Mencken's work. In the twenties he did not write solely for sophomores. He reflected and became a voice for values superior to those which had had such wide currency, not only among the species "boobus Americanus" but also on college campuses and in editorial offices and the realm of the so-called mighty. This might be obscured because of Mencken's ex-cathedra manner, because of his over-generalizations, his humor, and his frequent reliance on the argument of *reductio ad absurdum,* which he often handled not only cleverly but even brilliantly. Furthermore, a realization of Mencken's role in fighting for major values can easily be lost by those who react quickly to his anti-democratic views.

Mencken continually declared that he wrote for "the civilized minority." He meant those who believed in and were interested in ideas and the play of the mind. He meant those whose taste for literature was for books in which you could find truth, a sense of reality, a feeling for the complexities and inexplicableness of men and of their varied destinies. He held the eighteenth century in high esteem, and undoubtedly associated himself with it. In 1931, when writing in *The American Mercury* on "The New Architecture," he stated:

"The Eighteenth Century . . . had its defects, but they were vastly overshadowed by its merits. It got rid of religion. It lifted music to first place among the arts. It introduced urbanity into manners, and made even war relatively gracious and decent. It took eating and drinking out of the stable and put them into the parlor. It found the sciences childish curiosities, and bent them to the service of men, and elevated them above metaphysics for all time."

His idea of "the civilized minority," of an intellectual aristocracy, was as definitely influenced by the eighteenth century as it was by the Nietzschean idea of the superman. The ideal of reason or rationality and of impersonal causation is at the core of Mencken's thought and his writing. He was a far-off derivative of the Enlightenment, and in twentieth-century America he played something of the role of a Voltaire. In addition, he was a convinced Darwinian. And, despite the rather freewheeling manner in which he made blanket, all-inclusive statements, Mencken could and did think well. Those who declare that he was a great humorist, but minimize his capacities of ratiocination are, I believe, not quite accurate about him. Many of these *Prejudices* show us a man with a strong mind as well as a vigorous, virile spirit full of gusto. His ideas and views became fixed early in life, and, admittedly, he held to his biases and prejudices. He changed his opinions, but never his basic views. Thus, one of his gorgeous essays is "The Sahara of the Bozart," which is included in this selection. He later somewhat revised his views of the South and saw some changes in that region. After having characterized Hollywood as "Moronia," he met a number of intelligent people in the motion-picture industry and accordingly revised his opinion of it.

These essays reveal that Mencken had a ranging, curious mind. Also, while his basic views on democracy, on economics, liberty, and reason were firm and practically immovable, he was a reasonable man ready to recognize grounds for changing his mind on many matters of interpretation. People who knew him and corresponded with him encountered many instances of this.

Mencken's views, so challengingly and excitingly expressed in these essays, were well-formed in the early 1900's. From then on, he largely saw in American life evidence to confirm his own ideas. The attitudes from a Victorian-Puritan past were still powerful in America during the early years of this century. Many sentimentalities, pieties, childish and banal simplicities of McGuffey's Readers remained gospel for millions. A colonialized Victorianism with its moral piety was still exerting a suffocating influence in the literary world. Liberation of the mind from the vestiges of this colonialism and the taboos of an over-conventionalized moralism was far from complete. We frequently read of the American tradition as a liberal one of fair play and tolerance. This is but a partial truth. From the frontier and through Lincoln, Mark Twain, and Walt Whitman, as well as from the Founding Fathers, we do derive a tradition that is liberal. It should be added here that Mencken rejected the ideas of the historian Frederick Jackson Turner. He saw anew that there was much illiberalism, intolerance, and bigotry in the American past. Especially in small towns and the countryside, narrow-mindedness was rampant. America is so vast that almost everything said about it is likely to be true, and the opposite is probably equally true. Mencken in these *Prejudices* recognized and described much that is true about American life.

From the final years of the nineteenth century onward, America received new and fresh whiffs from Europe. In the arts, one of the agents of this influence was James Huneker, a friend and to some degree an inspirer of Mencken. Also, this was a period when the city triumphed over the country. The superiority of the values of the city over those of the rural areas is crucial and central in these essays, as well as in much of Mencken's other writing. He saw issues of freedom of speech, scientific truth versus superstition, and even the phenomenon of Prohibition as part of the conflict between city and country. This explains one of the wittiest essays of this collection, "The Husbandman." And a recent volume of Mencken's journalistic articles on politics, *A Carnival of Buncombe,* reiterates this point. Thus, he wrote in 1928:

"But the battle for Prohibition was more than a struggle for a moral reform: it was also a clear-cut combat between cities and the country, between the civilized centers and the areas of cornbread and revival."

Above all else, you will find here Mencken as a liberating voice. These essays originally strengthened the will of a generation to think independently, to write with greater truth and conviction. He challenged those forces in American life which would have repressed honesty. He dramatically satirized the preposterous, including the malignantly preposterous. He handled and manhandled manners and pieties which stood as barriers to a free development. In addition, his writing is just plain good fun and excitement.

III

"Carlyle was right. The only solution is work." This was a remark which Mencken often made to his friends. With all his vigor and ribaldry, Mencken was, in fact, a strongly pessimistic man. Something of that deep pessimism which intelligent men drew as a conclusion from Darwinism and nineteenth-century determinism was fixed in his nature. He was a rebel in spirit, but not a reformer. He did not believe that either man or society could be much improved. He regarded this life as all that man can ever know, and he had no illusions about it. In his long and rather famous essay "On the National Letters," published in 1919, Mencken criticized popular American fiction of the time on the ground that its usual hero was a second-rate man who struggled to achieve inferior and unsatisfactory ends of material success. In contrast to "the typical American hero" of the success

novel, he wrote of the hero of first-class or great fiction
as a "man of reflective habits." And "what interests this
man is the . . . poignant and significant conflict between
a salient individual and the harsh and meaningless fiats
of destiny, the indestructible mandates and vagaries of
God." Here Mencken was actually referring to more
than the hero of significant fiction: he was writing of
his own inner feeling about life. This, I believe, is the
reason why he was so frequently prompted to remark
that work was the only solution. At the same time, he
was a man who loved his work. He loved writing and
reading. He liked writers, too, even though he poked
fun at them. He saw them as part of "the civilized
minority," and infinitely superior to politicians. He also
genuinely enjoyed helping them. In his "Notebooks,"
published posthumously as *Minority Report,* he jotted
down the following:

"I know a great many more people than most men,
and in wider and more diverse circles, yet my life is essentially one of isolation, and so is that of every other
man. We not only have to die alone; we also, save for a
few close associates, have to live alone. I have been able,
in my time, to give help to a good many young authors,
male and female, and some of them have turned out
very well. I often think of the immense number of others
that I might have aided if I had only known of them."

I was the last, or at least one of the last, younger
writers whom Mencken published in *The American
Mercury.* In April 1932, five days before my first novel,
Young Lonigan, was published, my wife and I arrived
in New York from Paris. We had about ten dollars,
which we spent on that first day. But the next morning
I learned that Mencken had bought a story of mine,
"Helen I Love You." I received one hundred dollars for
it, and it was published in *The American Mercury.*
From then on I corresponded with Mencken until he
was stricken in 1948. His letters always came promptly in
answer to mine. Many of them were brief, but he was
usually to the point. These letters covered a range of

subjects—literature, political oratory and style, Napoleon, language and slang. I first met Mencken one night in August 1935. I was passing the Hotel Brevoort with Hortense Alden, and she remarked that there was Mencken. He was sitting at a table with Edgar Lee Masters. I introduced myself, and he invited us to sit down. We drank beer and talked for about an hour. Mencken and Masters were good friends, and they enjoyed each other's company. They liked to joke about Bryan, the Fundamentalists, and the yokels, and they did so that evening. Perhaps because I was a younger man, Mencken spoke of his own earlier days. He mentioned Richard Harding Davis as a great reporter of that era, and talked of the Kipling of *Barrack Room Ballads*. And he predicted that Huey Long would be assassinated. It was a most pleasant evening.

I next saw Mencken at the Republican National Convention in Cleveland in 1936. As conventions go, it was a very dull one. But it was my first, and I lapped it up, undoubtedly because I had been influenced by Mencken's descriptions. No one but the Kansans took Governor Landon seriously. But they, endlessly singing "Oh Susannah," believed as firmly that Landon would be the next President of the United States as William Jennings Bryan believed in the tenets of Fundamentalism.

At a convention Mencken was not as flamboyant as he is sometimes said to have been. He worked seriously and stayed longer at his seat in the press section than many of the other working reporters. If he had to get his story off when a session closed, he would not stop to drink, but would go to his typewriter. When I watched him, he didn't take many notes. At Cleveland, and again at the 1936 Democratic Convention in Philadelphia, I happened to sit next to him at a number of the sessions. Usually wearing a seersucker suit, he would look out at the swarm of delegates with his glasses sliding down on his nose, his eyes twinkling, and his face lighted up with amusement and interest. In Philadelphia in 1936 I sat next to him on the hot, dull day when President

Roosevelt was renominated. The platform was crowded with politicians from every corner of the land. One after another, they got in on the act with seconding speeches. This went on for hours and hours and was carried into the night. The floor emptied of delegates, who went off to the ball game, to the saloons, to any place less depressing and boring than the Convention Hall. For on that day the record for an all-time low in the history of political oratory was undoubtedly established. Not one cliché was missed. The platitudes were deadly. The English language was raped. One after another, the politicians came to the rostrum and contributed their bits to the obscene ritual. Included among them was Happy Chandler; no one outdid him. This was a Mencken day, a Mencken scene on the convention floor. Like the delegates, the newspapermen had flown the coop. They were paid to work, but this was too much for them. But I sat it out with Mencken, fascinated. Perhaps the writings of Mencken back in the twenties impelled me. We listened in glee and amazement. He kept shaking his head, peering at the crowd of politicians on the platform. Finally he nudged me.

"Farrell, do you see all of those politicians up there?" He pointed.

"Every one of them thinks that he can be President of the United States."

In 1945 my brother and I went from Washington to Baltimore to have lunch with Mencken. As he took us to his club, he half apologized, explaining that he had lambasted it and the other members but that he had found it more convenient to meet people for lunch there than at home. He was, needless to say, most gracious in his concern about what we ate and how we liked the food. He was a genuine gentleman.

Mencken was a good and fluent talker, and he had much to say that day. Because my brother was a doctor, Mencken spoke of medicine and insanity. He asserted his belief that eventually science would prove that insanity was caused by a condition in the blood; he expatiated on this theory. He also spoke of Ezra Pound, then but recently committed to St. Elizabeth's Hospital.

Mencken had visited Pound, taking along an armful of books of poetry. He'd told the doctor that the books were all poetry, "as bad as Ezra's." Mencken did not admire most poetry, as is well known. However, he was one of the first writers to visit Pound. This was characteristic of him. He would often do such things. He never knew Leon Trotsky and had no great respect for the man. However, when Trotsky was in exile in Prinkipo, Mencken read that there had been a fire in his home and that Trotsky's library was said to have been destroyed. Mencken wrote to Trotsky, offering to send him some books. Later, in Mexico, I discussed American writers with Trotsky, and he mentioned Mencken and that letter. Asking about Mencken, Trotsky said that he had never answered the letter. Why should he have accepted books from Mencken? The letter to Trotsky came into our conversation at Baltimore. Mencken made little of it. Trotsky's not having replied did not trouble him. He said that, having read of the fire, he had offered to send Trotsky some books that he might need for his work. But Trotsky, so often a gracious and impeccably polite man in personal relationships, was too haughty to respond to what was a friendly and impersonal gesture.

At that time, blood and blood pressure were on Mencken's mind. For, after having spoken of blood as the possible source or cause of insanity, he mentioned President Roosevelt, who had died two months previously.

"Jesus, his blood pressure must have been way up," Mencken said.

A few moments later he again mentioned Roosevelt's blood pressure. And then, after about five minutes more, he said:

"In four years I'll have a stroke and die."

I laughed at him and said that I didn't believe it. He insisted that this would happen. His stroke came about six months short of four years later, and it almost killed him.

He also spoke of books and writers, and remarked that, in the end, perhaps only scenes remained as great literature. This was the case, he said, with *Babbitt* and also with what he considered to be Dreiser's best work. Mencken had affection for Dreiser, but regarded the man as a peasant. He remarked that if Dreiser became ill, and walked along a street where there were two signs, one reading Dr. Osler and the other Dr. Quack, you could bet all your money that Dreiser would go in to Dr. Quack every time.

It was when we were walking back to the railroad station that he suddenly asked:

"Farrell, how old are you?"

I told him forty-one. He said that I was young, had a wonderful future, and would possibly still write my best books.

"Farrell, if you want to develop further as a writer, there are three things to stay away from. Booze . . . women . . . and politics."

These, he insisted, killed a literary talent. He mentioned Ring Lardner, whom he had seen often. Lardner, he said, would sit for hours, drinking in a morose silence.

Luncheon with Mencken was always a happy event.

IV

It was a gray fall afternoon in the period after Mencken had had a cerebral hemorrhage. I stopped off in Baltimore and took a cab to his house in Hollins Street. Mencken, wearing a blue suit, met me at the door. He did not look ill. In fact, he appeared hale and healthy. But then I realized definitely that he had become an old man. The first question he asked was:

"How are my friends?"

We went to his office or workroom and talked.

"I'm out of it. I'm finished. I wish I were dead."

He explained that he could no longer work. He was unable to read or write. The only thing he could do was help his secretary, who was arranging his correspondence, which was to go to a library.

Mencken's stroke, suffered in the fall of 1948, destroyed or affected the association tracts in his brain. He had great difficulty in remembering proper nouns or names. While I was with him on this occasion and later, he said that he knew me and remembered my books. But he didn't know my name; after I told it to him, he said he remembered.

"If I could read and write, I'd be content," he said. "I'm out of it."

He described how he lived. In spring he did some work in his garden. He and his brother August collected boxes and pieces of wood in the alley, and he broke them up. He went to some movies. During the first years he could go to Florida or be driven around Baltimore. Later he could not go out much. He would look out at the park or square in front of his home, watch the people in it, watch the children coming home from school, guess and speculate about them and their ages. He would walk around and talk to the Negro children in the neighborhood. Every afternoon he took a nap, and he went to bed early.

"I listen to the machine, the machine upstairs," he said, pointing upward. "The machine, they're all morons."

He meant the radio.

And people. He spoke of "the publisher." He meant Alfred Knopf, who would visit him. And "his friend," the "drama critic." It was George Jean Nathan. So it went. As soon as the name was supplied him, his memory functioned. He also mentioned books he'd like to reread. And there was the refrain in his conversation: he was out of it. And the second refrain: he would just as soon be dead. But, considering what had happened to him, his condition was good.

His voice was just a bit thick. Sometimes the wrong word would come. After a period of conversation his thoughts would wander. He was aware of this, and even commented on it. For two or three minutes we would speak of another subject. Then he would pick up the threads of the conversation.

He spoke, also, of the night when he had his stroke while at a restaurant in Baltimore. His description conveyed a sense of sick agony. But he was realistic and resigned about his condition. He had, in a sense, suggested his own final days, years before, when he had written of the hero of major fiction, a superior man, "a salient individual" in conflict with "harsh and meaningless fiats of destiny." His biological tragedy, this harshness of his destiny, was all the more cruel and punishing because he was deprived of his main surcease—his work.

On that first visit after his stroke, we talked for a long time, perhaps two hours. It was dark out when I left. He accompanied me to the door and reminded me to tell his friends that he was doing well. But after a pause he added:

"Remember me to my friends. Tell them I'm a hell of a mess."

Such were the last days of H. L. Mencken. He bore them with courage.

V

It should be clear to the reader that the preparation of this volume was to me a joy, a labor of love, and a privilege. These selections are all taken from Mencken's six volumes of *Prejudices,* which were published between 1919 and 1927. A number of them, however, appeared first in *The Smart Set* or *The American Mercury.* They represent Mencken when he was at the peak of his influence and had, in fact, become a legend. Here is some of his wittiest and most buoyant writing. Something of his wide range of interests and his broad field of reference is to be found in these essays. Many of them are unforgettable. Here, in my opinion, is some of the very best of H. L. Mencken.

I was not guided by any one principle of selection. I chose what I liked and what I think and hope will be enjoyable to old and new readers of Mencken. It had been my desire to avoid any duplication of the selection in Alistair Cooke's excellently edited *The Vintage Mencken*. However, there are a few duplications of pieces just too good and impressive to omit. The Cooke volume, let me add, unlike this one, draws from the entire body of Mencken's writings. Also, I should like to call special attention to the essays on George Jean Nathan and James Huneker. These men were his friends. His name is bound up with theirs. In addition, in a couple of instances I have made small deletions, but wherever this was done I have placed dots. I wish to express gratitude to my wife, Dorothy B. Farrell, my secretary, Mrs. Luna Wolf, and Mrs. Louise Richmond for assisting me in the editing and mechanical preparation of this book.

Here, then, is a selection from Mencken's *Prejudices*. I hope these writings may give others as much pleasure as they have given me over the years stretching back to my own youth.

JAMES T. FARRELL

H. L. MENCKEN

PREJUDICES

A SELECTION

CRITICISM OF CRITICISM OF
CRITICISM

Every now and then, a sense of the futility
of their daily endeavors falling suddenly upon them, the
critics of Christendom turn to a somewhat sour and depressing consideration of the nature and objects of their
own craft. That is to say, they turn to criticizing criticism. What is it in plain words? What is its aim, exactly
stated in legal terms? How far can it go? What good
can it do? What is its normal effect upon the artist and
the work of art?

Such a spell of self-searching has been in progress for
several years past, and the critics of various countries
have contributed theories of more or less lucidity and
plausibility to the discussion. Their views of their own
art, it appears, are quite as divergent as their views of
the arts they more commonly deal with. One group
argues, partly by direct statement and partly by attacking
all other groups, that the one defensible purpose of the

critic is to encourage the virtuous and oppose the sinful—
in brief, to police the fine arts and so hold them in tune
with the moral order of the world. Another group, re-
pudiating this constabulary function, argues hotly that
the arts have nothing to do with morality whatsoever—
that their concern is solely with pure beauty. A third
group holds that the chief aspect of a work of art, particularly in the field of literature, is its aspect as psychological document—that if it doesn't help men to know
themselves it is nothing. A fourth group reduces the
thing to an exact science, and sets up standards that
resemble algebraic formulæ—this is the group of metrists,
of contrapuntists and of those who gabble of light-waves.
And so, in order, follow groups five, six, seven, eight,
nine, ten, each with its theory and its proofs.

Against the whole corps, moral and æsthetic, psychological and algebraic, stands Major J. E. Spingarn,
U. S. A. Major Spingarn lately served formal notice
upon me that he had abandoned the life of the academic
grove for that of the armed array, and so I give him his
military title, but at the time he wrote his "Creative
Criticism" he was a professor in Columbia University,
and I still find myself thinking of him, not as a soldier
extraordinarily literate, but as a professor in rebellion.
For his notions, whatever one may say in opposition to
them, are at least magnificently unprofessorial—they fly
violently in the face of the principles that distinguish
the largest and most influential group of campus critics.
As witness: "To say that poetry is moral or immoral is as
meaningless as to say that an equilateral triangle is
moral and an isosceles triangle immoral." Or, worse:
"It is only conceivable in a world in which dinner-table
conversation runs after this fashion: 'This cauliflower
would be good if it had only been prepared in accordance
with international law.'" One imagines, on hearing such
atheism flying about, the amazed indignation of Prof.
Dr. William Lyon Phelps, with his discovery that Joseph
Conrad preaches "the axiom of the moral law"; the
"Hey, what's that!" of Prof. Dr. W. C. Brownell, the

4

Amherst Aristotle, with his eloquent plea for standards as iron-clad as the Westminster Confession; the loud, patriotic alarm of the gifted Prof. Dr. Stuart P. Sherman, of Iowa, with his maxim that Puritanism is the official philosophy of America, and that all who dispute it are enemy aliens and should be deported. Major Spingarn, in truth, here performs a treason most horrible upon the reverend order he once adorned, and having achieved it, he straightway performs another and then another. That is to say, he tackles all the antagonistic groups of orthodox critics seriatim, and knocks them about unanimously —first the aforesaid agents of the sweet and pious; then the advocates of unities, meters, all rigid formulæ; then the experts in imaginary psychology; then the historical comparers, pigeonholers and makers of categories; finally, the professors of pure æsthetic. One and all, they take their places upon his operating table, and one and all they are stripped and anatomized.

But what is the anarchistic ex-professor's own theory? —for a professor must have a theory, as a dog must have fleas. In brief, what he offers is a doctrine borrowed from the Italian, Benedetto Croce, and by Croce filched from Goethe—a doctrine anything but new in the world, even in Goethe's time, but nevertheless long buried in forgetfulness—to wit, the doctrine that it is the critic's first and only duty, as Carlyle once put it, to find out "what the poet's aim really and truly was, how the task he had to do stood before his eye, and how far, with such materials as were afforded him, he has fulfilled it." For poet, read artist, or, if literature is in question, substitute the Germanic word *Dichter*—that is, the artist in words, the creator of beautiful letters, whether in verse or in prose. Ibsen always called himself a *Digter,* not a *Dramatiker* or *Skuespiller.* So, I daresay, did Shakespeare. . . . Well, what is this generalized poet trying to do? asks Major Spingarn, and how has he done it? That, and no more, is the critic's quest. The morality of the work does not concern him. It is not his business to determine whether it heeds Aristotle or flouts Aristotle.

He passes no judgment on its rhyme scheme, its length and breadth, its iambics, its politics, its patriotism, its piety, its psychological exactness, its good taste. He may note these things, but he may not protest about them—he may not complain if the thing criticized fails to fit into a pigeonhole. Every sonnet, every drama, every novel is *sui generis;* it must stand on its own bottom; it must be judged by its own inherent intentions. "Poets," says Major Spingarn, "do not really write epics, pastorals, lyrics, however much they may be deceived by these false abstractions; they express *themselves, and this expression is their only form.* There are not, therefore, only three or ten or a hundred literary kinds; there are as many kinds as there are individual poets." Nor is there any valid appeal *ad hominem.* The character and background of the poet are beside the mark; the poem itself is the thing. Oscar Wilde, weak and swine-like, yet wrote beautiful prose. To reject that prose on the ground that Wilde had filthy habits is as absurd as to reject "What Is Man?" on the ground that its theology is beyond the intelligence of the editor of the New York *Times.*

This Spingarn-Croce-Carlyle-Goethe theory, of course, throws a heavy burden upon the critic. It presupposes that he is a civilized and tolerant man, hospitable to all intelligible ideas and capable of reading them as he runs. This is a demand that at once rules out nine-tenths of the grown-up sophomores who carry on the business of criticism in America. Their trouble is simply that they lack the intellectual resilience necessary for taking in ideas, and particularly new ideas. The only way they can ingest one is by transforming it into the nearest related formula —usually a harsh and devastating operation. This fact accounts for their chronic inability to understand all that is most personal and original and hence most forceful and significant in the emerging literature of the country. They can get down what has been digested and re-digested, and so brought into forms that they know, and carefully labeled by predecessors of their own sort—but they exhibit alarm immediately they come into the presence of the extraordinary. Here we have an explanation of Brownell's loud appeal for a tightening of standards—*i.e.*, a larger respect for precedents, patterns, rubber stamps—and here we have an explanation of Phelps's inability to comprehend the colossal phenomenon of Dreiser, and of Boynton's childish nonsense about realism, and of Sherman's effort to apply the Espionage Act to the arts, and of More's querulous enmity to romanticism, and of all the fatuous pigeonholing that passes for criticism in the more solemn literary periodicals.

As practiced by all such learned and diligent but essentially ignorant and unimaginative men, criticism is little more than a branch of homiletics. They judge a work of art, not by its clarity and sincerity, not by the force and charm of its ideas, not by the technical virtuosity of the artist, not by his originality and artistic courage, but simply and solely by his orthodoxy. If he is what is called a "right thinker," if he devotes himself to advocating the transient platitudes in a sonorous manner, then he is worthy of respect. But if he lets fall the slightest hint that he is in doubt about any of them, or, worse still, that he is indifferent, then he is a scoundrel, and hence, by their theory, a bad artist. Such pious piffle is horribly familiar among us. I do not exaggerate its terms. You will find it running through the critical writings of practically all the dull fellows who combine criticism with tutoring; in the words of many of them it is stated in the plainest way and defended with much heat, theological and pedagogical. In its baldest form it shows itself in the doctrine that it is scandalous for an artist—say a dramatist or a novelist—to depict vice as attractive. The fact that vice, more often than not, undoubtedly *is* attractive—else why should it ever gobble any of us?—is disposed of with a lofty gesture. What of it? say these birchmen. The artist is not a reporter, but a Great Teacher. It is not his business to depict the world as it is, but as it ought to be.

Against this notion American criticism makes but feeble headway. We are, in fact, a nation of evangelists; every third American devotes himself to improving and lifting up his fellow-citizens, usually by force; the messianic delusion is our national disease. Thus the moral *Privatdozenten* have the crowd on their side, and it is difficult to shake their authority; even the vicious are still in favor of crying vice down. "Here is a novel," says the artist. "Why didn't you write a tract?" roars the professor—and down the chute go novel and novelist. "This girl is pretty," says the painter. "But she has left off her undershirt," protests the head-master—and off goes the poor dauber's head. At its mildest, this balderdash takes the form of the late Hamilton Wright Mabie's "White List of Books"; at its worst, it is comstockery, an idiotic and abominable thing. Genuine criticism is as impossible to such inordinately narrow and cocksure men as music is to a man who is tone-deaf. The critic, to interpret his artist, even to understand his artist, must be able to get into the mind of his artist; he must feel and comprehend the vast pressure of the creative passion; as Major Spingarn says, "æsthetic judgment and artistic creation are instinct with the same vital life." This is why all the best criticism of the world has been written by men who have had within them, not only the reflective and analytical faculty of critics, but also the gusto of artists—Goethe, Carlyle, Lessing, Schlegel, Saint-Beuve, and, to drop a story or two, Hazlitt, Hermann Bahr, Georg Brandes and James Huneker. Huneker, tackling "Also sprach Zarathustra," revealed its content in illuminating flashes. But tackled by Paul Elmer More, it became no more than a dull student's exercise, ill-naturedly corrected. . . .

So much for the theory of Major J. E. Spingarn, U. S. A., late professor of modern languages and literatures in Columbia University. Obviously, it is a far sounder and more stimulating theory than any of those cherished by the other professors. It demands that the critic be a man of intelligence, of toleration, of wide information, of genuine hospitality to ideas, whereas the others only demand that he have learning, and accept anything as learning that has been said before. But once he has stated his doctrine, the ingenious ex-professor,

professor-like, immediately begins to corrupt it by claiming too much for it. Having laid and hatched, so to speak, his somewhat stale but still highly nourishing egg, he begins to argue fatuously that the resultant flamingo is the whole mustering of the critical *Aves*. But the fact is, of course, that criticism, as humanly practiced, must needs fall a good deal short of this intuitive recreation of beauty, and what is more, it must go a good deal further. For one thing, it must be interpretation in terms that are not only exact but are also comprehensible to the reader, else it will leave the original mystery as dark as before—and once interpretation comes in, paraphrase and transliteration come in. What is recondite must be made plainer; the transcendental, to some extent at least, must be done into common modes of thinking. Well, what are morality, trochaics, hexameters, movements, historical principles, psychological maxims, the dramatic unities—what are all these save common modes of thinking, short cuts, rubber stamps, words of one syllable? Moreover, beauty as we know it in this world is by no means the apparition *in vacuo* that Dr. Spingarn seems to see. It has its social, its political, even its moral implications. The finale of Beethoven's C minor symphony is not only colossal as music; it is also colossal as revolt; it says something against something. Yet more, the springs of beauty are not within itself alone, nor even in genius alone, but often in things without. Brahms wrote his Deutsches Requiem, not only because he was a great artist, but also because he was a good German. And in Nietzsche there are times when the divine afflatus takes a back seat, and the *spirochaetae* have the floor.

Major Spingarn himself seems to harbor some sense of this limitation on his doctrine. He gives warning that "the poet's intention must be judged at the moment of the creative act"—which opens the door enough for many an ancient to creep in. But limited or not, he at least clears off a lot of moldy rubbish, and gets further toward the truth than any of his former colleagues. They waste themselves upon theories that only conceal the

9

poet's achievement the more, the more diligently they are applied; he, at all events, grounds himself upon the sound notion that there should be free speech in art, and no protective tariffs, and no *a priori* assumptions, and no testing of ideas by mere words. The safe ground probably lies between the contestants, but nearer Spingarn. The critic who really illuminates starts off much as he starts off, but with a due regard for the prejudices and imbecilities of the world. I think the best feasible practice is to be found in certain chapters of Huneker, a critic of vastly more solid influence and of infinitely more value to the arts than all the prating pedagogues since Rufus Griswold. Here, as in the case of Poe, a sensitive and intelligent artist recreates the work of other artists, but there also comes to the ceremony a man of the world, and the things he has to say are apposite and instructive too. To denounce moralizing out of hand is to pronounce a moral judgment. To dispute the categories is to set up a new anti-categorical category. And to admire the work of Shakespeare is to be interested in his handling of blank verse, his social aspirations, his shot-gun marriage and his frequent concessions to the bombastic frenzy of his actors, and to have some curiosity about Mr. W. H. The really competent critic must be an empiricist. He must conduct his exploration with whatever means lie within the bounds of his personal limitation. He must produce his effects with whatever tools will work. If pills fail, he gets out his saw. If the saw won't cut, he seizes a club. . . .

Perhaps, after all, the chief burden that lies upon Major Spingarn's theory is to be found in its label. The word "creative" is a bit too flamboyant; it says what he wants to say, but it probably says a good deal more. In this emergency, I propose getting rid of the misleading label by pasting another over it. That is, I propose the substitution of "catalytic" for "creative," despite the fact that "catalytic" is an unfamiliar word, and suggests the dog-Latin of the seminaries. I borrow it from chemistry, and its meaning is really quite simple. A catalyzer, in chemistry, is a substance that helps two other substances to react. For example, consider the case of ordinary cane sugar and water. Dissolve the sugar in the water and nothing happens. But add a few drops of acid and the sugar changes into glucose and fructose. Meanwhile, the acid itself is absolutely unchanged. All it does is to stir up the reaction between the water and the sugar. The process is called catalysis. The acid is a catalyzer.

Well, this is almost exactly the function of a genuine critic of the arts. It is his business to provoke the reaction between the work of art and the spectator. The spectator, untutored, stands unmoved; he sees the work of art, but it fails to make any intelligible impression on him; if he were spontaneously sensitive to it, there would be no need for criticism. But now comes the critic with his catalysis. He makes the work of art live for the spectator; he makes the spectator live for the work of art. Out of the process comes understanding, appreciation, intelligent enjoyment —and that is precisely what the artist tried to produce.

GEORGE ADE

When, after the Japs and their vassals conquer us and put us to the sword, and the republic descends into hell, some literary don of Oxford or Mittel-Europa proceeds to the predestined autopsy upon our Complete Works, one of the things he will surely notice, reviewing our literary history, is the curious persistence with which the dons native to the land have overlooked its emerging men of letters. I mean, of course, its genuine men of letters, its salient and truly original men, its men of intrinsic and unmistakable distinction. The fourth-raters have fared well enough, God knows. Go back to any standard literature book of ten, or twenty, or thirty, or fifty years ago, and you will be amazed by its praise of shoddy mediocrities, long since fly-blown and forgotten. George William Curtis, now seldom heard of at all, save perhaps in the reminiscences of senile publishers, was treated in his day with all the deference due to a prince of the blood. Artemus Ward, Petroleum V. Nasby and half a dozen other such hollow buffoons were ranked with Mark Twain, and even above him. Frank R. Stockton, for thirty years, was the delight of all right-thinking reviewers. Richard Henry Stoddard and Edmund Clarence Stedman were eminent personages, both as critics and as poets. And Donald G. Mitchell, to make an end of dull names, bulked so grandly in the academic eye that he was snatched from his tear-jugs and his teapots to become a charter member of the National Institute of Arts and Letters, and actually died a member of the American Academy!

Meanwhile, three of the five indubitably first-rate artists that America has produced went quite without orthodox recognition at home until either foreign enthusiasm or domestic clamor from below forced them into a belated and grudging sort of notice. I need not say that I allude to Poe, Whitman and Mark Twain. If it ever occurred to any American critic of position, during Poe's lifetime, that he was a greater man than either Cooper or Irving, then I have been unable to find any trace of the fact in the critical literature of the time. The truth is that he was looked upon as a facile and somewhat dubious journalist, too cocksure by half, and not a man to be encouraged. Lowell praised him in 1845 and at the same time denounced the current over-praise of lesser men, but later on this encomium was diluted with very important reservations, and there the matter stood until Baudelaire discovered the poet and his belated fame came winging home. Whitman, as every one knows, fared even worse. Emerson first hailed him and then turned tail upon him, eager to avoid any share in his ill-repute among blockheads. No other critic of any influence gave him help. He was carried through his dark days of poverty and persecution by a few private enthusiasts, none of them with the ear of the public, and in the end it was Frenchmen and Englishmen who lifted him into the light. Imagine a Harvard professor lecturing upon him in 1865! As for Mark Twain, the story of his first fifteen years has been admirably told by Prof. Dr. William Lyon Phelps, of Yale. The dons were unanimously against him. Some sneered at him as a feeble mountebank; others refused to discuss him at all; not one harbored the slightest suspicion that he was a man of genius, or even one leg of a man of genius. Phelps makes merry over this academic attempt to dispose of Mark by putting him into Coventry —and himself joins the sanctimonious brethren who essay the same enterprise against Dreiser. . . .

I come by this route to George Ade—who perhaps fails to fit into the argument doubly, for on the one hand he is certainly not a literary artist of the first rank, and on the other hand he has long enjoyed a meed of appreciation and even of honor, for the National Institute of Arts and Letters elevated him to its gilt-edged purple in its first days, and he is still on its roll of men of "notable achievement in art, music or literature," along with Robert W. Chambers, Henry Sydnor Harrison, Oliver Herford, E. S. Martin and E. W. Townsend, author of "Chimmie Fadden." Nevertheless, he does not fall too far outside, after all, for if he is not of the first rank then he surely deserves a respectable place in the second rank, and if the National Institute broke the spell by admitting him then it was probably on the theory that he was a second Chambers or Herford, or maybe even a second Martin or Townsend. As for the text-book dons, they hold resolutely to the doctrine that he scarcely exists, and is not worth noticing at all. For example, there is Prof. Fred Lewis Pattee, author of "A History of American Literature Since 1870." Prof. Pattee notices Chambers, Marion Harland, Herford, Townsend, Amélie Rives, R. K. Munkittrick and many other such ornaments of the national letters, and even has polite bows for Gelett Burgess, Carolyn Wells and John Kendrick Bangs, but the name of Ade is missing from his index, as is that of Dreiser. So with the other pedagogues. They are unanimously shy of Ade in their horn-books for sophomores, and they are gingery in their praise of him in their innumerable review articles. He is commended, when at all, much as the late Joseph Jefferson used to be commended—that is, to the accompaniment of reminders that even a clown is one of God's creatures, and may have the heart of a Christian under his motley. The most laudatory thing ever said of him by any critic of the apostolic succession, so far as I can discover, is that he is clean—that he does not import the lewd buffooneries of the barroom, the smoking-car and the wedding reception into his books. . . .

But what are the facts? The facts are that Ade is one of the few genuinely original literary craftsmen now in practice among us; that he comes nearer to making literature, when he has full steam up, than any save a scant half-dozen of our current novelists, and that the whole body of his work, both in books and for the stage, is as thoroughly American, in cut and color, in tang and savor, in structure and point of view, as the work of Howells, E. W. Howe or Mark Twain. No single American novel that I can think of shows half the sense of nationality, the keen feeling for national prejudice and peculiarity, the sharp and pervasive Americanism of such Adean fables as "The Good Fairy of the Eighth Ward and the Dollar Excursion of the Steam-Fitters," "The Mandolin Players and the Willing Performer," and "The Adult Girl Who Got Busy Before They Could Ring the Bell on Her." Here, amid a humor so grotesque that it almost tortures the midriff, there is a startlingly vivid and accurate evocation of the American scene. Here, under all the labored extravagance, there are brilliant flashlight pictures of the American people, and American ways of thinking, and the whole of American *Kultur*. Here the veritable Americano stands forth, lacking not a waggery, a superstition, a snuffle or a wen.

Ade himself, for all his story-teller's pretense of remoteness, is as absolutely American as any of his prairie-town traders and pushers, Shylocks and Dogberries, beaux and belles. No other writer of our generation, save perhaps Howe, is more unescapably national in his every gesture and trick of mind. He is as American as buckwheat cakes, or the Knights of Pythias, or the chautauqua, or Billy Sunday, or a bull by Dr. Wilson. He fairly reeks of the national Philistinism, the national respect for respectability, the national distrust of ideas. He is a marcher, one fancies, in parades; he joins movements, and movements against movements; he knows no language save his own; he regards a Roosevelt quite seriously and a Mozart or an Ibsen as a joke; one would not be surprised to hear that, until he went off to his fresh-water college, he slept in his underwear and read the *Epworth Herald*. But, like Dreiser, he is a peasant touched by the divine fire; somehow, a great instinctive artist got himself born out there on that lush Indiana farm. He has the rare faculty of seeing accurately, even when the thing seen is directly under his nose, and he has the still rarer faculty of recording vividly, of making the thing seen move with life. One often doubts a character in a novel, even in a good novel, but who ever doubted Gus in "The Two Mandolin Players," or Mae in "Sister Mae," or, to pass from the fables, Payson in "Mr. Payson's Satirical Christmas"? Here, with strokes so crude and obvious that they seem to be laid on with a broom, Ade achieves what O. Henry, with all his ingenuity, always failed to achieve: he fills his bizarre tales with human beings. There is never any artfulness on the surface. The tale itself is never novel, or complex; it never surprises; often it is downright banal. But underneath there is an artfulness infinitely well wrought, and that is the artfulness of a story-teller who dredges his story out of his people, swiftly and skillfully, and does not squeeze his people into his story, laboriously and unconvincingly.

Needless to say, a moralist stands behind the comedian. He would teach; he even grows indignant. Roaring like a yokel at a burlesque show over such wild and lighthearted jocosities as "Paducah's Favorite Comedians" and "Why 'Gondola' Was Put Away," one turns with something of a start to such things as "Little Lutie," "The Honest Money Maker" and "The Corporation Director and the Mislaid Ambition." Up to a certain point it is all laughter, but after that there is a flash of the knife, a show of teeth. Here a national limitation often closes in upon the satirist. He cannot quite separate the unaccustomed from the abominable; he is unable to avoid rattling his Philistine trappings a bit proudly; he must prove that he, too, is a right-thinking American, a solid citizen and a patriot, unshaken in his lofty rectitude by such poisons as aristocracy, adultery, *hors d'œuvres* and the sonata form. But in other directions this thorough-going nationalism helps him rather than hinders him. It enables him, for one thing, to see into sentimentality, and to comprehend it and project it accurately. I know of no book which displays the mooniness of youth with more feeling and sympathy than "Artie," save it be Frank Norris' forgotten "Blix." In such fields Ade achieves a success that is rare and indubitable. He makes the thing charming and he makes it plain.

But all these fables and other compositions of his are mere sketches, inconsiderable trifles, impromptus in bad English, easy to write and of no importance! Are they, indeed? Do not believe it for a moment. Fifteen or twenty years ago, when Ade was at the height of his celebrity as a newspaper Sganarelle, scores of hack comedians tried to imitate him—and all failed. I myself was of the number. I operated a so-called funny column in a daily newspaper, and like my colleagues near and far, I essayed to manufacture fables in slang. What miserable botches they were! How easy it was to imitate Ade's manner—and how impossible to imitate his matter! No; please don't get the notion that it is a simple thing to write such a fable as that of "The All-Night Seance and the Limit That Ceased to Be," or that of "The Preacher Who Flew His Kite, But Not Because He Wished to Do So," or that of "The Roystering Blades."

Far from it! On the contrary, the only way you will ever accomplish the feat will be by first getting Ade's firm grasp upon American character, and his ability to think out a straightforward, simple, amusing story, and his alert feeling for contrast and climax, and his extraordinary talent for devising novel, vivid and unforgettable phrases. Those phrases of his sometimes wear the external vestments of a passing slang, but they are no more commonplace and vulgar at bottom than Gray's "mute, inglorious Milton" or the "somewheres East of Suez" of Kipling. They reduce an idea to a few pregnant syllables. They give the attention a fillip and light up a whole scene in a flash. They are the running evidences of an eye that sees clearly and of a mind that thinks shrewdly. They give distinction to the work of a man who has so well concealed a highly complex and efficient artistry that few have ever noticed it.

THE GENEALOGY OF ETIQUETTE

Barring sociology (which is yet, of course, scarcely a science at all, but rather a monkeyshine which happens to pay, like play-acting or theology), psychology is the youngest of the sciences, and hence chiefly guesswork, empiricism, hocus-pocus, poppycock. On the one hand, there are still enormous gaps in its data, so that the determination of its simplest principles remains difficult, not to say impossible; and, on the other hand, the very hollowness and nebulosity of it, particularly around its edges, encourages a horde of quacks to invade it, sophisticate it and make nonsense of it. Worse, this state of affairs tends to such confusion of effort and direction that the quack and the honest inquirer are often found in the same man. It is, indeed, a commonplace to encounter a

17

professor who spends his days in the laborious accumulation of psychological statistics, sticking pins into babies and platting upon a chart the ebb and flow of their yells, and his nights chasing poltergeists and other such celestial fauna over the hurdles of a spiritualist's atelier, or gazing into a crystal in the privacy of his own chamber. The Binét test and the buncombe of mesmerism are alike the children of what we roughly denominate psychology, and perhaps of equal legitimacy. Even so ingenious and competent an investigator as Prof. Dr. Sigmund Freud, who has told us a lot that is of the first importance about the materials and machinery of thought, has also told us a lot that is trivial and dubious. The essential doctrines of Freudism, no doubt, come close to the truth, but many of Freud's remoter deductions are far more scandalous than sound, and many of the professed Freudians, both American and European, have grease-paint on their noses and bladders in their hands and are otherwise quite indistinguishable from evangelists and circus clowns.

In this condition of the science it is no wonder that we find it wasting its chief force upon problems that are petty and idle when they are not downright and palpably insoluble, and passing over problems that are of immediate concern to all of us, and that might be quite readily solved, or, at any rate, considerably illuminated, by an intelligent study of the data already available. After all, not many of us care a hoot whether Sir Oliver Lodge and the Indian chief Wok-a-wok-a-mok are happy in heaven, for not many of us have any hope or desire to meet them there. Nor are we greatly excited by the discovery that, of twenty-five freshmen who are hit with clubs, 17¾ will say "Ouch!" and 22⅕ will say "Damn!"; nor by a table showing that 38.2 per centum of all men accused of homicide confess when locked up with the carcasses of their victims, including 23.4 per centum who are innocent; nor by plans and specifications, by Cagliostro out of Lucrezia Borgia, for teaching poor, Godforsaken school children to write before they can read and to multiply before they can add; nor by endless disputes between half-witted pundits as to the precise difference between perception and cognition; nor by even longer feuds, between pundits even crazier, over free will, the subconscious, the endoneurium, the functions of the corpora quadrigemina, and the meaning of dreams in which one is pursued by hyenas, process-servers or grass-widows.

Nay; we do not bubble with rejoicing when such fruits of psychological deep-down-diving and much-mud-upbringing researches are laid before us, for after all they do not offer us any nourishment, there is nothing in them to engage our teeth, they fail to make life more comprehensible, and hence more bearable. What we yearn to know something about is the process whereby the ideas of everyday are engendered in the skulls of those about us, to the end that we may pursue a straighter and a safer course through the muddle that is life. Why do the great majority of Presbyterians (and, for that matter, of Baptists, Episcopalians, and Swedenborgians as well) regard it as unlucky to meet a black cat and lucky to find a pin? What are the logical steps behind the theory that it is indecent to eat peas with a knife? By what process does an otherwise sane man arrive at the conclusion that he will go to hell unless he is baptized by total immersion in water? What causes men to be faithful to their wives: habit, fear, poverty, lack of imagination, lack of enterprise, stupidity, religion? What is the psychological basis of commercial morality? What is the true nature of the vague pooling of desires that Rousseau called the social contract? Why does an American regard it as scandalous to wear dress clothes at a funeral, and a Frenchman regard it as equally scandalous *not* to wear them? Why is it that men trust one another so readily, and women trust one another so seldom? Why are we all so greatly affected by statements that we know are not true?—*e.g.* in Lincoln's Gettysburg speech, the Declaration of Independence and the CIII Psalm. What is the origin of the so-called double standard of morality? Why are women forbidden to take off their hats in church? What is happiness? Intelligence? Sin? Courage? Virtue? Beauty?

All these are questions of interest and importance to all of us, for their solution would materially improve the accuracy of our outlook upon the world, and with it our mastery of our environment, but the psychologists, busily engaged in chasing their tails, leave them unanswered, and, in most cases, even unasked. The late William James, more acute than the general, saw how precious little was known about the psychological inwardness of religion, and to the illumination of this darkness he addressed himself in his book, "The Varieties of Religious Experience." But life being short and science long, he got little beyond the statement of the problem and the marshaling of the grosser evidence—and even at this business he allowed himself to be constantly interrupted by spooks, hobgoblins, seventh sons of seventh sons and other such characteristic pets of psychologists. In the same way one Gustav le Bon, a Frenchman, undertook a psychological study of the crowd mind—and then blew up. Add the investigations of Freud and his school, chiefly into abnormal states of mind, and those of Lombroso and his school, chiefly quackish and for the yellow journals, and the idle romancing of such inquirers as Prof. Dr. Thorstein Veblen, and you have exhausted the list of contributions to what may be called practical and everyday psychology. The rev. professors, I daresay, have been doing some useful plowing and planting. All of their meticulous pin-sticking and measuring and chart-making, in the course of time, will enable their successors to approach the real problems of mind with more assurance than is now possible, and perhaps help to their solution. But in the meantime the public and social utility of psychology remains very small, for it is still unable to differentiate accurately between the true and the false, or to give us any effective protection against the fallacies, superstitions, crazes and hysterias which rage in the world.

In this emergency it is not only permissible but even laudable for the amateur to sniff inquiringly through the psychological pasture, essaying modestly to uproot things that the myopic (or, perhaps more accurately, hyper-metropic) professionals have overlooked. The late Friedrich Wilhelm Nietzsche did it often, and the usufructs were many curious and daring guesses, some of them probably close to accuracy, as to the genesis of this, that or the other common delusion of man—*i.e.,* the delusion that the law of the survival of the fittest may be repealed by an act of Congress. Into the same field several very interesting expeditions have been made by Dr. Elsie Clews Parsons, a lady once celebrated by Park Row for her invention of trial marriage—an invention, by the way, in which the Nietzsche aforesaid preceded her by at least a dozen years. The records of her researches are to be found in a brief series of books: "The Family," "The Old-Fashioned Woman" and "Fear and Conventionality." Apparently they have wrung relatively little esteem from the learned, for I seldom encounter a reference to them, and Dr. Parsons herself is denied the very modest reward of mention in "Who's Who in America." Nevertheless, they are extremely instructive books, particularly "Fear and Conventionality." I know of no other work, indeed, which offers a better array of observations upon that powerful complex of assumptions, prejudices, instinctive reactions, racial emotions and unbreakable vices of mind which enters so massively into the daily thinking of all of us. The author does not concern herself, as so many psychologists fall into the habit of doing, with thinking as a purely laboratory phenomenon, a process in vacuo. What she deals with is thinking as it is done by men and women in the real world—thinking that is only half intellectual, the other half being as automatic and unintelligent as swallowing, blinking the eye or falling in love. . . .

It is the business of Dr. Parsons, in "Fear and Conventionality," to prod into certain of the ideas which thus pour into every man's mind from the circumambient air, sweeping away, like some huge cataract, the feeble resistance that his own powers of ratiocination can offer. In particular, she devotes herself to an examination of those general ideas which condition the thought and action of man as a social being—those general ideas which govern his everyday attitude toward his fellow-men and his prevailing view of himself. In one direction they lay upon us the bonds of what we call etiquette, *i.e.*, the duty of considering the habits and feelings of those around us—and in another direction they throttle us with what we call morality—*i.e.*, the rules which protect the life and property of those around us. But, as Dr. Parsons shows, the boundary between etiquette and morality is very dimly drawn, and it is often impossible to say of a given action whether it is downright immoral or merely a breach of the punctilio. Even when the moral law is plainly running, considerations of mere amenity and politeness may still make themselves felt. Thus, as Dr. Parsons points out, there is even an etiquette of adultery. "The *ami de la famille* vows not to kiss his mistress in her husband's house"—not in fear, but "as an expression of conjugal consideration," as a sign that he has not forgotten the thoughtfulness expected of a gentleman. And in this delicate field, as might be expected, the differences in racial attitudes are almost diametrical. The Englishman, surprising his wife with a lover, sues the rogue for damages and has public opinion behind him, but for an American to do it would be for him to lose caste at once and forever. The plain and only duty of the American is to open upon the fellow with artillery, hitting him if the scene is south of the Potomac and missing him if it is above.

I confess to an endless interest in such puzzling niceties, and to much curiosity as to their origins and meaning. Why do we Americans take off our hats when we meet a flapper on the street, and yet stand covered before a male of the highest eminence? A Continental would regard this last as boorish to the last degree; in greeting any equal or superior, male or female, actual or merely conventional, he lifts his head-piece. Why does it strike us as ludicrous to see a man in dress clothes before 6 P.M.? The Continental puts them on whenever he has a solemn visit to make, whether the hour be six or noon. Why do we regard it as indecent to tuck the napkin between the waistcoat buttons—or into the neck!—at meals? The Frenchman does it without thought of crime. So does the Italian. So does the German. All three are punctilious men—far more so, indeed, than we are. Why do we snicker at the man who wears a wedding ring? Most Continentals would stare askance at the husband who didn't. Why is it bad manners in Europe and America to ask a stranger his or her age, and a friendly attention in China? Why do we regard it as absurd to distinguish a woman by her husband's title—*e.g.,* Mrs. Judge Jones, Mrs. Professor Smith? In Teutonic and Scandinavian Europe the omission of the title would be looked upon as an affront.

Such fine distinctions, so ardently supported, raise many interesting questions, but the attempt to answer them quickly gets one bogged. Several years ago I ventured to lift a sad voice against a custom common in America: that of married men, in speaking of their wives, employing the full panoply of "Mrs. Brown." It was my contention—supported, I thought, by logical considerations of the loftiest order—that a husband, in speaking of his wife to his equals, should say "my wife"—that the more formal mode of designation should be reserved for inferiors and for strangers of undetermined position. This contention, somewhat to my surprise, was vigorously combated by various volunteer experts. At first they rested their case upon the mere authority of custom, forgetting that this custom was by no means universal. But finally one of them came forward with a more analytical and cogent defense—the defense, to wit, that "my wife" connoted proprietorship and was thus offensive to a wife's *amour propre.* But what of "my sister" and "my mother"? Surely it is nowhere the custom for a man, addressing an equal, to speak of his sister as "Miss Smith." . . . The discussion, however, came to nothing. It was impossible to carry it on logically. The essence of all such inquiries lies in the discovery that there is a force within the liver and lights of man that is infinitely more potent than logic. His reflections, perhaps, may take on intellectually recognizable forms, but they seldom lead to intellectually recognizable conclusions.

Nevertheless, Dr. Parsons offers something in her book that may conceivably help to a better understanding of them, and that is the doctrine that the strange persistence of these rubber-stamp ideas, often unintelligible and sometimes plainly absurd, is due to fear, and that this fear is the product of a very real danger. The safety of human society lies in the assumption that every individual composing it, in a given situation, will act in a manner hitherto approved as seemly. That is to say, he is expected to react to his environment according to a fixed pattern, not necessarily because that pattern is the best imaginable, but simply because it is determined and understood. If he fails to do so, if he reacts in a novel manner—conducive, perhaps, to his better advantage or to what he thinks is his better advantage—then he disappoints the expectation of those around him, and forces them to meet the new situation he has created by the exercise of independent thought. Such independent thought, to a good many men, is quite impossible, and to the overwhelming majority of men, extremely painful. "To all of us," says Dr. Parsons, "to the animal, to the savage and to the civilized being, few demands are as uncomfortable, . . . disquieting or fearful, as the call to innovate. . . . Adaptations we all of us dislike or hate. We dodge or shirk them as best we may." And the man who compels us to make them against our wills we punish by withdrawing from him that understanding and friendliness which he, in turn, looks for and counts upon. In other words, we set him apart as one who is anti-social and not to be dealt with, and according as his rebellion has been small or great, we call him a boor or a criminal.

This distrust of the unknown, this fear of doing something unusual, is probably at the bottom of many ideas and institutions that are commonly credited to other motives. For example, monogamy. The orthodox explanation of monogamy is that it is a manifestation of the desire to have and to hold property—that the husband defends his solitary right to his wife, even at the cost of his own freedom, because she is the pearl among his chattels. But Dr. Parsons argues, and with a good deal of plausibility, that the real moving force, both in the husband and the wife, may be merely the force of habit, the antipathy to experiment and innovation. It is easier and safer to stick to the one wife than to risk adventures with another wife—and the immense social pressure that I have just described is all on the side of sticking. Moreover, the indulgence of a habit automatically strengthens its bonds. What we have done once or thought once, we are more apt than we were before to do and think again. Or, as the late Prof. William James put it, "the selection of a particular hole to live in, of a particular mate, . . . a particular anything, in short, out of a possible multitude . . . carries with it an insensibility to *other* opportunities and occasions—an insensibility which can only be described physiologically as an inhibition of new impulses by the habit of old ones already formed. The possession of homes and wives of our own makes us strangely insensible to the charms of other people. . . . The original impulse which got us homes, wives, . . . seems to exhaust itself in its first achievements and to leave no surplus energy for reacting on new cases." Thus the benedict looks no more on women (at least for a while), and the post-honeymoon bride, as the late David Graham Phillips once told us, neglects the bedizenments which got her a man.

In view of the popular or general character of most of the taboos which put a brake upon personal liberty in thought and action—that is to say, in view of their enforcement by people in the mass, and not by definite specialists in conduct—it is quite natural to find that they are of extra force in democratic societies, for it is the distinguishing mark of democratic societies that they exalt the powers of the majority almost infinitely, and tend to deny the minority any rights whatever. Under a society dominated by a small caste the revolutionist in custom, despite the axiom to the contrary, has a relatively easy time of it, for the persons whose approval he seeks for his innovation are relatively few in number, and most of them are already habituated to more or less intelligible and independent thinking. But under a democracy he is opposed by a horde so vast that it is a practical impossibility for him, without complex and expensive machinery, to reach and convince all of its members, and even if he could reach them he would find most of them quite incapable of rising out of their accustomed grooves. They cannot understand innovations that are genuinely novel and they don't want to understand them; their one desire is to put them down. Even at this late day, with enlightenment raging through the republic like a pestilence, it would cost the average Southern or Middle Western Congressman his seat if he appeared among his constituents in spats, or wearing a wrist-watch. And if a Justice of the Supreme Court of the United States, however gigantic his learning and his juridic rectitude, were taken in crim. con. with the wife of a Senator, he would be destroyed instanter. And if, suddenly revolting against the democratic idea, he were to propose, however gingerly, its abandonment, he would be destroyed with the same dispatch. . . .

But here I wander into political speculation and no doubt stand in contumacy of some statute of Congress. Dr. Parsons avoids politics in her very interesting book. She confines herself to the purely social relations, *e.g.,* between man and woman, parent and child, host and guest, master and servant. The facts she offers are vastly interesting, and their discovery and coördination reveal a tremendous industry, but of even greater interest are the facts that lie over the margin of her inquiry. Here is a golden opportunity for other investigators: I often wonder that the field is so little explored. Perhaps the Freudians, once they get rid of their sexual obsession, will enter it and chart it. No doubt the inferiority complex described by Prof. Dr. Alfred Adler will one day provide

an intelligible explanation of many of the puzzling phenomena of mob thinking. In the work of Prof. Dr. Freud
himself there is, perhaps, a clew to the origin and
anatomy of Puritanism, that worst of intellectual nephri-
tises. I live in hope that the Freudians will fall upon the
business without much further delay. Why do otherwise
sane men believe in spirits? What is the genesis of the
American axiom that the fine arts are unmanly? What
is the precise machinery of the process called falling in
love? Why do people believe newspapers? . . . Let there
be light!

THE ULSTER POLONIUS

A good half of the humor of the late Mark
Twain consisted of admitting frankly the possession of
vices and weaknesses that all of us have and few of us
care to acknowledge. Practically all of the sagacity of
George Bernard Shaw consists of bellowing vociferously
what every one knows. I think I am as well acquainted
with his works, both hortatory and dramatic, as the next
man. I wrote the first book ever devoted to a discussion
of them, and I read them pretty steadily, even to-day,
and with endless enjoyment. Yet, so far as I know, I
have never found an original idea in them—never a single
statement of fact or opinion that was not anteriorly
familiar, and almost commonplace. Put the thesis of any
of his plays into a plain proposition, and I doubt that you
could find a literate man in Christendom who had not
heard it before, or who would seriously dispute it. The
roots of each one of them are in platitude; the roots of
every effective stage-play are in platitude; that a dramatist
is inevitably a platitudinarian is itself a platitude double
damned. But Shaw clings to the obvious even when he is

27

not hampered by the suffocating conventions of the stage. His Fabian tracts and his pamphlets on the war are veritable compendiums of the undeniable; what is seriously stated in them is quite beyond logical dispute. They have excited a great deal of ire, they have brought down upon him a great deal of amusing abuse, but I have yet to hear of any one actually controverting them. As well try to controvert the Copernican astronomy. They are as bullet-proof in essence as the multiplication table, and vastly more bullet-proof than the Ten Commandments or the Constitution of the United States.

Well, then, why does the Ulsterman kick up such a pother? Why is he regarded as an arch-heretic, almost comparable to Galileo, Nietzsche or Simon Magnus? For the simplest of reasons. Because he practices with great zest and skill the fine art of exhibiting the obvious in unexpected and terrifying lights—because he is a master of the logical trick of so matching two apparently safe premises that they yield an incongruous and inconvenient conclusion—above all, because he is a fellow of the utmost charm and address, quick-witted, bold, limber-tongued, persuasive, humorous, iconoclastic, ingratiating—in brief, a true Kelt, and so the exact antithesis of the solemn Sassenachs who ordinarily instruct and exhort us. Turn to his "Man and Superman," and you will see the whole Shaw machine at work. What he starts out with is the self-evident fact, disputed by no one not idiotic, that a woman has vastly more to gain by marriage, under Christian monogamy, than a man. That fact is as old as monogamy itself; it was, I daresay, the admitted basis of the palace revolution which brought monogamy into the world. But now comes Shaw with an implication that the sentimentality of the world chooses to conceal—with a deduction plainly resident in the original proposition, but kept in safe silence there by a preposterous and hypocritical taboo—to wit, the deduction that women are well aware of the profit that marriage yields for them, and that they are thus much more eager to marry than men are, and ever alert to take the lead in the business. This second fact, to any man who has passed through the terrible years between twenty-five and forty, is as plain as the first, but by a sort of general consent it is not openly stated. Violate that general consent and you are guilty of *scandalum magnatum*. Shaw is simply one who is guilty of *scandalum magnatum* habitually, a professional criminal in that department. It is his life work to announce the obvious in terms of the scandalous.

What lies under the horror of such blabbing is the deepest and most widespread of human weaknesses, which is to say, intellectual cowardice, the craven appetite for mental ease and security, the fear of thinking things out. All men are afflicted by it more or less; not even the most courageous and frank of men likes to admit, in specific terms, that his wife is fat, or that she seduced him to the altar by a transparent trick, or that their joint progeny resemble her brother or father, and are thus cads. A few extraordinary heroes of logic and evidence may do it occasionally, but only occasionally. The average man never does it at all. He is eternally in fear of what he knows in his heart; his whole life is made up of efforts to dodge it and conceal it; he is always running away from what passes for his intelligence and taking refuge in what pass for his higher feelings, *i.e.*, his stupidities, his delusions, his sentimentalities. Shaw is devoted to the art of hauling this recreant fellow up. He is one who, for purposes of sensation, often for the mere joy of outraging the tender-minded, resolutely and mercilessly thinks things out—sometimes with the utmost ingenuity and humor, but often, it must be said, in the same muddled way that the average right-thinker would do it if he ever got up the courage. Remember this formula, and all of the fellow's alleged originality becomes no more than a sort of bad-boy audacity, usually in bad taste. He drags skeletons from their closet and makes them dance obscenely—but every one, of course, knew that they were there all the while. He would produce an excitement of exactly the same kind (though perhaps superior in intensity) if he should walk down the Strand bared to the waist, and so

remind the shocked Londoners of the unquestioned fact
(though conventionally concealed and forgotten) that
he is a mammal, and has an umbilicus.

Turn to a typical play-and-preface of his later canon,
say "Androcles and the Lion." Here the complete Shaw
formula is exposed. On the one hand there is a mass
of platitudes; on the other hand there is the air of a
peep-show. On the one hand he rehearses facts so stale
that even Methodist clergymen have probably heard of
them; on the other hand he states them so scandalously
that the pious get all of the thrills out of the business
that would accompany a view of the rector in liquor
in the pulpit. Here, for example, are some of his con-
tentions:

(a) That the social and economic doctrines preached
by Jesus were indistinguishable from what is now called
Socialism.

(b) That the Pauline transcendentalism visible in the
Acts and the Epistles differs enormously from the simple
humanitarianism set forth in the Four Gospels.

(c) That the Christianity on tap to-day would be almost
as abhorrent to Jesus, supposing Him returned to earth,
as the theories of Nietzsche, Hindenburg or Clemenceau,
and vastly more abhorrent than those of Emma Goldman.

(d) That the rejection of the Biblical miracles, and even
of the historical credibility of the Gospels, by no means
disposes of Christ Himself.

(e) That the early Christians were persecuted, not because their theology was regarded as unsound, but because
their public conduct constituted a nuisance.

It is unnecessary to go on. Could any one imagine a
more abject surrender to the undeniable? Would it be
possible to reduce the German exegesis of a century
and a half to a more depressing series of platitudes?
But his discussion of the inconsistencies between the
Four Gospels is even worse; you will find all of its
points set forth in any elemental treatise upon New
Testament criticism—even in so childish a tract as
Ramsden Balmforth's. He actually dishes up, with a

heavy air of profundity, the news that there is a glaring
conflict between the genealogy of Jesus in Matthew i,
1–17, and the direct claim of divine paternity in Matthew
i, 18. More, he breaks out with the astounding discovery
that Jesus was a good Jew, and that Paul's repudiation
of circumcision (now a cardinal article of the so-called
Christian faith) would have surprised Him and perhaps
greatly shocked Him. The whole preface, running to
114 pages, is made up of just such shop-worn stuff.
Searching it from end to end with eagle eye, I have
failed to find a single fact or argument that was not
previously familiar to me, despite the circumstance that
I ordinarily give little attention to the sacred sciences
and thus might have been expected to be surprised by
their veriest commonplaces.

Nevertheless, this preface makes bouncing reading—
and therein lies the secret of the continued vogue of
Shaw. He has a large and extremely uncommon capacity
for provocative utterance; he knows how to get a touch
of bellicosity into the most banal of doctrines; he is forever on tiptoe, forever challenging, forever *sforzando*.
His matter may be from the public store, even from
the public junk-shop, but his manner is always all his
own. The tune is old, but the words are new. Consider,
for example, his discussion of the personality of Jesus.
The idea is simple and obvious: Jesus was not a long-
faced prophet of evil, like John the Baptist, nor was He
an ascetic, or a mystic. But here is the Shaw way of
saying it: "He was . . . what we call an artist and a
Bohemian in His manner of life." The fact remains
unchanged, but in the extravagant statement of it there
is a shock for those who have been confusing the sour
donkey they hear of a Sunday with the tolerant, likable
Man they profess to worship—and perhaps there is even
a genial snicker in it for their betters. So with his treatment of the Atonement. His objections to it are time-
worn, but suddenly he gets the effect of novelty by
pointing out the quite manifest fact that acceptance of
it is apt to make for weakness, that the man who rejects

it is thrown back upon his own courage and circumspection, and is hence stimulated to augment them. The first argument—that Jesus was of free and easy habits —is so commonplace that I have heard it voiced by a bishop. The second suggests itself so naturally that I myself once employed it against a chance Christian encountered in a Pullman smoking-room. This Christian was at first shocked as he might have been by reading Shaw, but in half an hour he was confessing that he had long ago thought of the objection himself, and put it away as immoral. I well remember his fascinated interest as I showed him how my inability to accept the doctrine put a heavy burden of moral responsibility upon me, and forced me to be more watchful of my conduct than the elect of God, and so robbed me of many pleasant advantages in finance, the dialectic and amour. . . .

A double jest conceals itself in the Shaw legend. The first half of it I have already disclosed. The second half has to do with the fact that Shaw is not at all the wholesale agnostic his fascinated victims see him, but an orthodox Scotch Presbyterian of the most cocksure and bilious sort—in fact, almost the archetype of the blue-nose. In the theory that he is Irish I take little stock. His very name is as Scotch as haggis, and the part of Ireland from which he springs is peopled almost exclusively by Scots. The true Irishman is a romantic. He senses life as a mystery, a thing of wonder, an experience of passion and beauty. In politics he is not logical, but emotional. In religion his interest centers, not in the commandments, but in the sacraments. The Scot, on the contrary, is almost devoid of romanticism. He is a materialist, a logician, a utilitarian. Life to him is not a poem, but a series of police regulations. God is not an indulgent father, but a hanging judge. There are no saints, but only devils. Beauty is a lewdness, redeemable only in the service of morality. It is more important to get on in the world than to be brushed by angels' wings. Here Shaw runs exactly true to type.

Read his critical writings from end to end, and you will not find the slightest hint that objects of art were passing before him as he wrote. He founded, in England, the superstition that Ibsen was no more than a tin-pot evangelist—a sort of brother to General Booth, Mrs. Pankhurst and the syndics of the Sex Hygiene Society. He turned Shakespeare into a bird of evil, croaking dismally in a rain-barrel. He even injected a moral content (by dint of herculean straining) into the music dramas of Richard Wagner—surely the most colossal sacrifices of moral ideas ever made on the altar of beauty! Always the ethical obsession, the hall-mark of the Scotch Puritan, is visible in him. His politics is mere moral indignation. His æsthetic theory is cannibalism upon æsthetics. And in his general writing he is forever discovering an atrocity in what was hitherto passed as no more than a human weakness; he is forever inventing new sins, and demanding their punishment; he always sees his opponent, not only as wrong, but also as a scoundrel. I have called him a Presbyterian. Need I add that he flirts with predestination under the quasi-scientific *nom de guerre* of determinism—that he seems to be convinced that, while men may not be responsible for their virtues, they are undoubtedly responsible for their offendings, and deserve to be clubbed therefor? . . .

And this is Shaw the revolutionist, the heretic! Next, perhaps, we shall be hearing of Benedict XV, the atheist. . . .

GEORGE JEAN NATHAN

One thinks of Gordon Craig, not as a jester, but as a very serious and even solemn fellow. For a dozen years past all the more sober dramatic critics of America have approached him with the utmost politeness, and to the gushing old maids and autointoxicated professors of the Drama League of America he has stood for the last word in theatrical æstheticism. Moreover, a good deal of this veneration has been deserved, for Craig has done excellent work in the theater, and is a man of much force and ingenuity and no little originality. Nevertheless, there must be some flavor of low, barroom wit in him, some echo of Sir Toby Belch and the Captain of Köpenick, for a year or so ago he shook up his admirers with a joke most foul. Need I say that I refer to the notorious Nathan affair? Imagine the scene: the campus Archers and Walkleys in ponderous conclave, perhaps preparing their monthly cablegram of devotion to Maeterlinck. Arrives now a messenger with dreadful news. Gordon Craig, from his far-off Italian retreat, has issued a bull praising Nathan! Which Nathan? George Jean, of course. What! The *Smart Set* scaramouche, the ribald fellow, the raffish mocker, with his praise of Florenz Ziegfeld, his naughty enthusiasm for pretty legs, his contumacious scoffing at Brieux, Belasco, Augustus Thomas, Mrs. Fiske? Aye; even so. And what has Craig to say of him? . . . In brief, that he is the *only* American dramatic critic worth reading, that he knows far more about the theater than all the honorary pallbearers of criticism rolled together, that he is immeasurably the superior, in learning, in sense, in shrewdness, in candor, in plausibility, in skill at writing, of—

But names do not matter. Craig, in fact, did not bother to rehearse them. He simply made a clean sweep of the board, and then deftly placed the somewhat disconcerted Nathan in the center of the vacant space. It was a sad day for the honest donkeys who, for half a decade, had been laboriously establishing Craig's authority in America, but it was a glad day for Knopf, the publisher. Knopf, at the moment, had just issued Nathan's "The Popular Theater." At once he rushed to a job printer in Eighth avenue, ordered 100,000 copies of the Craig encomium, and flooded the country with them. The result was amusing, and typical of the republic. Nathan's previous books, when praised at all, had been praised faintly and with reservations. The fellow, it appeared, was too spoofish; he lacked the sobriety and dignity necessary to a True Critic; he was entertaining but not to be taken seriously. But now, with foreign backing, and particularly English backing, he suddenly began to acquire merit and even a certain vague solemnity —and "The Popular Theater" was reviewed more lavishly and more favorably than I have ever seen any other theater book reviewed, before or since. The phenomenon, as I say, was typical. The childish mass of superstitions passing for civilized opinion in America was turned inside out overnight by one authoritative foreign voice. I have myself been a figure in the same familiar process. All of my books up to "The American Language" were, in the main, hostilely noticed. "A Book of Prefaces," in particular, was manhandled by the orthodox reviewers. Then, just before "The American Language" was issued, the *Mercure de France* printed an article commending "A Book of Prefaces" in high, astounding terms. The consequence was that "The American Language," a far inferior work, was suddenly discovered to be full of merit, and critics of the utmost respectability, who had ignored all my former books, printed extremely friendly reviews of it. . . .

But to return to Nathan. What deceived the Drama Leaguers and other such imposing popinjays for so long, causing them to mistake him for a mere sublimated Alan Dale, was his refusal to take imbecilities seriously, his easy casualness and avoidance of pedagogics, his frank delight in the theater as a show-shop—above all, his bellicose iconoclasm and devastating wit. What Craig, an intelligent man, discerned underneath was his extraordinary capacity for differentiating between sham and reality, his catholic freedom from formulæ and prejudice, his astonishing acquaintance with the literature of the practical theater, his firm grounding in rational æsthetic theory—above all, his capacity for making the thing he writes of interesting, his uncommon craftsmanship. This craftsmanship had already got him a large audience; he had been for half a dozen years, indeed, one of the most widely read of American dramatic critics. But the traditional delusion that sagacity and dullness are somehow identical had obscured the hard and accurate thinking that made the show. What was so amusing seemed necessarily superficial. It remained for Craig to show that this appearance of superficiality was only an appearance, that the Nathan criticism was well planned and soundly articulated, that at the heart of it there was a sound theory of the theater, and of the literature of the theater no less.

And what was that theory? You will find it nowhere put into a ready formula, but the outlines of it must surely be familiar to any one who has read "Another Book on the Theater," "The Popular Theater" and "Mr. George Jean Nathan Presents." In brief, it is the doctrine preached with so much ardor by Benedetto Croce and his disciple, Dr. J. E. Spingarn, and by them borrowed from Goethe and Carlyle—the doctrine, to wit, that every work of art is, at bottom, unique, and that it is the business of the critic, not to label it and pigeonhole it, but to seek for its inner intent and content, and to value it according as that intent is carried out and that content is valid and worth while. This is the precise opposite of the academic critical attitude. The professor is nothing if not a maker of card-indexes; he must classify or be damned. His masterpiece is the dictum that "it is excellent, but it is not a play." Nathan has a far more intelligent and hospitable eye. His criterion, elastic and undefined, is inimical only to the hollow, the meretricious, the fraudulent. It bars out the play of flabby and artificial sentiment. It bars out the cheap melodrama, however gaudily set forth. It bars out the moony mush of the bad imitators of Ibsen and Maeterlinck. It bars out all mere clap-trap and sensation-monging. But it lets in every play, however conceived or designed, that contains an intelligible idea well worked out. It lets in every play by a dramatist who is ingenious, and original, and genuinely amusing. And it lets in every other sort of theatrical spectacle that has an honest aim, and achieves that aim passably, and is presented frankly for what it is.

Bear this theory in mind, and you have a clear explanation of Nathan's actual performances—first, his merciless lampooning of the trade-goods of Broadway and the pifflings of the Drama League geniuses, and secondly, his ardent championing of such widely diverse men as Avery Hopwood, Florenz Ziegfeld, Ludwig Thoma, Lord Dunsany, Sasha Guitry, Lothar Schmidt, Ferenz Molnar, Roberto Bracco and Gerhart Hauptmann, all of whom have one thing in common: they are intelligent and full of ideas and know their trade. In Europe, of course, there are many more such men than in America, and some of the least of them are almost as good as our best. That is why Nathan is forever announcing them and advocating the presentation of their works—not because he favors foreignness for its own sake, but because it is so often accompanied by sound achievement and by stimulating example to our own artists. And that is why, when he tackles the maudlin flubdub of the Broadway dons, he does it with the weapons of comedy, and even of farce. Does an Augustus Thomas rise up with his corn-doctor magic and Sunday-school platitudes, proving heavily that love is mightier than the sword, that a pure heart will baffle the electric chair, that the eye is quicker than the hand? Then Nathan proceeds against him with a slapstick, and makes excellent practice upon his pantaloons. Does a Belasco, thumb on forelock, posture before the yeomanry as a Great Artist, the evidence being a large chromo of a Childs' restaurant, and a studio like a Madison avenue antique-shop? Then Nathan flings a laugh at him and puts him in his place. And does some fat rhinoceros of an actress, unearthing a smutty play by a corn-fed Racine, loose its banal obscenities upon the vulgar in the name of Sex Hygiene, presuming thus to teach a Great Lesson, and break the Conspiracy of Silence, and carry on the Noble Work of Brieux and company, and so save impatient flappers from the Moloch's Sacrifice of the Altar—does such a bumptious and preposterous baggage fill the newspapers with her pishposh and the largest theater in Manhattan with eager dunderheads? Then the ribald Jean has at her with a flour-sack filled with the pollen of the *Ambrosia artemisiaefolia,* driving her from the scene to the tune of her own unearthly sneezing.

Necessarily, he has to lay on with frequency. For one honest play, honestly produced and honestly played, Broadway sees two dozen that are simply so much green-goods. To devote serious exposition to the badness of such stuff would be to descend to the donkeyish futility of William Winter. Sometimes, indeed, even ridicule is not enough; there must be a briefer and more dramatic display of the essential banality. Well, then, why not re-create it in the manner of Croce—but touching up a line here, a color there? The result is burlesque, but burlesque that is the most searching and illuminating sort of criticism. Who will forget Nathan's demonstration that a platitudinous play by Thomas would be better if played backward? A superb bravura piece, enormously beyond the talents of any other American writer on the theater, it smashed the Thomas legend with one stroke. In the little volume called "Bottoms Up" you will find many other such annihilating waggeries.

Nathan does not denounce melodrama with a black cap upon his head, painfully demonstrating its inferiority to the drama of Ibsen, Scribe and Euripides; he simply sits down and writes a little melodrama so extravagantly ludicrous that the whole genus collapses. And he does not prove in four columns of a Sunday paper that French plays done into American are spoiled; he simply shows the spoiling in six lines.

This method, of course, makes for broken heads; it outrages the feelings of tender theatrical mountebanks; it provokes reprisals more or less furtive and behind the door. The theater in America, as in most other countries, is operated chiefly by bounders. Men so constantly associated with actors tend to take on the qualities of the actor—his idiotic vanity, his herculean stupidity, his chronic underrating of his betters. The miasma spreads to dramatists and dramatic critics; the former drift into charlatanery and the latter into a cowardly and disgusting dishonesty. Amid such scenes a man of positive ideas, of civilized tastes and of unshakable integrity is a stranger, and he must face all the hostility that the lower orders of men display to strangers. There is, so far as I know, no tripe-seller in Broadway who has not tried, at one time or another, to dispose of Nathan by *attentat.* He has been exposed to all the measures ordinarily effective against rebellious reviewers, and, resisting them, he has been treated to special treatment with infernal machines of novel and startling design. No writer for the theater has been harder beset, and none has been less incommoded by the onslaught. What is more, he has never made the slightest effort to capitalize this drum-fire—the invariable device of lesser men. So far as I am aware, and I have been in close association with him for ten years, it has had not the slightest effect upon him whatsoever. A thoroughgoing skeptic, with no trace in him of the messianic delusion, he has avoided timorousness on the one hand and indignation on the other. No man could be less a public martyr of the Metcalfe type; it would probably amuse him vastly to hear it argued that his unbreakable independence (and often somewhat high and mighty sniffishness) has been of any public usefulness. I sometimes wonder what keeps such a man in the theater, breathing bad air nightly, gaping at prancing imbeciles, sitting cheek by jowl with cads. Perhaps there is, at bottom, a secret romanticism—a lingering residuum of a boyish delight in pasteboard and spangles, gaudy colors and soothing sounds, preposterous heroes and appetizing wenches. But more likely it is a sense of humor—the zest of a man to whom life is a spectacle that never grows dull—a show infinitely surprising, amusing, buffoonish, vulgar, obscene. The theater, when all is said and done, is not life in miniature, but life enormously magnified, life hideously exaggerated. Its emotions are ten times as powerful as those of reality, its ideas are twenty times as idiotic as those of real men, its lights and colors and sounds are forty times as blinding and deafening as those of nature, its people are grotesque burlesques of every one we know. Here is diversion for a cynic. And here, it may be, is the explanation of Nathan's fidelity.

Whatever the cause of his enchantment, it seems to be lasting. To a man so fertile in ideas and so facile in putting them into words there is a constant temptation to make experiments, to plunge into strange waters, to seek self-expression in ever-widening circles. And yet, at the brink of forty years, Nathan remains faithful to the theater; of his half dozen books, only one does not deal with it, and that one is a very small one. In four or five years he has scarcely written of aught else. I doubt that anything properly describable as enthusiasm is at the bottom of this assiduity; perhaps the right word is curiosity. He is interested mainly, not in the staple fare of the playhouse, but in what might be called its fancy goods—in its endless stream of new men, its restless innovations, the radical overhauling that it has been undergoing in our time. I do not recall, in any of his books or articles, a single paragraph appraising the classics of the stage, or more than a brief note or two on their interpretation. His attention is always turned in a quite opposite direction. He is intensely interested in novelty of whatever sort, if it be only free from sham. Such experimentalists as Max Reinhardt, George Bernard Shaw, Sasha Guitry and the daring nobodies of the Grand Guignol, such divergent originals as Dunsany, Ziegfeld, George M. Cohan and Schnitzler, have enlisted his eager partisanship. He saw something new to our theater in the farces of Hopwood before any one else saw it; he was quick to welcome the novel points of view of Eleanor Gates and Clare Kummer; he at once rescued what was sound in the Little Theatre movement from what was mere attitudinizing and pseudo-intellectuality. In the view of Broadway, an exigent and even malignant fellow, wielding a pen dipped in *aqua fortis,* he is actually amiable to the last degree, and constantly announces pearls in the fodder of the swine. Is the new play in Forty-second Street a serious work of art, as the press-agents and the newspaper reviewers say? Then so are your grandmother's false teeth! Is Maeterlinck a Great Thinker? Then so is Dr. Frank Crane! Is Belasco a profound artist? Then so is the man who designs the ceilings of hotel dining rooms! But let us not weep too soon. In the play around the corner there is a clever scene. Next door, amid sickening dullness, there are two buffoons who could be worse: one clouts the other with a *Blutwurst* filled with mayonnaise. And a block away there is a girl in the second row with a very charming twist of the *vastus medialis.* Let us sniff the roses and forget the thorns!

What this attitude chiefly wars with, even above cheapness, meretriciousness and banality, is the fatuous effort to turn the theater, a place of amusement, into a sort of outhouse to the academic grove—the Maeterlinck-Brieux-Barker complex. No critic in America, and none in England save perhaps Walkley, has combated this movement more vigorously than Nathan. He is under no illusion as to the functions and limitations of the stage. He knows, with Victor Hugo, that the best it can do, in the domain of ideas, is to "turn thoughts into food for the crowd," and he knows that only the simplest and shakiest ideas may undergo that transformation. Coming upon the scene at the height of the Ibsen mania of half a generation ago, he ranged himself against its windy pretenses from the start. He saw at once the high merit of Ibsen as a dramatic craftsman and welcomed him as a reformer of dramatic technique, but he also saw how platitudinous was the ideational content of his plays and announced the fact in terms highly offensive to the Ibsenites. . . . But the Ibsenites have vanished and Nathan remains. He has survived, too, the Brieux hubbub. He has lived to preach the funeral sermon of the Belasco legend. He has himself sworded Maeterlinck and Granville Barker. He has done frightful execution upon many a poor mime. And meanwhile, breasting the murky tide of professorial buncombe, of solemn pontificating, of Richard-Burtonism, Clayton-Hamiltonism and other such decaying forms of William-Winterism, he has rescued dramatic criticism among us from its exile with theology, embalming and obstetrics, and given it a place among what Nietzsche called the gay sciences, along with war, fiddle-playing and laparotomy. He has made it amusing, stimulating, challenging, even, at times, a bit startling. And to the business, artfully concealed, he has brought a sound and thorough acquaintance with the heavy work of the pioneers, Lessing, Schlegel, Hazlitt, Lewes *et al*—and an even wider acquaintance, lavishly displayed, with every nook and corner of the current theatrical scene across the water. And to discharge this extraordinarily copious mass of information he has hauled and battered the English language into new and often astounding forms, and when English has failed he has helped it out with French, German, Italian, American, Swedish, Russian, Turkish, Latin, Sanskrit and Old Church Slavic, and with algebraic symbols, chemical formulæ, musical notation and the signs of the Zodiac. . . .

This manner, of course, is not without its perils. A

man so inordinately articulate is bound to succumb, now and then, to the seductions of mere virtuosity. The average writer, and particularly the average critic of the drama, does well if he gets a single new and racy phrase into an essay; Nathan does well if he dilutes his inventions with enough commonplaces to enable the average reader to understand his discourse at all. He carries the avoidance of the *cliché* to the length of an *idée fixe*. It would be difficult, in all his books, to find a dozen of the usual rubber stamps of criticism; I daresay it would kill him, or, at all events, bring him down with cholera morbus, to discover that he had called a play "convincing" or found "authority" in the snorting of an English actor-manager. At best, this incessant flight from the obvious makes for a piquant and arresting style, a procession of fantastic and often highly pungent neologisms—in brief, for Nathanism. At worst, it becomes artificiality, pedantry, obscurity. I cite an example from an essay on Eleanor Gates' "The Poor Little Rich Girl," prefaced to the printed play:

> As against the not unhollow symbolic strut and gasconade of such over-pæaned pieces as, let us for example say, "The Blue Bird" of Maeterlinck, so simple and unaffected a bit of stage writing as this—of school dramatic intrinsically the same—cajoles the more honest heart and satisfies more plausibly and fully those of us whose thumbs are ever being pulled professionally for a native stage less smeared with the snobberies of empty, albeit high-sounding, nomenclatures from overseas.

Fancy that, Hedda!—and in praise of a "simple and unaffected bit of stage writing"! I denounced it at the time, *circa* 1916, and perhaps with some effect. At all events, I seem to notice a gradual disentanglement of the parts of speech. The old florid invention is still there; one encounters startling coinages in even the most casual of reviews; the thing still flashes and glitters; the tune is yet upon the E string. But underneath I hear a more sober rhythm than of old. The fellow, in fact, takes on a sedater habit, both in style and in point of view. Without abandoning anything essential, without making the slightest concession to the orthodox opinion that he so magnificently disdains, he yet begins to yield to the middle years. The mere shocking of the stupid is no longer as charming as it used to be. What he now offers is rather more *gemütlich;* sometimes it even verges upon the instructive. . . . But I doubt that Nathan will ever become a professor, even if he enjoys the hideously prolonged senility of a William Winter. He will be full of surprises to the end. With his last gasp he will make a phrase to flabbergast a dolt.

THREE AMERICAN IMMORTALS

1. *Aristotelean Obsequies*

I take the following from the Boston *Herald* of May 1, 1882:

> A beautiful floral book stood at the left of the pulpit, being spread out on a stand. . . . Its last page was composed of white carnations, white daisies and light-colored immortelles. On the leaf was displayed, in neat letters of purple immortelles, the word "Finis." This device was about two feet square, and its border was composed of different colored tea-roses. The other portion of the book was composed of dark and light-colored flowers. . . . The front of the large pulpit was covered with a mass of white pine boughs laid on loosely. In the center of this mass of boughs appeared a large harp composed of yellow jonquils. . . . Above this harp was a handsome bouquet of dark pansies. On each side appeared large clusters of calla lilies.

Well, what have we here? The funeral of a Grand Exalted Pishposh of the Odd Fellows, of an East Side Tammany leader, of an aged and much respected brothel-keeper? Nay. What we have here is the funeral of Ralph Waldo Emerson. It was thus that New England lavished the loveliest fruits of the Puritan æsthetic upon the bier of her greatest son. It was thus that Puritan *Kultur* mourned a philosopher.

2. *Edgar Allan Poe*

The myth that there is a monument to Edgar Allan Poe in Baltimore is widely believed; there are even persons who, stopping off in Baltimore to eat oysters, go to look at it. As a matter of fact, no such monument exists. All that the explorer actually finds is a cheap and hideous tombstone in the corner of a Presbyterian church-yard—a tombstone quite as bad as the worst in Père La Chaise. For twenty-six years after Poe's death there was not even this: the grave remained wholly unmarked. Poe had surviving relatives in Baltimore, and they were well-to-do. One day one of them ordered a local stone-cutter to put a plain stone over the grave. The stonecutter hacked it out and was preparing to haul it to the church-yard when a runaway freight-train smashed into his stoneyard and broke the stone to bits. Thereafter the Poes seem to have forgotten Cousin Edgar; at all events, nothing further was done.

The existing tombstone was erected by a committee of Baltimore schoolmarms, and cost about $1,000. It took the dear girls ten long years to raise the money. They started out with a "literary entertainment" which yielded $380. This was in 1865. Six years later the fund had made such slow progress that, with accumulated interest, it came to but $587.02. Three years more went by: it now reached $627.55. Then some anonymous Poeista came down with $100, two others gave $50 each, one of the devoted schoolmarms raised $52 in nickels and dimes, and George W. Childs agreed to pay any re-maining deficit. During all this time not a single Ameri-can author of position gave the project any aid. And when, finally, a stone was carved and set up and the time came for the unveiling, the only one who appeared at the ceremony was Walt Whitman. All the other persons present were Baltimore nobodies—chiefly school-

teachers and preachers. There were three set speeches—
one by the principal of a local high school, the second by
a teacher in the same seminary, and the third by a man
who was invited to give his "personal recollections" of
Poe, but who announced in his third sentence that "I
never saw Poe but once, and our interview did not last
an hour."

This was the gaudiest Poe celebration ever held in
America. The poet has never enjoyed such august posthu-
mous attentions as those which lately flattered the shade
of James Russell Lowell. At his actual burial, in 1849,
exactly eight persons were present, of whom six were
relatives. He was planted, as I have said, in a Presbyterian
churchyard, among generations of honest believers in
infant damnation, but the officiating clergyman was a
Methodist. Two days after his death a Baptist gentleman
of God, the illustrious Rufus W. Griswold, printed a
defamatory article upon him in the New York *Tribune,*
and for years it set the tone of native criticism of him.
And so he rests: thrust among Presbyterians by a
Methodist and formally damned by a Baptist.

3. *Memorial Service*

Let us summon from the shades the immortal soul
of James Harlan, born in 1820, entered into rest in 1899.
In the year 1865 this Harlan resigned from the United
States Senate to enter the cabinet of Abraham Lincoln
as Secretary of the Interior. One of the clerks in that
department, at $600 a year, was Walt Whitman, lately
emerged from three years of hard service as an army
nurse during the Civil War. One day, discovering that
Whitman was the author of a book called "Leaves of
Grass," Harlan ordered him incontinently kicked out,
and it was done forthwith. Let us remember this event
and this man; he is too precious to die. Let us repair,
once a year, to our accustomed houses of worship and
there give thanks to God that one day in 1865 brought
together the greatest poet that America has ever produced
and the damndest ass.

ROOSEVELT: AN AUTOPSY

One thinks of Dr. Woodrow Wilson's biography of George Washington as one of the strangest of all the world's books. Washington: the first, and perhaps also the last American gentleman. Wilson: the self-bamboozled Presbyterian, the right-thinker, the great moral statesman, the perfect model of the Christian cad. It is as if the Rev. Dr. Billy Sunday should do a biography of Charles Darwin—almost as if Dr. Wilson himself should dedicate his senility to a life of the Chevalier Bayard, or the Cid, or Christ. . . . But such phenomena, of course, are not actually rare in the republic; here everything happens that is forbidden by the probabilities and the decencies. The chief native critic of beautiful letters, for a whole generation, was a Baptist clergyman; he was succeeded by a literary Wall Street man, who gave way, in turn, to a soviet of ninth-rate pedagogues; this very curious apostolic succession I have already discussed. The dean of the music critics, even to-day, is a translator of grand opera libretti, and probably one of the worst that ever lived. Return, now, to political biography. Who can think of anything in American literature comparable to Morley's life of Gladstone, or Trevelyan's life of Macaulay, or Carlyle's Frederick, or even Winston Churchill's life of his father? I dredge my memory hopelessly; only William Graham Sumner's study of Andrew Jackson emerges—an extraordinarily astute and careful piece of work by one of the two most underestimated Americans of his generation, the other being Daniel Coit Gilman. But where is the first-rate biography of Washington—sound, fair, penetrating, honest, done by a man capable of comprehending the English gentry of the eighteenth century? And how long must we wait for adequate treatises upon Jefferson, Hamilton, Sam Adams, Aaron Burr, Henry Clay, Calhoun, Webster, Sumner, Grant, Sherman, Lee?

Even Lincoln is yet to be got vividly between the covers of a book. The Nicolay-Hay work is quite impossible; it is not a biography, but simply a huge storehouse of biographical raw materials; whoever can read it can also read the official Records of the Rebellion. All the other standard lives of old Abe—for instance, those of Lamon, Herndon and Weil, Stoddard, Morse and Miss Tarbell—fail still worse; when they are not grossly preachy and disingenuous they are trivial. So far as I can make out, no genuinely scientific study of the man has ever been attempted. The amazing conflict of testimony about him remains a conflict; the most elemental facts are yet to be established; he grows vaguer and more fabulous as year follows year. One would think that, by this time, the question of his religious views (to take one example) ought to be settled, but apparently it is not, for no longer than a year ago there came a reverend author, Dr. William E. Barton, with a whole volume upon the subject, and I was as much in the dark after reading it as I had been before I opened it. All previous biographers, it appeared by this author's evidence, had either dodged the problem, or lied. The official doctrine, in this as in other departments, is obviously quite unsound. One hears in the Sunday-schools that Abe was an austere and pious fellow, constantly taking the name of God in whispers, just as one reads in the school history-books that he was a shining idealist, holding all his vast powers by the magic of an inner and ineffable virtue. Imagine a man getting on in American politics, interesting and enchanting the boobery, sawing off the horns of other politicians, elbowing his way through primaries and conventions, by the magic of virtue! As well talk of fetching the mob by hawking exact and arctic justice! Abe, in fact, must have been a fellow highly skilled at the great democratic art of gum-shoeing. I like to think of him as one who defeated such politicians as Stanton, Douglas and Sumner with their own weapons—deftly leading them into ambuscades, boldly pulling their noses, magnificently hamstringing and hornswoggling them—in brief, as a politician of extraordinary talents, who loved the game for its own sake, and had the measure of the crowd. His official portraits, both in prose and in daguerreotype, show him wearing the mien of a man about to be hanged; one never sees him smiling. Nevertheless, one hears that, until he emerged from Illinois, they always put the women, children and clergy to bed when he got a few gourds of corn aboard, and it is a matter of unescapable record that his career in the State Legislature was indistinguishable from that of a Tammany Nietzsche.

But, as I say, it is hopeless to look for the real man in the biographies of him: they are all full of distortion, chiefly pious and sentimental. The defect runs through the whole of American political biography, and even through the whole of American history. Nearly all our professional historians are poor men holding college posts, and they are ten times more cruelly beset by the ruling politico-plutocratic-social oligarchy than ever the Prussian professors were by the Hohenzollerns. Let them diverge in the slightest from what is the current official doctrine, and they are turned out of their chairs with a ceremony suitable for the expulsion of a drunken valet. During the recent war a herd of two thousand and five hundred such miserable slaves was organized by Dr. Creel to lie for their country, and they at once fell upon the congenial task of rewriting American history to make it accord with the ideas of H. P. Davison, Admiral Sims, Nicholas Murray Butler, the Astors, Barney Baruch and Lord Northcliffe. It was a committee of this herd that solemnly pledged the honor of American scholarship to the authenticity of the celebrated Sisson documents. . . .

In the face of such acute miliary imbecility it is not

49

surprising to discover that all of the existing biographies of the late Colonel Roosevelt—and they have been rolling off the presses at a dizzy rate since his death—are feeble, inaccurate, ignorant and preposterous. I have read, I suppose, at least ten of these tomes during the past year or so, and in all of them I have found vastly more gush than sense. Lawrence Abbott's "Impressions of Theodore Roosevelt" and William Roscoe Thayer's "Theodore Roosevelt" may well serve as specimens. Abbott's book is the composition, not of an unbiased student of the man, but of a sort of groom of the hero. He is so extremely eager to prove that Roosevelt was the perfect right-thinker, according to the transient definitions of right-thinking, that he manages to get a flavor of dubiousness into his whole chronicle. I find myself doubting him even when I know that he is honest and suspect that he is right. As for Thayer, all he offers is a hasty and hollow pot-boiler—such a work as might have been well within the talents of, say, the late Murat Halstead or the editor of the New York *Times*. This Thayer has been heavily praised of late as the Leading American Biographer, and one constantly hears that some new university has made him *Legum Doctor,* or that he has been awarded a medal by this or that learned society, or that the post has brought him a new ribbon from some literary potentate in foreign parts. If, in fact, he is actually the cock of the walk in biography, then all I have said against American biographers is too mild and mellow. What one finds in his book is simply the third-rate correctness of a Boston colonial. Consider, for example, his frequent discussions of the war—a necessity in any work on Roosevelt. In England there is the mob's view of the war, and there is the view of civilized and intelligent men, *e.g.,* Lansdowne, Loreburn, Austin Harrison, Morel, Keynes, Haldane, Hirst, Balfour, Robert Cecil. In New England, it would appear, the two views coalesce, with the first outside. There is scarcely a line on the subject in Thayer's book that might not have been written by Horatio Bottomley. . . .

Obviously, Roosevelt's reaction to the war must occupy a large part of any adequate biography of him, for that reaction was probably more comprehensively typical of the man than any other business of his life. It displayed not only his whole stock of political principles, but also his whole stock of political tricks. It plumbed, on the one hand, the depths of his sagacity, and on the other hand the depths of his insincerity. Fundamentally, I am convinced, he was quite out of sympathy with, and even quite unable to comprehend the body of doctrine upon which the Allies, and later the United States, based their case. To him it must have seemed insane when it was not hypocritical, and hypocritical when it was not insane. His instincts were profoundly against a new loosing of democratic fustian upon the world; he believed in strongly centralized states, founded upon power and devoted to enterprises far transcending mere internal government; he was an imperialist of the type of Cecil Rhodes, Treitschke and Delcassé. But the fortunes of domestic politics jockeyed him into the position of standing as the spokesman of an almost exactly contrary philosophy. The visible enemy before him was Wilson. What he wanted as a politician was something that he could get only by wresting it from Wilson, and Wilson was too cunning to yield it without making a tremendous fight, chiefly by chicane—whooping for peace while preparing for war, playing mob fear against mob fear, concealing all his genuine motives and desires beneath clouds of chautauqual rhetoric, leading a mad dance whose tune changed at every swing. Here was an opponent that more than once puzzled Roosevelt, and in the end flatly dismayed him. Here was a mob-master with a technique infinitely more subtle and effective than his own. So lured into an unequal combat, the Rough Rider got bogged in absurdities so immense that only the democratic anæsthesia to absurdity saved him. To make any progress at all he was forced into fighting against his own side. He passed from the scene bawling piteously for a cause that, at bottom, it is impossible to imagine him believing in, and in terms of a philosophy that was as foreign to his true faith as it was to the faith of Wilson. In the whole affair there was a colossal irony. Both contestants were intrinsically frauds.

The fraudulence of Wilson is now admitted by all save a few survivors of the old corps of official press-agents, most of them devoid of both honesty and intelligence. No unbiased man, in the presence of the revelations of Bullitt, Keynes and a hundred other witnesses, and of the Russian and Shantung performances, and of innumerable salient domestic phenomena, can now believe that the *Doctor dulcifluus* was ever actually in favor of any of the brummagem ideals he once wept for, to the edification of a moral universe. They were, at best, no more than ingenious *ruses de guerre,* and even in the day of their widest credit it was the Espionage Act and the Solicitor-General to the Postoffice, rather than any plausibility in their substance, that got them their credit. In Roosevelt's case the imposture is less patent; he died before it was fully unmasked. What is more, his death put an end to whatever investigation of it was under way, for American sentimentality holds that it is indecent to inquire into the weaknesses of the dead, at least until all the flowers have withered on their tombs. When, a year ago, I ventured in a magazine article to call attention to Roosevelt's philosophical kinship to the Kaiser I received letters of denunciation from all parts of the United States, and not a few forthright demands that I recant on penalty of lynch law. Prudence demanded that I heed these demands. We live in a curious and often unsafe country. Haled before a Roosevelt judge for speeding my automobile, or spitting on the sidewalk, or carrying a jug, I might have been railroaded for ten years under some constructive corollary of the Espionage Act. But there were two things that supported me in my contumacy to the departed. One was a profound reverence for and fidelity to the truth, sometimes almost amounting to fanaticism. The other was the support of my venerable brother in epistemology, the eminent Iowa right-thinker and patriot, Prof. Dr. S. P. Sherman. Writing in the *Nation,* where he survives from more seemly days than these, Prof. Dr. Sherman put the thing in plain terms. "With the essentials in the religion of the militarists of Germany," he said, "Roosevelt was utterly in sympathy."

Utterly? Perhaps the adverb is a bit too strong. There was in the man a certain instinctive antipathy to the concrete aristocrat and in particular to the aristocrat's private code—the product, no doubt, of his essentially *bourgeois* origin and training. But if he could not go with the Junkers all the way, he could at least go the whole length of their distrust of the third order—the undifferentiated masses of men below. Here, I daresay, he owed a lot to Nietzsche. He was always reading German books, and among them, no doubt, were "Also sprach Zarathustra" and "Jenseits von Gut und Böse." In fact, the echoes were constantly sounding in his own harangues. Years ago, as an intellectual exercise while confined to hospital, I devised and printed a give-away of the Rooseveltian philosophy in parallel columns—in one column, extracts from "The Strenuous Life"; in the other, extracts from Nietzsche. The borrowings were numerous and unescapable. Theodore had swallowed Friedrich as a peasant swallows Peruna—bottle, cork, label and testimonials. Worse, the draft whetted his appetite, and soon he was swallowing the Kaiser of the *Garde-Kavallerie*-mess and battleship-launching speeches —another somewhat defective Junker. In his palmy days it was often impossible to distinguish his politico-theological bulls from those of Wilhelm; during the war, indeed, I suspect that some of them were boldly lifted by the British press bureau, and palmed off as felonious imprudences out of Potsdam. Wilhelm was his model in *Weltpolitik,* and in sociology, exegetics, administration, law, sport and connubial polity no less. Both roared for doughty armies, eternally prepared—for the theory that the way to prevent war is to make all conceivable enemies think twice, thrice, ten times. Both dreamed

53

of gigantic navies, with battleships as long as Brooklyn Bridge. Both preached incessantly the duty of the citizen to the state, with the soft pedal upon the duty of the state to the citizen. Both praised the habitually gravid wife. Both delighted in the armed pursuit of the lower fauna. Both heavily patronized the fine arts. Both were intimates of God, and announced His desires with authority. Both believed that all men who stood opposed to them were prompted by the devil and would suffer for it in hell.

If, in fact, there was any difference between them, it was all in favor of Wilhelm. For one thing, he made very much fewer speeches; it took some colossal event, such as the launching of a dreadnaught or the birthday of a colonel-general, to get him upon his legs; the Reichstag was not constantly deluged with his advice and upbraiding. For another thing, he was a milder and more modest man—one more accustomed, let us say, to circumstance and authority, and hence less intoxicated by the greatness of his state. Finally, he had been trained to think, not only of his own immediate fortunes, but also of the remote interests of a family that, in his most expansive days, promised to hold the throne for many years, and so he cultivated a certain prudence, and even a certain ingratiating suavity. He could, on occasion, be extremely polite to an opponent. But Roosevelt was never polite to an opponent; perhaps a gentleman, by American standards, he was surely never a gentle man. In a political career of nearly forty years he was never even fair to an opponent. All of his gabble about the square deal was merely so much protective coloration, easily explicable on elementary Freudian grounds. No man, facing Roosevelt in the heat of controversy, ever actually got a square deal. He took extravagant advantages; he played to the worst idiocies of the mob; he hit below the belt almost habitually. One never thinks of him as a duelist, say of the school of Disraeli, Palmerston and, to drop a bit, Blaine. One always thinks of him as a glorified longshoreman engaged eternally in cleaning out bar-rooms—and not too proud to gouge when the inspiration came to him, or to bite in the clinches, or to oppose the relatively fragile brass knuckles of the code with chair-legs, bung-starters, cuspidors, demijohns, and ice-picks.

Abbott and Thayer, in their books, make elaborate efforts to depict their hero as one born with a deep loathing of the whole Prussian scheme of things, and particularly of the Prussian technique in combat. Abbott even goes so far as to hint that the attentions of the Kaiser, during Roosevelt's historic tour of Europe on his return from Africa, were subtly revolting to him. Nothing could be more absurd. Prof. Dr. Sherman, in the article I have mentioned, blows up that nonsense by quoting from a speech made by the tourist in Berlin—a speech arguing for the most extreme sort of militarism in a manner that must have made even some of the Junkers blow their noses dubiously. The disproof need not be piled up; the America that Roosevelt dreamed of was always a sort of swollen Prussia, truculent without and regimented within. There was always a clank of the saber in his discourse; he could not discuss the tamest matter without swaggering in the best dragoon fashion. Abbott gets into yet deeper waters when he sets up the doctrine that the invasion of Belgium threw his darling into an instantaneous and tremendous fit of moral indignation, and that the curious delay in the public exhibition thereof, so much discussed since, was due to his (Abbott's) fatuous interference—a *faux pas* later regretted with much bitterness. Unluckily, the evidence he offers leaves me full of doubts. What the doctrine demands that one believe is simply this: that the man who, for mere commercial advantage and (in Frederick's famous phrase) "to make himself talked of in the world," tore up the treaty of 1848 between the United States and Colombia (*geb.* New Grenada), whereby the United States forever guaranteed the "sovereignty and ownership" of the Colombians in the isthmus of Panama—that this same man, thirteen years later, was horrified into a fever when Germany, facing powerful foes on two fronts, tore up the treaty of 1832, guaranteeing, not the sovereignty, but the bald neutrality of Belgium—a neutrality already destroyed, according to the evidence before the Germans, by Belgium's own acts.

It is hard, without an inordinate strain upon the credulity, to believe any such thing, particularly in view of the fact that this instantaneous indignation of the most impulsive and vocal of men was diligently concealed for at least six weeks, with reporters camped upon his doorstep day and night, begging him to say the very thing that he left so darkly unsaid. Can one imagine Roosevelt, with red-fire raging within him and sky-rockets bursting in his veins, holding his peace for a month and a half? I have no doubt whatever that Abbott, as he says, desired to avoid embarrassing Dr. Wilson— but think of Roosevelt showing any such delicacy! For one, I am not equal to the feat. All that unprecedented reticence, in fact, is far more readily explicable on other and less lofty grounds. What really happened I presume to guess. My guess is that Roosevelt, like the great majority of other Americans, was *not* instantly and automatically outraged by the invasion of Belgium. On the contrary, he probably viewed it as a regrettable, but not unexpected or unparalleled device of war—if anything, as something rather thrillingly gaudy and effective—a fine piece of virtuosity, pleasing to a military connoisseur. But then came the deluge of Belgian atrocity stories, and the organized campaign to enlist American sympathies. It succeeded very quickly. By the middle of August the British press bureau was in full swing; by the beginning of September the country was flooded with inflammatory stuff; six weeks after the war opened it was already hazardous for a German in America to state his country's case. Meanwhile, the Wilson administration had declared for neutrality, and was still making a more or less sincere effort to practice it, at least on the surface. Here was Roosevelt's opportunity, and he leaped to it with sure instinct. On the one side was the administration that he detested, and that all his self-interest (*e.g.,* his yearning to get back his old leadership and to become President again in 1917) prompted him to deal a mortal blow, and on the other side was a ready-made issue, full of emotional possibilities, stupendously pumped up by extremely clever propaganda, and so far unembraced by any other rabble-rouser of the first magnitude. Is it any wonder that he gave a whoop, jumped upon his cayuse, and began screaming for war? In war lay the greatest chance of his life. In war lay the confusion and destruction of Wilson, and the melodramatic renaissance of the Rough Rider, the professional hero, the national Barbarossa.

In all this, of course, I strip the process of its plumes and spangles, and expose a chain of causes and effects that Roosevelt himself, if he were alive, would denounce as grossly contumelious to his native purity of spirit—and perhaps in all honesty. It is not necessary to raise any doubts as to that honesty. No one who has given any study to the development and propagation of political doctrine in the United States can have failed to notice how the belief in issues among politicians tends to run in exact ratio to the popularity of those issues. Let the populace begin suddenly to swallow a new panacea or to take fright at a new bugaboo, and almost instantly nine-tenths of the master-minds of politics begin to believe that the panacea is a sure cure for all the malaises of the republic, and the bugaboo an immediate and unbearable menace to all law, order and domestic tranquillity. At the bottom of this singular intellectual resilience, of course, there is a good deal of hard calculation; a man must keep up with the procession of crazes, or his day is swiftly done. But in it there are also considerations a good deal more subtle, and maybe less discreditable. For one thing, a man devoted professionally to patriotism and the wisdom of the fathers is very apt to come to a resigned sort of acquiescence in all the doctrinaire rubbish that lies beneath the national scheme of things—to believe, let us say, if not that the plain people are gifted with an infallible sagacity, then at least that they have an inalienable right to see their follies executed. Poll-parroting nonsense as a matter of daily routine, the politician ends by assuming that it is sense, even though he doesn't believe it. For another thing, there is the contagion of mob enthusiasm—a much underestimated murrain. We all saw what it could do during the war—college professors taking their tune from the yellow journals, the rev. clergy performing in the pulpit like so many Liberty Loan orators in five-cent moving-picture houses, hysteria grown epidemic like the influenza. No man is so remote and arctic that he is wholly safe from that contamination; it explains many extravagant phenomena of a democratic society; in particular, it explains why the mob leader is so often a victim to his mob.

Roosevelt, a perfectly typical politician, devoted to the trade, not primarily because he was gnawed by ideals, but because he frankly enjoyed its rough-and-tumble encounters and its gaudy rewards, was probably moved in both ways—and also by the hard calculation that I have mentioned. If, by any ineptness of the British press-agents, tear-squeezers and orphan-exhibitors, indignation over the invasion of Belgium had failed to materialize—if, worse still, some gross infringement of American rights by the English had caused it to be forgotten completely—if, finally, Dr. Wilson had been whooping for war with the populace firmly against him—in such event it goes without saying that the moral horror of Dr. Roosevelt would have stopped short at a very low amperage, and that he would have refrained from making it the center of his polity. But with things as they were, lying neatly to his hand, he permitted it to take on an extraordinary virulence, and before long all his old delight in German militarism had been converted into a lofty detestation of German militarism, and its chief spokesman on this side of the Atlantic became its chief opponent. Getting rid of that old delight, of course, was not easily achieved. The concrete enthusiasm could be throttled, but the habit of mind remained. Thus one beheld the curious spectacle of militarism belabored in terms of militarism—of the Kaiser arraigned in unmistakably *kaiserliche* tones.

Such violent swallowings and regurgitations were no novelties to the man. His whole political career was marked, in fact, by performances of the same sort. The issues that won him most votes were issues that, at bottom, he didn't believe in; there was always a mental reservation in his rhetoric. He got into politics, not as a tribune of the plain people, but as an amateur reformer of the snobbish type common in the eighties, by the *Nation* out of the Social Register. He was a young Harvard man scandalized by the discovery that his town was run by men with such names as Michael O'Shaunnessy and Terence Googan—that his social inferiors were his political superiors. His sympathies were essentially anti-democratic. He had a high view of his private position as a young fellow of wealth and education. He believed in strong centralization—the concentration of power in a few hands, the strict regimentation of the nether herd, the abandonment of democratic platitudes. His heroes were such Federalists as Morris and Hamilton; he made his first splash in the world by writing about them and praising them. Worse, his daily associations were with the old Union League crowd of high-tariff Republicans—men almost apoplectically opposed to every movement from below—safe and sane men, highly conservative and suspicious men—the profiteers of peace, as they afterward became the profiteers of war. His early adventures in politics were not very fortunate, nor did they reveal any capacity for leadership. The bosses of the day took him in rather humorously, played him for what they could get out of him, and then turned him loose. In a few years he became disgusted and went West. Returning after a bit, he encountered catastrophe: as a candidate for Mayor of New York he was drubbed unmercifully. He went back to the West. He was, up to this time, a comic figure —an anti-politician victimized by politicians, a pseudo-aristocrat made ridiculous by the mob-masters he detested.

But meanwhile something was happening that changed the whole color of the political scene, and was destined, eventually, to give Roosevelt his chance. That something was a shifting in what might be called the foundations of reform. Up to now it had been an essentially aristocratic movement—superior, sniffish and anti-democratic. But hereafter it took on a strongly democratic color and began to adopt democratic methods. More, the change gave it new life. What Harvard, the Union League Club and the *Nation* had failed to accomplish, the plain people now undertook to accomplish. This invasion of the old citadel of virtue was first observed in the West, and its manifestations out there must have given Roosevelt a good deal more disquiet than satisfaction. It is impossible to imagine him finding anything to his taste in the outlandish doings of the Populists, the wild schemes of the pre-Bryan dervishes. His instincts were against all that sort of thing. But as the movement spread toward the East it took on a certain urbanity, and by the time it reached the seaboard it had begun to be quite civilized. With this new brand of reform Roosevelt now made terms. It was full of principles that outraged all his pruderies, but it at least promised to work. His entire political history thereafter, down to the day of his death, was a history of compromises with the new forces—of a gradual yielding, for strategic purposes, to ideas that were intrinsically at odds with his congenital prejudices. When, after a generation of that sort of compromising, the so-called Progressive party was organized and he seized the leadership of it from the Westerners who had founded it, he performed a feat of wholesale englutination that must forever hold a high place upon the roll of political prodigies. That is to say, he swallowed at one gigantic gulp, and out of the same herculean jug, the most amazing mixture of social, political and economic perunas ever got down by one hero, however valiant, however athirst—a cocktail made up of all the elixirs hawked among the boobery in his time, from woman suffrage to the direct primary, and from the initiative and referendum to the short ballot, and from prohibition to public ownership, and from trust-busting to the recall of judges.

This homeric achievement made him the head of the

most tatterdemalion party ever seen in American politics
—a party composed of such incompatible ingredients and
hung together so loosely that it began to disintegrate the
moment it was born. In part it was made up of mere
disordered enthusiasts—believers in anything and everything, pathetic victims of the credulity complex, habitual
followers of jitney messiahs, incurable hopers and snuf-
flers. But in part it was also made up of rice converts like
Roosevelt himself—men eager for office, disappointed by
the old parties, and now quite willing to accept any aid
that half-idiot doctrinaires could give them. I have no
doubt that Roosevelt himself, carried away by the emotional storms of the moment and especially by the quasi-
religious monkey-shines that marked the first Progressive
convention, gradually convinced himself that at least
some of the doctrinaires, in the midst of all their imbecility, yet preached a few ideas that were workable, and
perhaps even sound. But at bottom he was against them,
and not only in the matter of their specific sure cures,
but also in the larger matter of their childish faith in the
wisdom and virtue of the plain people. Roosevelt, for all
his fluent mastery of democratic counter-words, democratic gestures and all the rest of the armamentarium of
the mob-master, had no such faith in his heart of hearts.
He didn't believe in democracy; he believed simply in
government. His remedy for all the great pangs and
longings of existence was not a dispersion of authority,
but a hard concentration of authority. He was not in
favor of unlimited experiment; he was in favor of a rigid
control from above, a despotism of inspired prophets and
policemen. He was not for democracy as his followers
understood democracy, and as it actually is and must be;
he was for a paternalism of the true Bismarckian pattern,
almost of the Napoleonic or Ludendorffian pattern—a
paternalism concerning itself with all things, from the
regulation of coal-mining and meat-packing to the regulation of spelling and marital rights. His instincts were
always those of the property-owning Tory, not those of
the romantic Liberal. All the fundamental objects of

Liberalism—free speech, unhampered enterprise, the least possible governmental interference—were abhorrent to him. Even when, for campaign purposes, he came to terms with the Liberals his thoughts always ranged far afield. When he tackled the trusts the thing that he had in his mind's eye was not the restoration of competition but the subordination of all private trusts to one great national trust, with himself at its head. And when he attacked the courts it was not because they put their own prejudice before the law but because they refused to put *his* prejudices before the law.

In all his career no one ever heard him make an argument for the rights of the citizen; his eloquence was always expended in expounding the duties of the citizen. I have before me a speech in which he pleaded for "a spirit of kindly justice toward every man and woman," but that seems to be as far as he ever got in that direction —and it was the gratuitous justice of the absolute monarch that he apparently had in mind, not the autonomous and inalienable justice of a free society. The duties of the citizen, as he understood them, related not only to acts, but also to thoughts. There was, to his mind, a simple body of primary doctrine, and dissent from it was the foulest of crimes. No man could have been more bitter against opponents, or more unfair to them, or more ungenerous. In this department, indeed, even so gifted a specialist in dishonorable controversy as Dr. Wilson has seldom surpassed him. He never stood up to a frank and chivalrous debate. He dragged herrings across the trail. He made seductive faces at the gallery. He capitalized his enormous talents as an entertainer, his rank as a national hero, his public influence and consequence. The two great law-suits in which he was engaged were screaming burlesques upon justice. He tried them in the newspapers before ever they were called; he befogged them with irrelevant issues; his appearances in court were not the appearances of a witness standing on a level with other witnesses, but those of a comedian sure of his crowd. He was, in his dealings with concrete men as in his dealings with men in the mass, a charlatan of the very highest skill—and there was in him, it goes without saying, the persuasive charm of the charlatan as well as the daring deviousness, the humanness of naïveté as well as the humanness of chicane. He knew how to woo—and not only boobs. He was, for all his ruses and ambuscades, a jolly fellow.

It seems to be forgotten that the current American theory that political heresy should be put down by force, that a man who disputes whatever is official has no rights in law or equity, that he is lucky if he fares no worse than to lose his constitutional benefits of free speech, free assemblage and the use of the mails—it seems to be forgotten that this theory was invented, not by Dr. Wilson, but by Roosevelt. Most Liberals, I suppose, would credit it, if asked, to Wilson. He has carried it to extravagant lengths; he is the father superior of all the present advocates of it; he will probably go down into American history as its greatest prophet. But it was first clearly stated, not in any Wilsonian bull to the right-thinkers of all lands, but in Roosevelt's proceedings against the so-called Paterson anarchists. You will find it set forth at length in an opinion prepared for him by his Attorney-General, Charles J. Bonaparte, another curious and almost fabulous character, also an absolutist wearing the false whiskers of a democrat. Bonaparte furnished the law, and Roosevelt furnished the blood and iron. It was an almost ideal combination; Bonaparte had precisely the touch of Italian finesse that the Rough Rider always lacked. Roosevelt believed in the Paterson doctrine —in brief, that the Constitution does not throw its cloak around heretics—to the end of his days. In the face of what he conceived to be contumacy to revelation his fury took on a sort of lyrical grandeur. There was nothing too awful for the culprit in the dock. Upon his head were poured denunciations as violent as the wildest interdicts of a mediæval pope.

The appearance of such men, of course, is inevitable under a democracy. Consummate showmen, they arrest the wonder of the mob, and so put its suspicions to sleep. What they actually believe is of secondary consequence; the main thing is what they say; even more, the way they say it. Obviously, their activity does a great deal of damage to the democratic theory, for they are standing refutations of the primary doctrine that the common folk choose their leaders wisely. They damage it again in another and more subtle way. That is to say, their ineradicable contempt for the minds they must heat up and bamboozle leads them into a fatalism that shows itself in a cynical and opportunistic politics, a deliberate avoidance of fundamentals. The policy of a democracy thus becomes an eternal improvisation, changing with the private ambitions of its leaders and the transient and often unintelligible emotions of its rank and file. Roosevelt, incurably undemocratic in his habits of mind, often found it difficult to gauge those emotional oscillations. The fact explains his frequent loss of mob support, his periodical journeys into Coventry. There were times when his magnificent talents as a public comedian brought the proletariat to an almost unanimous groveling at his feet, but there were also times when he puzzled and dismayed it, and so awakened its hostility. When he assaulted Wilson on the neutrality issue, early in 1915, he made a quite typical mistake. That mistake consisted in assuming that public indignation over the wrongs of the Belgians would maintain itself at a high temperature— that it would develop rapidly into a demand for intervention. Roosevelt made himself the spokesman of that demand, and then found to his consternation that it was waning—that the great masses of the plain people, prospering under the Wilsonian neutrality, were inclined to preserve it, at no matter what cost to the Belgians. In 1915, after the *Lusitania* affair, things seemed to swing his way again, and he got vigorous support from the British press bureau. But in a few months he found himself once more attempting to lead a mob that was fast slipping away. Wilson, a very much shrewder politician, with little of Roosevelt's weakness for succumbing to his own rhetoric, discerned the truth much more quickly and clearly. In 1916 he made his campaign for reëlection on a flatly anti-Roosevelt peace issue, and not only got himself reëlected, but also drove Roosevelt out of the ring.

What happened thereafter deserves a great deal more careful study than it will ever get from the timorous eunuchs who posture as American historians. At the moment, it is the official doctrine in England, where the thing is more freely discussed than at home, that Wilson was forced into the war by an irresistible movement from below—that the plain people compelled him to abandon neutrality and move reluctantly upon the Germans. Nothing could be more untrue. The plain people, at the end of 1916, were in favor of peace, and they believed that Wilson was in favor of peace. How they were gradually worked up to complaisance and then to enthusiasm and then to hysteria and then to acute mania—this is a tale to be told in more leisurely days and by historians without boards of trustees on their necks. For the present purpose it is sufficient to note that the whole thing was achieved so quickly and so neatly that its success left Roosevelt surprised and helpless. His issue had been stolen from directly under his nose. He was left standing daunted and alone, a boy upon a burning deck. It took him months to collect his scattered wits, and even then his attack upon the administration was feeble and ineffective. To the plain people it seemed a mere ill-natured snapping at a successful rival, which in fact it was, and so they paid no heed to it, and Roosevelt found himself isolated once more. Thus he passed from the scene in the shadows, a broken politician and a disappointed man.

I have a notion that he died too soon. His best days were probably not behind him, but ahead of him. Had he lived ten years longer, he might have enjoyed a great rehabilitation, and exchanged his old false leadership of the inflammatory and fickle mob for a sound and true leadership of the civilized minority. For the more one studies his mountebankeries as mob-master, the more one is convinced that there was a shrewd man beneath the

65

motley, and that his actual beliefs were anything but non-sensical. The truth of them, indeed, emerges more clearly day by day. The old theory of a federation of free and autonomous states has broken down by its own weight, and we are moved toward centralization by forces that have long been powerful and are now quite irresistible. So with the old theory of national isolation: it, too, has fallen to pieces. The United States can no longer hope to lead a separate life in the world, undisturbed by the pressure of foreign aspirations. We came out of the war to find ourselves hemmed in by hostilities that no longer troubled to conceal themselves, and if they are not as close and menacing to-day as those that have hemmed in Germany for centuries they are none the less plainly there and plainly growing. Roosevelt, by whatever route of reflection or intuition, arrived at a sense of these facts at a time when it was still somewhat scandalous to state them, and it was the capital effort of his life to reconcile them, in some dark way or other, to the prevailing platitudes, and so get them heeded. To-day no one seriously maintains, as all Americans once maintained, that the states can go on existing together as independent commonwealths, each with its own laws, its own legal theory and its own view of the common constitutional bond. And to-day no one seriously maintains, as all Americans once maintained, that the nation may safely potter on without adequate means of defense. However unpleasant it may be to contemplate, the fact is plain that the American people, during the next century, will have to fight to maintain their place in the sun.

Roosevelt lived just long enough to see his notions in these directions take on life, but not long enough to see them openly adopted. To the extent of his prevision he was a genuine leader of the nation, and perhaps in the years to come, when his actual ideas are disentangled from the demagogic fustian in which he had to wrap them, his more honest pronunciamentoes will be given canonical honors, and he will be ranked among the prophets. He saw clearly more than one other thing that was by no means obvious to his age—for example, the inevitability of frequent wars under the new world-system of extreme nationalism; again, the urgent necessity, for primary police ends, of organizing the backward nations into groups of vassals, each under the hoof of some first-rate power; yet again, the probability of the breakdown of the old system of free competition; once more, the high social utility of the Spartan virtues and the grave dangers of sloth and ease; finally, the incompatibility of free speech and democracy. I do not say that he was always quite honest, even when he was most indubitably right. But in so far as it was possible for him to be honest and exist at all politically, he inclined toward the straightforward thought and the candid word. That is to say, his instinct prompted him to tell the truth, just as the instinct of Dr. Wilson prompts him to shift and dissimulate. What ailed him was the fact that his lust for glory, when it came to a struggle, was always vastly more powerful than his lust for the eternal verities. Tempted sufficiently, he would sacrifice anything and everything to get applause. Thus the statesman was debauched by the politician, and the philosopher was elbowed out of sight by the popinjay.

Where he failed most miserably was in his remedies. A remarkably penetrating diagnostician, well-read, unprejudiced and with a touch of genuine scientific passion, he always stooped to quackery when he prescribed a course of treatment. For all his sensational attacks upon the trusts, he never managed to devise a scheme to curb them —and even when he sought to apply the schemes of other men he invariably corrupted the business with timorousness and insincerity. So with his campaign for national preparedness. He displayed the disease magnificently, but the course of medication that he proposed was vague and unconvincing; it was not, indeed, without justification that the plain people mistook his advocacy of an adequate army for a mere secret yearning to prance upon a charger at the head of huge hordes. So, again, with his eloquent plea for national solidarity and an end of hyphenism. The dangers that he pointed out were very real and very menacing, but his plan for abating them only made them worse. His objurgations against the Germans surely accomplished nothing; the hyphenate of 1915 is still a hyphenate in his heart—with bitter and unforgettable grievances to support him. Roosevelt, very characteristically, swung too far. In denouncing German hyphenism so extravagantly he contrived to give an enormous impetus to English hyphenism, a far older and more perilous malady. It has already gone so far that a large and influential party endeavors almost openly to convert the United States into a mere vassal state of England's. Instead of national solidarity following the war, we have only a revival of Know-Nothingism; one faction of hyphenates tries to exterminate another faction. Roosevelt's error here was one that he was always making. Carried away by the ease with which he could heat up the mob, he tried to accomplish instantly and by *force majeure* what could only be accomplished by a long and complex process, with more good will on both sides than ever so opinionated and melodramatic a pseudo-Junker was capable of. But though he thus made a mess of the cure, he was undoubtedly right about the disease.

The talented Sherman, in the monograph that I have praised, argues that the chief contribution of the dead gladiator to American life was the example of his gigantic gusto, his delight in toil and struggle, his superb aliveness. The fact is plain. What he stood most clearly in opposition to was the superior pessimism of the three Adams brothers—the notion that the public problems of a democracy are unworthy the thought and effort of a civilized and self-respecting man—the sad error that lies in wait for all of us who hold ourselves above the general. Against this suicidal aloofness Roosevelt always hurled himself with brave effect. Enormously sensitive and resilient, almost pathological in his appetite for activity, he made it plain to every one that the most stimulating sort of sport imaginable was to be obtained in fighting, not for mere money, but for ideas. There was no aristocratic reserve about him. He was not, in fact, an aristocrat at all, but a quite typical member of the upper *bourgeoisie;* his people were not *patroons* in New Amsterdam, but simple traders; he was himself a social pusher, and eternally tickled by the thought that he had had a Bonaparte in his cabinet. The marks of the thoroughbred were simply not there. The man was blatant, crude, overly confidential, devious, tyrannical, vainglorious, sometimes quite childish. One often observed in him a certain pathetic wistfulness, a reaching out for a grand manner that was utterly beyond him. But the sweet went with the bitter. He had all the virtues of the fat and complacent burgher. His disdain of affectation and prudery was magnificent. He hated all pretension save his own pretension. He had a sound respect for hard effort, for loyalty, for thrift, for honest achievement.

His worst defects, it seems to me, were the defects of his race and time. Aspiring to be the leader of a nation of third-rate men, he had to stoop to the common level. When he struck out for realms above that level he always came to grief: this was the "unsafe" Roosevelt, the Roosevelt who was laughed at, the Roosevelt retired suddenly to cold storage. This was the Roosevelt who, in happier times and a better place, might have been. Well, one does what one can.

THE SAHARA OF THE BOZART

> Alas, for the South! Her books have grown fewer—
> She never was much given to literature.

In the lamented J. Gordon Coogler, author of these elegiac lines, there was the insight of a true poet. He was the last bard of Dixie, at least in the legitimate line. Down there a poet is now almost as rare as an oboe-player, a dry-point etcher or a metaphysician. It is, indeed, amazing to contemplate so vast a vacuity. One thinks of the interstellar spaces, of the colossal reaches of the now mythical ether. Nearly the whole of Europe could be lost in that stupendous region of fat farms, shoddy cities and paralyzed cerebrums: one could throw in France, Germany and Italy, and still have room for the British Isles. And yet, for all its size and all its wealth and all the "progress" it babbles of, it is almost as sterile, artistically, intellectually, culturally, as the Sahara Desert. There are single acres in Europe that house more first-rate men than all the states south of the Potomac; there are probably single square miles in America. If the whole of the late Confederacy were to be engulfed by a tidal wave tomorrow, the effect upon the civilized minority of men in the world would be but little greater than that of a flood on the Yang-tse-kiang. It would be impossible in all history to match so complete a drying-up of a civilization.

I say a civilization because that is what, in the old days, the south had, despite the Baptist and Methodist barbarism that reigns down there now. More, it was a civilization of manifold excellences—perhaps the best that the Western Hemisphere has ever seen—undoubtedly the best that These States have ever seen. Down to the middle of the last century, and even beyond, the main hatchery of ideas on this side of the water was across the Potomac bridges. The New England shopkeepers and theologians never really developed a civilization; all they ever developed was a government. They were, at their best, tawdry and tacky fellows, oafish in manner and devoid of imagination; one searches the books in vain for mention of a salient Yankee gentleman; as well look for a Welsh gentleman. But in the south there were men of delicate fancy, urbane instinct and aristocratic manner—in brief, superior men—in brief, gentry. To politics, their chief diversion, they brought active and original minds. It was there that nearly all the political theories we still cherish and suffer under came to birth. It was there that the crude dogmatism of New England was refined and humanized. It was there, above all, that some attention was given to the art of living—that life got beyond and above the state of a mere infliction and became an exhilarating experience. A certain noble spaciousness was in the ancient southern scheme of things. The *Ur-*Confederate had leisure. He liked to toy with ideas. He was hospitable and tolerant. He had the vague thing that we call culture.

But consider the condition of his late empire to-day. The picture gives one the creeps. It is as if the Civil War stamped out every last bearer of the torch, and left only a mob of peasants on the field. One thinks of Asia Minor, resigned to Armenians, Greeks and wild swine, of Poland abandoned to the Poles. In all that gargantuan paradise of the fourth-rate there is not a single picture gallery worth going into, or a single orchestra capable of playing the nine symphonies of Beethoven, or a single opera-house, or a single theater devoted to decent plays, or a single public monument (built since the war) that is worth looking at, or a single workshop devoted to the making of beautiful things. Once you have counted Robert Loveman (an Ohioan by birth) and John McClure (an Oklahoman) you will not find a single southern poet above the rank of a neighborhood rhymester. Once you have counted James Branch Cabell (a lingering survivor of the *ancien régime:* a scarlet dragonfly imbedded in opaque amber) you will not find a single southern prose writer who can actually write. And once you have—but when you come to critics, musical composers, painters, sculptors, architects and the like, you will have to give it up, for there is not even a bad one between the Potomac mud-flats and the Gulf. Nor an historian. Nor a sociologist. Nor a philosopher. Nor a theologian. Nor a scientist. In all these fields the south is an awe-inspiring blank—a brother to Portugal, Serbia and Esthonia.

Consider, for example, the present estate and dignity of Virginia—in the great days indubitably the premier American state, the mother of Presidents and statesmen, the home of the first American university worthy of the name, the *arbiter elegantiarum* of the western world. Well, observe Virginia to-day. It is years since a first-rate man, save only Cabell, has come out of it; it is years since an idea has come out of it. The old aristocracy went down the red gullet of war; the poor white trash are now in the saddle. Politics in Virginia are cheap, ignorant, parochial, idiotic; there is scarcely a man in office above the rank of a professional job-seeker; the political doctrine that prevails is made up of hand-me-downs from the bumpkinry of the Middle West—Bryanism, Prohibition, vice crusading, all that sort of filthy claptrap; the administration of the law is turned over to professors of Puritanism and espionage; a Washington or a Jefferson, dumped there by some act of God, would be denounced as a scoundrel and jailed overnight. Elegance, *esprit,* culture? Virginia has no art, no literature, no philosophy, no mind or aspiration of her own. Her education has sunk to the Baptist seminary level; not a single contribution to human knowledge has come out of her colleges in twenty-five years; she spends less than half upon her common schools, *per capita,* than any northern state spends. In brief, an intellectual Gobi or Lapland. Urbanity, *politesse,* chivalry? Go to! It was in Virginia that they invented the device of searching for contraband whisky in women's underwear. . . . There remains, at the top, a ghost of the old aristocracy, a bit wistful and infinitely charming. But it has lost all its old leadership to fabulous monsters from the lower depths; it is submerged in an industrial plutocracy that is ignorant and ignominious. The mind of the state, as it is revealed to the nation, is pathetically naïve and inconsequential. It no longer reacts with energy and elasticity to great problems. It has fallen to the bombastic trivialities of the camp-meeting and the chautauqua. Its foremost exponent—if so flabby a thing may be said to have an exponent—is a statesman whose name is synonymous with empty words, broken pledges and false pretenses. One could no more imagine a Lee or a Washington in the Virginia of to-day than one could imagine a Huxley in Nicaragua.

I choose the Old Dominion, not because I disdain it, but precisely because I esteem it. It is, by long odds, the most civilized of the southern states, now as always. It has sent a host of creditable sons northward; the stream kept running into our own time. Virginians, even the worst of them, show the effects of a great tradition. They hold themselves above other southerners, and with sound pretension. If one turns to such a commonwealth as Georgia the picture becomes far darker. There the liberated lower orders of whites have borrowed the worst commercial bounderism of the Yankee and superimposed it upon a culture that, at bottom, is but little removed from savagery. Georgia is at once the home of the cotton-mill sweater and of the most noisy and vapid sort of chamber of commerce, of the Methodist parson turned Savonarola and of the lynching bee. A self-respecting European, going there to live, would not only find intellectual stimulation utterly lacking; he would actually feel a certain insecurity, as if the scene were the Balkans or the China Coast. The Leo Frank affair was no isolated phenomenon. It fitted into its frame very snugly. It was a natural expression of Georgian notions of truth and justice. There is a state with more than half the area of Italy and more population than either Denmark or Norway, and yet in thirty years it has not produced a single idea. Once upon a time a Georgian printed a couple of books that attracted notice, but immediately it turned out that he was little more than an amanuensis for the local blacks—that his works were really the products, not of white Georgia, but of black Georgia. Writing afterward *as* a white man, he swiftly subsided into the fifth rank. And he is not only the glory of the literature of Georgia; he is, almost literally, the whole of the literature of Georgia—nay, of the entire art of Georgia.

Virginia is the best of the south to-day, and Georgia is perhaps the worst. The one is simply senile; the other is crass, gross, vulgar and obnoxious. Between lies a vast plain of mediocrity, stupidity, lethargy, almost of dead silence. In the north, of course, there is also grossness, crassness, vulgarity. The north, in its way, is also stupid and obnoxious. But nowhere in the north is there such complete sterility, so depressing a lack of all civilized gesture and aspiration. One would find it difficult to unearth a second-rate city between the Ohio and the Pacific that isn't struggling to establish an orchestra, or setting up a little theater, or going in for an art gallery, or making some other effort to get into touch with civilization. These efforts often fail, and sometimes they succeed rather absurdly, but under them there is at least an impulse that deserves respect, and that is the impulse to seek beauty and to experiment with ideas, and so to give the life of every day a certain dignity and purpose. You will find no such impulse in the south. There are no committees down there cadging subscriptions for orchestras; if a string quartet is ever heard there, the news of it has never come out; an opera troupe, when it roves the land, is a nine days' wonder. The little theater movement has swept the whole country, enormously augmenting the public interest in sound plays, giving new dramatists their chance, forcing reforms upon the commercial theater. Everywhere else the wave rolls high—but along the line of the Potomac it breaks upon a rock-bound shore. There is no little theater beyond. There is no gallery of pictures. No artist ever gives exhibitions. No one talks of such things. No one seems to be interested in such things.

As for the cause of this unanimous torpor and doltishness, this curious and almost pathological estrangement from everything that makes for a civilized culture, I have hinted at it already, and now state it again. The south has simply been drained of all its best blood. The vast bloodletting of the Civil War half exterminated and wholly paralyzed the old aristocracy, and so left the land to the harsh mercies of the poor white trash, now its masters. The war, of course, was not a complete massacre. It spared a decent number of first-rate southerners—perhaps even some of the very best. Moreover, other countries, notably France and Germany, have survived far more staggering butcheries, and even showed marked progress thereafter. But the war not only cost a great many valuable lives; it also brought bankruptcy, demoralization and despair in its train—and so the majority of the first-rate southerners that were left, broken in spirit and unable to live under the new dispensation, cleared out. A few went to South America, to Egypt, to the Far East. Most came north. They were fecund; their progeny is widely dispersed, to the great benefit of the north. A southerner of good blood almost always does well in the north. He finds, even in the big cities, surroundings fit for a man of condition. His peculiar qualities have a high social value, and are esteemed. He is welcomed by the codfish aristocracy as one palpably superior. But in the south he throws up his hands. It is impossible for him to stoop to the common level. He cannot brawl in politics with the grandsons of his grandfather's tenants. He is unable to share their fierce jealousy of the emerging black—the cornerstone of all their public thinking. He is anæsthetic to their theological and political enthusiasms. He finds himself an alien at their feasts of soul. And so he withdraws into his tower, and is heard of no more. Cabell is almost a perfect example. His eyes, for years, were turned toward the past; he became a professor of the grotesque genealogizing that decaying aristocracies affect; it was only by a sort of accident that he discovered himself to be an artist. The south is unaware of the fact to this day; it regards Woodrow Wilson and Col. John Temple Graves as much finer stylists, and Frank L. Stanton as an infinitely greater poet. If it has heard, which I doubt, that Cabell has been hoofed by the Comstocks, it unquestionably views that assault as a deserved rebuke to a fellow who indulges a lewd passion for fancy writing, and is a covert enemy to the Only True Christianity.

What is needed down there, before the vexatious public problems of the region may be intelligently approached, is a survey of the population by competent ethnologists and anthropologists. The immigrants of the north have been studied at great length, and any one who is interested may now apply to the Bureau of Ethnology for elaborate data as to their racial strains, their stature and cranial indices, their relative capacity for education, and the changes that they undergo under American *Kultur*. But the older stocks of the south, and particularly the emancipated and dominant poor white trash, have never been investigated scientifically, and most of the current generalizations about them are probably wrong. For example, the generalization that they are purely Anglo-Saxon in blood. This I doubt very seriously. The chief strain down there, I believe, is Celtic rather than Saxon, particularly in the hill country. French blood, too, shows itself here and there, and so does Spanish, and so does German. The last-named entered from the northward, by way of the limestone belt just east of the Alleghenies. Again, it is very likely that in some parts of the south a good many of the plebeian whites have more than a trace of negro blood. Interbreeding under concubinage produced some very light half-breeds at an early day, and no doubt appreciable numbers of them went over into the white race by the simple process of changing their abode. Not long ago I read a curious article by an intelligent negro, in which he stated that it is easy for a very light negro to pass as white in the south on account of the fact that large numbers of southerners accepted as white have distinctly negroid features. Thus it becomes a delicate and dangerous matter for a train conductor or a hotel-keeper to challenge a suspect. But the Celtic strain is far more obvious than any of these others. It not only makes itself visible in physical stigmata—*e.g.*, leanness and dark coloring—but also in mental traits. For example, the religious thought of the south is almost precisely identical with the religious thought of Wales. There is the same naïve belief in an anthropomorphic Creator but little removed, in manner and desire, from an evangelical bishop; there is the same submission to an ignorant and impudent sacerdotal tyranny, and there is the same sharp contrast between doctrinal orthodoxy and private ethics. Read Caradoc Evans' ironical picture of the Welsh

Wesleyans in his preface to "My Neighbors," and you will be instantly reminded of the Georgia and Carolina Methodists. The most booming sort of piety, in the south, is not incompatible with the theory that lynching is a benign institution. Two generations ago it was not incompatible with an ardent belief in slavery.

It is highly probable that some of the worst blood of western Europe flows in the veins of the southern poor whites, now poor no longer. The original strains, according to every honest historian, were extremely corrupt. Philip Alexander Bruce (a Virginian of the old gentry) says in his "Industrial History of Virginia in the Seventeenth Century" that the first native-born generation was largely illegitimate. "One of the most common offenses against morality committed in the lower ranks of life in Virginia during the seventeenth century," he says, "was bastardy." The mothers of these bastards, he continues, were chiefly indentured servants, and "had belonged to the lowest class in their native country." Fanny Kemble Butler, writing of the Georgia poor whites of a century later, described them as "the most degraded race of human beings claiming an Anglo-Saxon origin that can be found on the face of the earth—filthy, lazy, ignorant, brutal, proud, penniless savages." The Sunday-school and the chautauqua, of course, have appreciably mellowed the descendants of these "savages," and their economic progress and rise to political power have done perhaps even more, but the marks of their origin are still unpleasantly plentiful. Every now and then they produce a political leader who puts their secret notions of the true, the good and the beautiful into plain words, to the amazement and scandal of the rest of the country. That amazement is turned into downright incredulity when news comes that his platform has got him high office, and that he is trying to execute it.

In the great days of the south the line between the gentry and the poor whites was very sharply drawn. There was absolutely no intermarriage. So far as I know there is not a single instance in history of a southerner of the upper class marrying one of the bondwomen described by Mr. Bruce. In other societies characterized by class distinctions of that sort it is common for the lower class to be improved by extra-legal crosses. That is to say, the men of the upper class take women of the lower class as mistresses, and out of such unions spring the extraordinary plebeians who rise sharply from the common level, and so propagate the delusion that all other plebeians would do the same thing if they had the chance —in brief, the delusion that class distinctions are merely economic and conventional, and not congenital and genuine. But in the south the men of the upper classes sought their mistresses among the blacks, and after a few generations there was so much white blood in the black women that they were considerably more attractive than the unhealthy and bedraggled women of the poor whites. This preference continued into our own time. A southerner of good family once told me in all seriousness that he had reached his majority before it ever occurred to him that a white woman might make quite as agreeable a mistress as the octaroons of his jejune fancy. If the thing has changed of late, it is not the fault of the southern white man, but of the southern mulatto women. The more sightly yellow girls of the region, with improving economic opportunities, have gained self-respect, and so they are no longer as willing to enter into concubinage as their grand-dams were.

As a result of this preference of the southern gentry for mulatto mistresses there was created a series of mixed strains containing the best white blood of the south, and perhaps of the whole country. As another result the poor whites went unfertilized from above, and so missed the improvement that so constantly shows itself in the peasant stocks of other countries. It is a commonplace that nearly all negroes who rise above the general are of mixed blood, usually with the white predominating. I know a great many negroes, and it would be hard for me to think of an exception. What is too often forgotten is that this white blood is not the blood of the poor whites but that of the old gentry. The mulatto girls of the early days despised the poor whites as creatures distinctly inferior to negroes, and it was thus almost unheard of for such a girl to enter into relations with a man of that submerged class. This aversion was based upon a sound instinct. The southern mulatto of to-day is a proof of it. Like all other half-breeds he is an unhappy man, with disquieting tendencies toward anti-social habits of thought, but he is intrinsically a better animal than the pure-blooded descendant of the old poor whites, and he not infrequently demonstrates it. It is not by accident that the negroes of the south are making faster progress, economically and culturally, than the masses of the whites. It is not by accident that the only visible æsthetic activity in the south is wholly in their hands. No southern composer has ever written music so good as that of half a dozen white-black composers who might be named. Even in politics, the negro reveals a curious superiority. Despite the fact that the race question has been the main political concern of the southern whites for two generations, to the practical exclusion of everything else, they have contributed nothing to its discussion that has impressed the rest of the world so deeply and so favorably as three or four books by southern negroes.

Entering upon such themes, of course, one must resign one's self to a vast misunderstanding and abuse. The south has not only lost its old capacity for producing ideas; it has also taken on the worst intolerance of ignorance and stupidity. Its prevailing mental attitude for several decades past has been that of its own hedge ecclesiastics. All who dissent from its orthodox doctrines are scoundrels. All who presume to discuss its ways realistically are damned. I have had, in my day, several experiences in point. Once, after I had published an article on some phase of the eternal race question, a leading southern newspaper replied by printing a column of denunciation of my father, then dead nearly twenty years—a philippic placarding him as an ignorant foreigner of dubious origin, inhabiting "the Baltimore ghetto" and speaking a dialect recalling that of Weber & Fields—two thousand words of incandescent nonsense, utterly false and beside the point, but exactly meeting the latter-day southern notion of effective controversy. Another time, I published a short discourse on lynching, arguing that the sport was popular in the south because the backward culture of the region denied the populace more seemly recreations. Among such recreations I mentioned those afforded by brass bands, symphony orchestras, boxing matches, amateur athletic contests, shoot-the-chutes, roof gardens, horse races, and so on. In reply another great southern journal denounced me as a man "of wineshop temperament, brass-jewelry tastes and pornographic predilections." In other words, brass bands, in the south, are classed with brass jewelry, and both are snares of the devil! To advocate setting up symphony orchestras is pornography! . . . Alas, when the touchy southerner attempts a greater urbanity, the result is often even worse. Some time ago a colleague of mine printed an article deploring the arrested cultural development of Georgia. In reply he received a number of protests from patriotic Georgians, and all of them solemnly listed the glories of the state. I indulge in a few specimens:

> Who has not heard of Asa G. Candler, whose name is synonymous with Coca-Cola, a Georgia product?
> The first Sunday-school in the world was opened in Savannah.
> Who does not recall with pleasure the writings of . . . Frank L. Stanton, Georgia's brilliant poet?
> Georgia was the first state to organize a Boys' Corn Club in the South—Newton county, 1904.
> The first to suggest a common United Daughters of the Confederacy badge was Mrs. Raynes, of Georgia.
> The first to suggest a state historian of the United Daughters of the Confederacy was Mrs. C. Helen Plane (Macon convention, 1896).
> The first to suggest putting to music Heber's "From

Greenland's Icy Mountains" was Mrs. F. R. Goulding, of Savannah.

And so on, and so on. These proud boasts came, remember, not from obscure private persons, but from "Leading Georgians"—in one case, the state historian. Curious sidelights upon the ex-Confederate mind! Another comes from a stray copy of a negro paper. It describes an ordinance lately passed by the city council of Douglas, Ga., forbidding any trousers presser, on penalty of forfeiting a $500 bond, to engage in "pressing for both white and colored." This in a town, says the negro paper, where practically all of the white inhabitants have "their food prepared by colored hands," "their babies cared for by colored hands," and "the clothes which they wear right next to their skins washed in houses where negroes live"—houses in which the said clothes "remain for as long as a week at a time." But if you marvel at the absurdity, keep it dark! A casual word, and the united press of the south will be upon your trail, denouncing you bitterly as a scoundrelly Yankee, a Bolshevik Jew, an agent of the Wilhelmstrasse. . . .

Obviously, it is impossible for intelligence to flourish in such an atmosphere. Free inquiry is blocked by the idiotic certainties of ignorant men. The arts, save in the lower reaches of the gospel hymn, the phonograph and the chautauqua harangue, are all held in suspicion. The tone of public opinion is set by an upstart class but lately emerged from industrial slavery into commercial enterprise—the class of "hustling" business men, of "live wires," of commercial club luminaries, of "drive" managers, of forward-lookers and right-thinkers—in brief, of third-rate southerners inoculated with all the worst traits of the Yankee sharper. One observes the curious effects of an old tradition of truculence upon a population now merely pushful and impudent, of an old tradition of chivalry upon a population now quite without imagination. The old repose is gone. The old romanticism is gone. The philistinism of the new type of town-boomer southerner is not only indifferent to the ideals of the old south; it is positively antagonistic to them. That philistinism regards human life, not as an agreeable adventure, but as a mere trial of rectitude and efficiency. It is overwhelmingly utilitarian and moral. It is inconceivably hollow and obnoxious. What remains of the ancient tradition is simply a certain charming civility in private intercourse—often broken down, alas, by the hot rages of Puritanism, but still generally visible. The southerner, at his worst, is never quite the surly cad that the Yankee is. His sensitiveness may betray him into occasional bad manners, but in the main he is a pleasant fellow—hospitable, polite, good-humored, even jovial. . . . But a bit absurd. . . . A bit pathetic.

THE CEREBRAL MIME

Of all actors, the most offensive to the higher cerebral centers is the one who pretends to intellectuality. His alleged intelligence, of course, is always purely imaginary: no man of genuinely superior intelligence has ever been an actor. Even supposing a young man of appreciable mental powers to be lured upon the stage, as philosophers are occasionally lured into bordellos, his mind would be inevitably and almost immediately destroyed by the gaudy nonsense issuing from his mouth every night. That nonsense enters into the very fiber of the actor. He becomes a grotesque boiling down of all the preposterous characters that he has ever impersonated. Their characteristics are seen in his manner, in his reactions to stimuli, in his point of view. He becomes a walking artificiality, a strutting dummy, a thematic catalogue of imbecilities.

There are, of course, plays that are not wholly nonsense, and now and then one encounters an actor who aspires to appear in them. This aspiration almost always overtakes the so-called actor-manager—that is to say, the actor who has got rich and is thus ambitious to appear as a gentleman. Such aspirants commonly tackle Shakespeare, and if not Shakespeare, then Shaw, or Hauptmann, or Rostand, or some other apparently intellectual dramatist. But this is seldom more than a passing madness. The actor-manager may do that sort of thing once in a while, but in the main he sticks to his garbage. Consider, for example, the late Henry Irving. He posed as an intellectual and was forever gabbling about his high services to the stage, and yet he appeared constantly in such puerile things as "The Bells," beside which the average newspaper editorial or college yell was literature. So with the late Mansfield. His pretension, deftly circulated by press-agents, was that he was a man of brilliant and polished mind. Nevertheless, he spent two-thirds of his life in the theater playing such abominable drivel as "A Parisian Romance" and "Dr. Jekyll and Mr. Hyde."

It is commonly urged in defense of certain actors that they are forced to appear in that sort of stuff by the public demand for it—that appearing in it painfully violates their secret pruderies. This defense is unsound and dishonest. An actor never disdains anything that gets him applause and money; he is almost completely devoid of that æsthetic conscience which is the chief mark of the genuine artist. If there were a large public willing to pay handsomely to hear him recite limericks, or to blow a cornet, or to strip off his underwear and dance a polonaise stark naked, he would do it without hesitation—and then convince himself that such buffooning constituted a difficult and elevated art, fully comparable to Wagner's or Dante's. In belief, the one essential, in his sight, is the chance to shine, the fat part, the applause. Who ever heard of an actor declining a fat part on the ground that it invaded his intellectual integrity? The thing is simply unimaginable.

THE CULT OF HOPE

Of all the sentimental errors which reign and rage in this incomparable republic, the worst, I often suspect, is that which confuses the function of criticism, whether æsthetic, political or social, with the function of reform. Almost invariably it takes the form of a protest: "The fellow condemns without offering anything better. Why tear down without building up?" So coo and snivel the sweet ones: so wags the national tongue. The messianic delusion becomes a sort of universal murrain. It is impossible to get an audience for an idea that is not "constructive"—*i.e.,* that is not glib, and uplifting, and full of hope, and hence capable of tickling the emotions by leaping the intermediate barrier of the intelligence.

In this protest and demand, of course, there is nothing but a hollow sound of words—the empty babbling of men who constantly mistake their mere feelings for thoughts. The truth is that criticism, if it were thus confined to the proposing of alternative schemes, would quickly cease to have any force or utility at all, for in the overwhelming majority of instances no alternative scheme of any intelligibility is imaginable, and the whole object of the critical process is to demonstrate it. The poet, if the victim is a poet, is simply one as bare of gifts as a herring is of fur: no conceivable suggestion will ever make him write actual poetry. The cancer cure, if one turns to popular swindles, is wholly and absolutely without merit—and the fact that medicine offers us no better cure does not dilute its bogusness in the slightest. And the plan of reform, in politics, sociology or what not, is simply beyond the pale of reason; no change in it or improvement of it will ever make it achieve the downright impossible. Here, precisely, is what is the matter with most of the notions that go floating about the country, particularly in the field of governmental reform. The trouble with them is not only that they won't and don't work; the trouble with them, more importantly, is that the thing they propose to accomplish is intrinsically, or at all events most probably, beyond accomplishment. That is to say, the problem they are ostensibly designed to solve is a problem that is insoluble. To tackle them with a proof of that insolubility, or even with a colorable argument of it, is sound criticism; to tackle them with another solution that is quite as bad, or even worse, is to pick the pocket of one knocked down by an automobile.

Unluckily, it is difficult for a certain type of mind to grasp the concept of insolubility. Thousands of poor dolts keep on trying to square the circle; other thousands keep pegging away at perpetual motion. The number of persons so afflicted is far greater than the records of the Patent Office show, for beyond the circle of frankly insane enterprise there lie circles of more and more plausible enterprise, and finally we come to a circle which embraces the great majority of human beings. These are the optimists and chronic hopers of the world, the believers in men, ideas and things. These are the advocates of leagues of nations, wars to make the world safe for democracy, political mountebanks, "clean-up" campaigns, laws, raids, Men and Religion Forward Movements, eugenics, sex hygiene, education, newspapers. It is the settled habit of such credulous folk to give ear to whatever is comforting; it is their settled faith that whatever is desirable will come to pass. A caressing confidence—but one, unfortunately, that is not borne out by human experience. The fact is that some of the things that men and women have desired most ardently for thousands of years are not nearer realization to-day than they were in the time of Rameses, and that there is not the slightest reason for believing that they will lose their coyness on any near to-morrow. Plans for hurrying them on have been tried since the beginning; plans for forcing them overnight are in copious and antagonistic operation to-day; and yet they continue to hold off and elude us, and the chances are that they will keep on holding off and eluding us until the angels get tired of the show, and the whole earth is set off like a gigantic bomb, or drowned, like a sick cat, between two buckets.

But let us avoid the grand and chronic dreams of the race and get down to some of the concrete problems of life under the Christian enlightenment. Let us take a look, say, at the so-called drink problem, a small sub-division of the larger problem of saving men from their inherent and incurable hoggishness. What is the salient feature of the discussion of the drink problem, as one observes it going on eternally in These States? The salient feature of it is that very few honest and intelligent men ever take a hand in the business—that the best men of the nation, distinguished for their sound sense in other fields, seldom show any interest in it. On the one hand it is labored by a horde of obvious jackasses, each confident that he can dispose of it overnight. And on the other hand it is sophisticated and obscured by a crowd of oblique fellows, hired by interested parties, whose secret desire is that it be kept unsolved. To one side, the professional gladiators of Prohibition; to the other side, the agents of the brewers and distillers. But why do all neutral and clear-headed men avoid it? Why does one hear so little about it from those who have no personal stake in it, and can thus view it fairly and accurately? Is it because they are afraid? Is it because they are not intrigued by it? I doubt that it would be just to accuse them in either way. The real reason why they steer clear of the gabble is simpler and more creditable. It is this: that none of them—that no genuinely thoughtful and prudent man—can imagine any solution which meets the tests of his own criticism—that no genuinely intelligent man believes the thing is soluble at all.

Here, of course, I generalize a bit heavily. Honest and intelligent men, though surely not many of them, occasionally come forward with suggestions. In the midst of so much debate it is inevitable that even a man of critical mind should sometimes lean to one side or the other—that some salient imbecility should make him react toward its rough opposite. But the fact still remains that not a single complete and comprehensive scheme has ever come from such a man, that no such man has ever said, in so many words, that he thought the problem could be solved, simply and effectively. All such schemes come from idiots or from sharpers disguised as idiots to win the public confidence. The whole discussion is based upon assumptions that even the most casual reflection must reject as empty balderdash.

And as with the drink problem, so with most of the other great questions that harass and dismay the helpless human race. Turn, for example, to the sex problem. There is no half-baked ecclesiastic, bawling in his galvanized-iron temple on a suburban lot, who doesn't know precisely how it ought to be dealt with. There is no fantoddish old suffragette, sworn to get her revenge on man, who hasn't a sovereign remedy for it. There is not a shyster of a district attorney, ambitious for higher office, who doesn't offer to dispose of it in a few weeks, given only enough help from the city editors. And yet, by the same token, there is not a man who has honestly studied it and pondered it, bringing sound information to the business, and understanding of its inner difficulties and a clean and analytical mind, who doesn't believe and hasn't stated publicly that it is intrinsically and eternally insoluble. I can't think of an exception, nor does a fresh glance through the literature suggest one. The latest expert to tell the disconcerting truth is Dr. Maurice Parmelee, the criminologist. His book, "Personality and Conduct," is largely devoted to demonstrating that the popular solutions, for all the support they get from vice crusaders, complaisant legislators and sensational newspapers, are unanimously imbecile and pernicious—that their only effect in practice is to make what was bad a good deal worse. His remedy is—what? An alternative solution? Not at all. His remedy, in brief, is to abandon all attempts at a solution, to let the whole thing go, to cork up all the reformers and try to forget it.

And in this proposal he merely echoes Havelock Ellis, undoubtedly the most diligent and scientific student of the sex problem that the world has yet seen—in fact, the one man who, above all others, has made a decorous and intelligent examination of it possible. Ellis' remedy is simply a denial of all remedies. He admits that the disease is bad, but he shows that the medicine is infinitely worse, and so he proposes going back to the plain disease, and advocates bearing it with philosophy, as we bear colds in the head, marriage, the noises of the city, bad cooking and the certainty of death. Man is inherently vile—but he is never so vile as when he is trying to disguise and deny his vileness. No prostitute was ever so costly to a community as a prowling and obscene vice crusader, or as the dubious legislator or prosecuting officer who jumps as he pipes.

Ellis, in all this, falls under the excommunication of the sentimentalists. He demolishes one scheme without offering an alternative scheme. He tears down without making any effort to build up. This explains, no doubt, his general unpopularity; into mouths agape for peruna, he projects only paralyzing streams of ice-water. And it explains, too, the curious fact that his books, the most competent and illuminating upon the subject that they discuss, are under the ban of the Comstocks in both England and America, whereas the hollow treatises of ignorant clerics and smutty old maids are merchanted with impunity, and even commended from the sacred desk. The trouble with Ellis is that he tells the truth, which is the unsafest of all things to tell. His crime is that he is a man who prefers facts to illusions, and knows what he is talking about. Such men are never popular. The public taste is for merchandise of a pre-

cisely opposite character. The way to please is to pro-
claim in a confident manner, not what is true, but what
is merely comforting. This is what is called building up.
This is constructive criticism.

ON BEING AN AMERICAN

1

Apparently there are those who begin to find
it disagreeable—nay, impossible. Their anguish fills the
Liberal weeklies, and every ship that puts out from
New York carries a groaning cargo of them, bound for
Paris, London, Munich, Rome and way points—anywhere to escape the great curses and atrocities that make
life intolerable for them at home. Let me say at once
that I find little to cavil at in their basic complaints.
In more than one direction, indeed, I probably go a
great deal further than even the Young Intellectuals. It
is, for example, one of my firmest and most sacred
beliefs, reached after an inquiry extending over a score
of years and supported by incessant prayer and medita-
tion, that the government of the United States, in both
its legislative arm and its executive arm, is ignorant,
incompetent, corrupt, and disgusting—and from this
judgment I except no more than twenty living lawmakers and no more than twenty executioners of their
laws. It is a belief no less piously cherished that the
administration of justice in the Republic is stupid, dishonest, and against all reason and equity—and from
this judgment I except no more than thirty judges, including two upon the bench of the Supreme Court of
the United States. It is another that the foreign policy of
the United States—its habitual manner of dealing with

other nations, whether friend or foe—is hypocritical, disingenuous, knavish, and dishonorable—and from this judgment I consent to no exceptions whatever, either recent or long past. And it is my fourth (and, to avoid too depressing a bill, final) conviction that the American people, taking one with another, constitute the most timorous, sniveling, poltroonish, ignominious mob of serfs and goose-steppers ever gathered under one flag in Christendom since the end of the Middle Ages, and that they grow more timorous, more sniveling, more poltroonish, more ignominious every day.

So far I go with the fugitive Young Intellectuals—and into the Bad Lands beyond. Such, in brief, are the cardinal articles of my political faith, held passionately since my admission to citizenship and now growing stronger and stronger as I gradually disintegrate into my component carbon, oxygen, hydrogen, phosphorus, calcium, sodium, nitrogen and iron. This is what I believe and preach, *in nomine Domini,* Amen. Yet I remain on the dock, wrapped in the flag, when the Young Intellectuals set sail. Yet here I stand, unshaken and undespairing, a loyal and devoted Americano, even a chauvinist, paying taxes without complaint, obeying all laws that are physiologically obeyable, accepting all the searching duties and responsibilities of citizenship unprotestingly, investing the sparse usufructs of my miserable toil in the obligations of the nation, avoiding all commerce with men sworn to overthrow the government, contributing my mite toward the glory of the national arts and sciences, enriching and embellishing the native language, spurning all lures (and even all invitations) to get out and stay out—here am I, a bachelor of easy means, forty-two years old, unhampered by debts or issue, able to go wherever I please and to stay as long as I please—here am I, contentedly and even smugly basking beneath the Stars and Stripes, a better citizen, I daresay, and certainly a less murmurous and exigent one, than thousands who put the Hon. Warren Gamaliel Harding beside Friedrich Barbarossa and

Charlemagne, and hold the Supreme Court to be directly inspired by the Holy Spirit, and belong ardently to every Rotary Club, Ku Klux Klan, and Anti-Saloon League, and choke with emotion when the band plays "The Star-Spangled Banner," and believe with the faith of little children that one of Our Boys, taken at random, could dispose in a fair fight of ten Englishmen, twenty Germans, thirty Frogs, forty Wops, fifty Japs, or a hundred Bolsheviki.

Well, then, why am I still here? Why am I so complacent (perhaps even to the point of offensiveness), so free from bile, so little fretting and indignant, so curiously happy? Why did I answer only with a few academic "Hear, Hears" when Henry James, Ezra Pound, Harold Stearns and the *émigrés* of Greenwich Village issued their successive calls to the corn-fed *intelligentsia* to flee the shambles, escape to fairer lands, throw off the curse forever? The answer, of course, is to be sought in the nature of happiness, which tempts to metaphysics. But let me keep upon the ground. To me, at least (and I can only follow my own nose), happiness presents itself in an aspect that is tripartite. To be happy (reducing the thing to its elementals) I must be:

a. Well-fed, unhounded by sordid cares, at ease in Zion.
b. Full of a comfortable feeling of superiority to the masses of my fellow-men.
c. Delicately and unceasingly amused according to my taste.

It is my contention that, if this definition be accepted, there is no country on the face of the earth wherein a man roughly constituted as I am—a man of my general weaknesses, vanities, appetites, prejudices, and aversions—can be so happy, or even one-half so happy, as he can be in these free and independent states. Going further, I lay down the proposition that it is a sheer physical impossibility for such a man to live in These States and *not* be happy—that it is as impossible to him

as it would be to a schoolboy to weep over the burning
down of his school-house. If he says that he isn't happy
here, then he either lies or is insane. Here the business
of getting a living, particularly since the war brought
the loot of all Europe to the national strong-box, is
enormously easier than it is in any other Christian land
—so easy, in fact, that an educated and forehanded man
who fails at it must actually make deliberate efforts to
that end. Here the general average of intelligence, of
knowledge, of competence, of integrity, of self-respect,
of honor is so low that any man who knows his trade,
does not fear ghosts, has read fifty good books, and
practices the common decencies stands out as brilliantly
as a wart on a bald head, and is thrown willy-nilly into
a meager and exclusive aristocracy. And here, more than
anywhere else that I know of or have heard of, the
daily panorama of human existence, of private and communal folly—the unending procession of governmental
extortions and chicaneries, of commercial brigandages
and throat-slittings, of theological buffooneries, or
æsthetic ribaldries, of legal swindles and harlotries, of
miscellaneous rogueries, villainies, imbecilities, gro-
tesqueries, and extravagances—is so inordinately gross and
preposterous, so perfectly brought up to the highest
conceivable amperage, so steadily enriched with an
almost fabulous daring and originality, that only the
man who was born with a petrified diaphragm can fail
to laugh himself to sleep every night, and to awake
every morning with all the eager, unflagging expectation
of a Sunday-school superintendent touring the Paris
peep-shows.

A certain sough of rhetoric may be here. Perhaps I
yield to words as a chautauqua lecturer yields to them,
belaboring and fermenting the hinds with his Message
from the New Jerusalem. But fundamentally I am quite
as sincere as he is. For example, in the matter of attain-
ing to ease in Zion, of getting a fair share of the national
swag, now piled so mountainously high. It seems to
me, sunk in my Egyptian night, that the man who fails

to do this in the United States to-day is a man who is somehow stupid—maybe not on the surface, but certainly deep down. Either he is one who cripples himself unduly, say by setting up a family before he can care for it, or by making a bad bargain for the sale of his wares, or by concerning himself too much about the affairs of other men; or he is one who endeavors fatuously to sell something that no normal American wants. Whenever I hear a professor of philosophy complain that his wife has eloped with some moving-picture actor or bootlegger who can at least feed and clothe her, my natural sympathy for the man is greatly corrupted by contempt for his lack of sense. Would it be regarded as sane and laudable for a man to travel the Soudan trying to sell fountain-pens, or Greenland offering to teach double-entry bookkeeping or counterpoint? Coming closer, would the judicious pity or laugh at a man who opened a shop for the sale of incunabula in Little Rock, Ark., or who demanded a living in McKeesport, Pa., on the ground that he could read Sumerian? In precisely the same way it seems to me to be nonsensical for a man to offer generally some commodity that only a few rare and dubious Americans want, and then weep and beat his breast because he is not patronized. One seeking to make a living in a country must pay due regard to the needs and tastes of that country. Here in the United States we have no jobs for grand dukes, and none for *Wirkliche Geheimräte,* and none for palace eunuchs, and none for masters of the buckhounds, and none (any more) for brewery *Todsaufer*—and very few for oboe-players, metaphysicians, astrophysicists, assyriologists, water-colorists, stylites and epic poets. . . . There may come a time when the composer of string quartettes is paid as much as a railway conductor, but it is not yet. Then why practice such trades—that is, as trades? The man of independent means may venture into them prudently; when he does so, he is seldom molested; it may even be argued that he performs a public service by adopting them. But the man who has a living to make is simply silly if he goes into them; he is like a soldier going over the top with a coffin strapped to his back. Let him abandon such puerile vanities, and take to the uplift instead, as, indeed, thousands of other victims of the industrial system have already done. Let him bear in mind that, whatever its neglect of the humanities and their monks, the Republic has never got half enough bond salesmen, quack doctors, ward leaders, phrenologists, Methodist evangelists, circus clowns, magicians, soldiers, farmers, popular song writers, moonshine distillers, forgers of gin labels, mine guards, detectives, spies, snoopers, and *agents provocateurs*. The rules are set by Omnipotence; the discreet man observes them. Observing them, he is safe beneath the starry bed-tick, in fair weather or foul. The *boobus Americanus* is a bird that knows no closed season—and if he won't come down to Texas oil stock, or one-night cancer cures, or building lots in Swampshurst, he will always come down to Inspiration and Optimism, whether political, theological, pedagogical, literary, or economic.

The doctrine that it is *infra digitatem* for an educated man to take a hand in the snaring of this goose is one in which I see nothing convincing. It is a doctrine chiefly voiced, I believe, by those who have tried the business and failed. They take refuge behind the childish notion that there is something honorable about poverty *per se*—the Greenwich Village complex. This is nonsense. Poverty may be an unescapable misfortune, but that no more makes it honorable than a cocked eye is made honorable by the same cause. Do I advocate, then, the ceaseless, senseless hogging of money? I do not. All I advocate—and praise as virtuous—is the hogging of enough to provide security and ease. Despite all the romantic superstitions to the contrary, the artist cannot do his best work when he is oppressed by unsatisfied wants. Nor can the philosopher. Nor can the man of science. The best and clearest thinking of the world is done and the finest art is produced, not by men who are hungry, ragged and harassed, but by men who are well-fed, warm and easy in mind. It is the artist's first duty to his art to achieve that tranquility for himself. Shakespeare tried to achieve it; so did Beethoven, Wagner, Brahms, Ibsen and Balzac. Goethe, Schopenhauer, Schumann and Mendelssohn were born to it. Joseph Conrad, Richard Strauss and Anatole France have got it for themselves in our own day. In the older countries, where competence is far more general and competition is thus more sharp, the thing is often cruelly difficult, and sometimes almost impossible. But in the United States it is absurdly easy, given ordinary luck. Any man with a superior air, the intelligence of a stockbroker, and the resolution of a hat-check girl—in brief, any man who believes in himself enough, and with sufficient cause, to be called a journeyman—can cadge enough money, in this glorious commonwealth of morons, to make life soft for him.

And if a lining for the purse is thus facilely obtainable, given a reasonable prudence and resourcefulness, then balm for the ego is just as unlaboriously got, given ordinary dignity and decency. Simply to exist, indeed, on the plane of a civilized man is to attain, in the Republic, to a distinction that should be enough for all save the most vain; it is even likely to be too much, as the frequent challenges of the Ku Klux Klan, the American Legion, the Anti-Saloon League, and other such vigilance committees of the majority testify. Here is a country in which all political thought and activity are concentrated upon the scramble for jobs—in which the normal politician, whether he be a President or a village road supervisor, is willing to renounce any principle, however precious to him, and to adopt any lunacy, however offensive to him, in order to keep his place at the trough. Go into politics, then, without seeking or wanting office, and at once you are as conspicuous as a red-haired blackamoor—in fact, a great deal more conspicuous, for red-haired blackamoors have been seen, but who has ever seen or heard of an American politician,

Democrat or Republican, Socialist or Liberal, Whig or
Tory, who did not itch for a job? Again, here is a
country in which it is an axiom that a business man
shall be a member of a Chamber of Commerce, an
admirer of Charles M. Schwab, a reader of the *Saturday
Evening Post,* a golfer—in brief, a vegetable. Spend
your hours of escape from *Geschäft* reading Remy
de Gourmont or practicing the violoncello, and the local
Sunday newspaper will infallibly find you out and
hymn the marvel—nay, your banker will summon you
to discuss your notes, and your rivals will spread the
report (probably truthful) that you were pro-German
during the war. Yet again, here is a land in which
women rule and men are slaves. Train your women to
get your slippers for you, and your ill fame will match
Galileo's or Darwin's. Once more, here is the Paradise
of back-slappers, of democrats, of mixers, of go-getters.
Maintain ordinary reserve, and you will arrest instant
attention—and have your hand kissed by multitudes who,
despite democracy, have all the inferior man's un-
quenchable desire to grovel and admire.

Nowhere else in the world is superiority more easily
attained or more eagerly admitted. The chief business
of the nation, as a nation, is the setting up of heroes,
mainly bogus. It admired the literary style of the late
Woodrow; it respects the theological passion of Bryan;
it venerates J. Pierpont Morgan; it takes Congress
seriously; it would be unutterably shocked by the proposition (with proof) that a majority of its judges
are ignoramuses, and that a respectable minority of
them are scoundrels. The manufacture of artificial
Durchlauchten, k.k. Hoheiten and even gods goes on
feverishly and incessantly; the will to worship never flags.
Ten iron-molders meet in the back-room of a near-beer
saloon, organize a lodge of the Noble and Mystic Order
of American Rosicrucians, and elect a wheelwright
Supreme Worthy Whimwham; a month later they send
a notice to the local newspaper that they have been
greatly honored by an official visit from that Whim-

wham, and that they plan to give him a jeweled fob for his watch-chain. The chief national heroes—Lincoln, Lee, and so on—cannot remain mere men. The mysticism of the mediæval peasantry gets into the communal view of them, and they begin to sprout haloes and wings. As I say, no intrinsic merit—at least, none commensurate with the mob estimate—is needed to come to such august dignities. Everything American is a bit amateurish and childish, even the national gods. The most conspicuous and respected American in nearly every field of endeavor, saving only the purely commercial (I exclude even the financial), is a man who would attract little attention in any other country. The leading American critic of literature, after twenty years of diligent exposition of his ideas, has yet to make it clear what he is in favor of, and why. The queen of the *haut monde,* in almost every American city, is a woman who regards Lord Reading as an aristocrat and her superior, and whose grandfather slept in his underclothes. The leading American musical director, if he went to Leipzig, would be put to polishing trombones and copying drum parts. The chief living American military man—the national heir to Frederick, Marlborough, Wellington, Washington and Prince Eugene—is a member of the Elks, and proud of it. The leading American philosopher (now dead, with no successor known to the average pedagogue) spent a lifetime erecting an epistemological defense for the national æsthetic maxim: "I don't know nothing about music, but I know what I like." The most eminent statesman the United States has produced since Lincoln was fooled by Arthur James Balfour, and miscalculated his public support by more than 5,000,000 votes. And the current Chief Magistrate of the nation—its defiant substitute for czar and kaiser—is a small-town printer who, when he wishes to enjoy himself in the Executive Mansion, invites in a homeopathic doctor, a Seventh Day Adventist evangelist, and a couple of moving-picture actresses.

2

All of which may be boiled down to this: that the United States is essentially a commonwealth of third-rate men—that distinction is easy here because the general level of culture, of information, of taste and judgment, of ordinary competence is so low. No sane man, employing an American plumber to repair a leaky drain, would expect him to do it at the first trial, and in precisely the same way no sane man, observing an American Secretary of State in negotiation with Englishmen and Japs, would expect him to come off better than second best. Third-rate men, of course, exist in all countries, but it is only here that they are in full control of the state, and with it of all the national standards. The land was peopled, not by the hardy adventurers of legend, but simply by incompetents who could not get on at home, and the lavishness of nature that they found here, the vast ease with which they could get livings, confirmed and augmented their native incompetence. No American colonist, even in the worst days of the Indian wars, ever had to face such hardships as ground down the peasants of Central Europe during the Hundred Years War, nor even such hardships as oppressed the English lower classes during the century before the Reform Bill of 1832. In most of the colonies, indeed, he seldom saw any Indians at all: the one thing that made life difficult for him was his congenital dunder-headedness. The winning of the West, so rhetorically celebrated in American romance, cost the lives of fewer men than the single battle of Tannenberg, and the victory was much easier and surer. The immigrants who have come in since those early days have been, if any-thing, of even lower grade than their forerunners. The old notion that the United States is peopled by the offspring of brave, idealistic and liberty loving minorities, who revolted against injustice, bigotry and mediævalism at home—this notion is fast succumbing to the alarmed study that has been given of late to the immigration of recent years. The truth is that the majority of non-Anglo-Saxon immigrants since the Revolution, like the majority of Anglo-Saxon immigrants before the Revolution, have been, not the superior men of their native lands, but the botched and unfit: Irishmen starving to death in Ireland, Germans unable to weather the *Sturm und Drang* of the post-Napoleonic reorganization, Italians weed-grown on exhausted soil, Scandinavians run to all bone and no brain, Jews too incompetent to swindle even the barbarous peasants of Russia, Poland and Roumania. Here and there among the immigrants, of course, there may be a bravo, or even a superman—*e.g.,* the ancestors of Volstead, Ponzi, Jack Dempsey, Schwab, Daugherty, Debs, Pershing—but the average newcomer is, and always has been, simply a poor fish.

Nor is there much soundness in the common assumption, so beloved of professional idealists and windmachines, that the people of America constitute "the youngest of the great peoples." The phrase turns up endlessly; the average newspaper editorial writer would be hamstrung if the Postoffice suddenly interdicted it, as it interdicted "the right to rebel" during the war. What gives it a certain specious plausibility is the fact that the American Republic, compared to a few other existing governments, is relatively young. But the American Republic is not necessarily identical with the American people; they might overturn it to-morrow and set up a monarchy, and still remain the same people. The truth is that, as a distinct nation, they go back fully three hundred years, and that even their government is older than that of most other nations, *e.g.,* France, Italy, Germany, Russia. Moreover, it is absurd to say that there is anything properly describable as youthfulness in the American outlook. It is not that of young men, but that of old men. All the characteristics of senescence are in it: a great distrust of ideas, an habitual timorousness, a harsh fidelity to a few fixed beliefs, a touch of mysticism. The average American is a prude and a Methodist under his skin, and the fact is never more evident than when he is trying to disprove it. His vices are not those of a healthy boy, but those of an ancient paralytic escaped from the *Greisenheim*. If you would penetrate to the causes thereof, simply go down to Ellis Island and look at the next shipload of immigrants. You will not find the spring of youth in their step; you will find the shuffling of exhausted men. From such exhausted men the American stock has sprung. It was easier for them to survive here than it was where they came from, but that ease, though it made them feel stronger, did not actually strengthen them. It left them what they were when they came: weary peasants, eager only for the comfortable security of a pig in a sty. Out of that eagerness has issued many of the noblest manifestations of American *Kultur*: the national hatred of war, the pervasive suspicion of the aims and intents of all other nations, the short way with heretics and disturbers of the peace, the unshakable belief in devils, the implacable hostility to every novel idea and point of view.

All these ways of thinking are the marks of the peasant—more, of the peasant long ground into the mud of his wallow, and determined at last to stay there —the peasant who has definitely renounced any lewd desire he may have ever had to gape at the stars. The habits of mind of this dull, sempiternal *fellah*—the oldest man in Christendom—are, with a few modifications, the habits of mind of the American people. The peasant has a great practical cunning, but he is unable to see any further than the next farm. He likes money and knows how to amass property, but his cultural development is but little above that of the domestic animals. He is intensely and cocksurely moral, but his morality and his self-interest are crudely identical. He is emotional and easy to scare, but his imagination cannot grasp an abstraction. He is a violent nationalist and patriot, but he admires rogues in office and always beats the tax-collector if he can. He has immovable opinions about all the great affairs of state, but nine-tenths of them are sheer imbecilities. He is violently jealous of what he conceives to be his rights, but brutally disregardful of the other fellow's. He is religious, but his religion is wholly devoid of beauty and dignity. This man, whether city or country bred, is the normal Americano—the 100 per cent. Methodist, Odd Fellow, Ku Kluxer, and Know Nothing. He exists in all countries, but here alone he rules—here alone his anthropoid fears and rages are accepted gravely as logical ideas, and dissent from them is punished as a sort of public offense. Around every one of his principal delusions—of the sacredness of democracy, of the feasibility of sumptuary law, of the incurable sinfulness of all other peoples, of the menace of ideas, of the corruption lying in all the arts—there is thrown a barrier of taboos, and woe to the anarchist who seeks to break it down!

The multiplication of such taboos is obviously not characteristic of a culture that is moving from a lower plane to a higher—that is, of a culture still in the full glow of its youth. It is a sign, rather, of a culture that is slipping downhill—one that is reverting to the most primitive standards and ways of thought. The taboo, indeed, is the trade-mark of the savage, and wherever it exists it is a relentless and effective enemy of civilized enlightenment. The savage is the most meticulously moral of men; there is scarcely an act of his daily life that is not conditioned by unyielding prohibitions and obligations, most of them logically unintelligible. The mob-man, a savage set amid civilization, cherishes a code of the same draconian kind. He believes firmly that right and wrong are immovable things—that they have an actual and unchangeable existence, and that any challenge of them, by word or act, is a crime against society. And with the concept of wrongness, of course, he always confuses the concept of mere differentness—to him the two are indistinguishable. Anything strange is to be combatted; it is of the Devil. The mob-man cannot grasp ideas in their native nakedness. They must be dramatized and personalized for him, and provided with either white wings or forked tails. All discussion of them, to interest him, must take the form of a pursuit and scotching of demons. He cannot think of a heresy without thinking of a heretic to be caught, condemned, and burned.

The Fathers of the Republic, I am convinced, had a great deal more prevision than even their most romantic worshipers give them credit for. They not only sought to create a governmental machine that would be safe from attack without; they also sought to create one that would be safe from attack within. They invented very ingenious devices for holding the mob in check, for protecting the national polity against its transient and illogical rages, for securing the determination of all the larger matters of state to a concealed but none the less real aristocracy. Nothing could have been further from the intent of Washington, Hamilton and even Jefferson than that the official doctrines of the nation, in the year 1922, should be identical with the nonsense heard in the chautauqua, from the evangelical pulpit, and on the stump. But Jackson and his merry men broke through the barbed wires thus so carefully strung, and ever since 1825 *vox populi* has been the true voice of the nation. To-day there is no longer any question of statesmanship, in any real sense, in our politics. The only way to success in American public life lies in flattering and kowtowing to the mob. A candidate for office, even the highest, must either adopt its current manias *en bloc,* or convince it hypocritically that he has done so, while cherishing reservations *in petto.* The result is that only two sorts of men stand any chance whatever of getting into actual control of affairs—first, glorified mob-men who genuinely believe what the mob believes, and secondly, shrewd fellows who are willing to make any sacrifice of conviction and self-respect in order to hold their jobs. One finds perfect examples of the first class in Jackson and Bryan. One finds hundreds of specimens of the second among the politicians who got themselves so affectingly converted to Prohibition, and who voted and blubbered for it with flasks in their pockets. Even on the highest planes our politics seems to be incurably mountebankish. The same Senators who raised such raucous alarms against the League of Nations voted for the Disarmament Treaty— a far more obvious surrender to English hegemony. And the same Senators who pleaded for the League on the ground that its failure would break the heart of the world were eloquently against the treaty. The few men who maintained a consistent course in both cases, voting either for or against both League and treaty, were denounced by the newspapers as deliberate marplots, and found their constituents rising against them. To such an extent had the public become accustomed to buncombe that simple honesty was incomprehensible to it, and hence abhorrent!

As I have pointed out in a previous work, this dominance of mob ways of thinking, this pollution of the whole intellectual life of the country by the prejudices and emotions of the rabble, goes unchallenged because the old landed aristocracy of the colonial era has been engulfed and almost obliterated by the rise of the industrial system, and no new aristocracy has arisen to take its place, and discharge its highly necessary functions. An upper class, of course, exists, and of late it has tended to increase in power, but it is culturally almost indistinguishable from the mob: it lacks absolutely anything even remotely resembling an aristocratic point of view. One searches in vain for any sign of the true *Junker* spirit in the Vanderbilts, Astors, Morgans, Garys, and other such earls and dukes of the plutocracy; their culture, like their aspiration, remains that of the pawnshop. One searches in vain, too, for the aloof air of the don in the official *intelligentsia* of the American universities; they are timorous and orthodox, and constitute a reptile Congregatio de Propaganda Fide to match Bismarck's *Reptilienpresse*. Everywhere else on earth, despite the rise of democracy, an organized minority of aristocrats survives from a more spacious day, and if its personnel has degenerated and its legal powers have decayed it has at least maintained some vestige of its old independence of spirit, and jealously guarded its old right to be heard without risk of penalty. Even in England, where the peerage has been debauched to the level of a political baptismal fount for Jewish money-lenders and Wesleyan soap-boilers, there is sanctuary for the old order in the two ancient universities, and a lingering respect for it in the peasantry. But in the United States it was paralyzed by Jackson and got its death blow from Grant, and since then no successor to it has been evolved. Thus there is no organized force to oppose the irrational vagaries of the mob. The legislative and executive arms of the government yield to them without resistance; the judicial arm has begun to yield almost as supinely, particularly when they take the form of witch-hunts; outside the official circle there is no opposition that is even dependably articulate. The worst excesses go almost without challenge. Discussion, when it is heard at all, is feeble and superficial, and girt about by the taboos that I have mentioned. The clatter about the so-called Ku Klux Klan, two or three years ago, was typical. The astounding program of this organization was discussed in the newspapers for months on end, and a committee of Congress sat in solemn state to investigate it, and yet not a single newspaper or Congressman, so far as I am aware, so much as mentioned the most patent and important fact about it, to wit, that the Ku Klux was, to all intents and purposes, simply the secular arm of the Methodist Church, and that its methods were no more than physical projections of the familiar extravagances of the Anti-Saloon League. The intimate relations between church and Klan, amounting almost to identity, must have been plain to every intelligent American, and yet the taboo upon the realistic consideration of ecclesiastical matters was sufficient to make every public soothsayer disregard it completely.

I often wonder, indeed, if there would be any intellectual life at all in the United States if it were not for the steady importation in bulk of ideas from abroad, and particularly, in late years, from England. What would become of the average American scholar if he could not borrow wholesale from English scholars? How could an inquisitive youth get beneath the surface of our politics if it were not for such anatomists as Bryce? Who would show our statesmen the dotted lines for their signatures if there were no Balfours and Lloyd-Georges? How could our young professors formulate æsthetic judgments, especially in the field of letters, if it were not for such gifted English mentors as Robertson Nicoll, Squire and Clutton-Brock? By what process, finally, would the true style of a visiting card be determined, and the *höflich* manner of eating artichokes, if there were no reports from Mayfair? On certain levels this naïve subservience must needs irritate every self-respecting American, and even dismay him. When he recalls the amazing feats of the English war propagandists between 1914 and 1917— and their even more amazing confessions of method since—he is apt to ask himself quite gravely if he belongs to a free nation or to a crown colony. The thing was done openly, shamelessly, contemptuously, cynically, and yet it was a gigantic success. The office of the American Secretary of State, from the end of Bryan's grotesque incumbency to the end of the Wilson administration, was little more than an antechamber of the British Foreign Office. Dr. Wilson himself, in the conduct of his policy, differed only legally from such colonial premiers as Hughes and Smuts. Even after the United States got into the war it was more swagger for a Young American blood to wear the British uniform than the American uniform. No American ever seriously questions an Englishman or Englishwoman of official or even merely fashionable position at home. Lord Birkenhead was accepted as a gentleman everywhere in the United States; Mrs. Asquith's almost unbelievable imbecilities were heard with hushed fascination; even Lady Astor, an American married to an expatriate German-American turned English viscount, was greeted with solemn effusiveness. During the latter part of 1917, when New York swarmed with British military missions, I observed in *Town Topics* a polite protest against a very significant habit of certain of their gallant members: that of going to dances wearing spurs, and so macerating the frocks and heels of the fawning fair. The protest, it appears, was not voiced by the hosts and hostesses of these singular officers: they would have welcomed their guests in trench boots. It was left to a dubious weekly, and it was made very gingerly.

The spectacle, as I say, has a way of irking the American touched by nationalistic weakness. Ever since the day of Lowell—even since the day of Cooper and Irving—there have been denunciations of it. But however unpleasant it may be, there is no denying that a chain of logical causes lies behind it, and that they are not to be disposed of by objecting to them. The average American of the Anglo-Saxon majority, in truth, is simply a second-rate Englishman, and so it is no wonder that he is spontaneously servile, despite all his democratic denial of superiorities, to what he conceives to be first-rate Englishmen. He corresponds, roughly, to an English Nonconformist of the better-fed variety, and he shows all the familiar characters of the breed. He is truculent and cocksure, and yet he knows how to take off his hat when a bishop of the Establishment passes. He is hot against the dukes, and yet the notice of a concrete duke is a singing in his heart. It seems to me that this inferior Anglo-Saxon is losing his old dominance in the United States—that is, biologically. But he will keep his cultural primacy for a long, long while, in spite of the overwhelming inrush of men of other races, if only because those newcomers are even more clearly inferior than he is. Nine-tenths of the Italians, for example, who have come to these shores in late years have brought no more of the essential culture of Italy with them than so many horned cattle would have brought. If they become civilized at all, settling here, it is the civilization of the Anglo-Saxon majority that they acquire, which is to say, the civilization of the English second table. So with the Germans, the Scandinavians, and even the Jews and Irish. The Germans, taking one with another, are on the cultural level of green-grocers. I have come into contact with a great many of them since 1914, some of them of considerable wealth and even of fashionable pretensions. In the whole lot I can think of but a score or two who could name offhand the principal works of Thomas Mann, Otto Julius Bierbaum, Ludwig Thoma or Hugo von Hofmannsthal. They know much more about Mutt and Jeff than they know about Goethe. The Scandinavians are even worse. The majority of them are mere clods, and they are sucked into the Knights of Pythias, the chautauqua and the Methodist Church almost as soon as they land; it is by no means a mere accident that the national Prohibition Enforcement Act bears the name of a man theoretically of the blood of Gustavus Vasa, Svend of the Forked Beard, and Eric the Red. The Irish in the United States are scarcely touched by the revival of Irish culture, despite their melodramatic concern with Irish politics. During the war they supplied diligent and dependable agents to the Anglo-Saxon White Terror, and at all times they are very susceptible to political and social bribery. As for the Jews, they change their names to Burton, Thompson and Cecil in order to qualify as true Americans, and when they are accepted and rewarded in the national coin they renounce Moses altogether and get themselves baptized in St. Bartholomew's Church.

Whenever ideas enter the United States from without they come by way of England. What the London *Times* says to-day, about Ukrainian politics, the revolt in India, a change of ministry in Italy, the character of the King of Norway, the oil situation in Mesopotamia, will be said week after next by the *Times* of New York, and a month or two later by all the other American newspapers. The extent of this control of American opinion by English news mongers is but little appreciated in the United States, even by professional journalists. Fully four-fifths of all the foreign news that comes to the American newspapers comes through London, and most of the rest is supplied either by Englishmen or by Jews (often American-born) who maintain close relations with the English.

During the years 1914–1917 so many English agents got into Germany in the guise of American correspondents —sometimes with the full knowledge of their Anglomaniac American employers—that the Germans, just before the United States entered the war, were considering barring American correspondents from their country altogether. I was in Copenhagen and Basel in 1917, and found both towns—each an important source of war news —full of Jews representing American journals as a sideline to more delicate and confidential work for the English department of press propaganda. Even to-day a very considerable proportion of the American correspondents in Europe are strongly under English influences, and in the Far East the proportion is probably still larger. But these men seldom handle really important news. All that is handled from London, and by trustworthy Britons. Such of it as is not cabled directly to the American newspapers and press associations is later clipped from English newspapers, and printed as bogus letters or cablegrams.

The American papers accept such very dubious stuff, not chiefly because they are hopelessly stupid or Anglomaniac, but because they find it impossible to engage competent American correspondents. If the native journalists who discuss our domestic politics avoid the fundamentals timorously, then those who venture to discuss foreign politics are scarcely aware of the fundamentals at all. We have simply developed no class of experts in such matters. No man comparable, say, to Dr. Dillon, Wickham Steed, Count zu Reventlow or Wilfrid Scawen Blunt exists in the United States. When, in the summer of 1920, the editors of the Baltimore *Sun* undertook plans to cover the approaching Disarmament Conference at Washington in a comprehensive and intelligent manner, they were forced, willy-nilly, into employing Englishmen to do the work. Such men as Brailsford and Bywater, writing from London, three thousand miles away, were actually better able to interpret the work of the conference than American correspondents on the spot, few of whom were capable of anything beyond the most trivial gossip.

During the whole period of the conference not a professional Washington correspondent—the flower of American political journalism—wrote a single article upon the proceedings that got further than their surface aspects. Before the end of the sessions this enforced dependence upon English opinion had an unexpected and significant result. Facing the English and the Japs in an unyielding alliance, the French turned to the American delegation for assistance. The issue specifically before the conference was one on which American self-interest was obviously identical with French self-interest. Nevertheless, the English had such firm grip upon the machinery of news distribution that they were able, in less than a week, to turn American public opinion against the French, and even to set up an active Francophobia. No American, not even any of the American delegates, was able to cope with their propaganda. They not only dominated the conference and pushed through a set of treaties that were extravagantly favorable to England; they even established the doctrine that all opposition to those treaties was immoral!

When Continental ideas, whether in politics, in metaphysics or in the fine arts, penetrate to the United States they nearly always travel by way of England. Emerson did not read Goethe; he read Carlyle. The American people, from the end of 1914 to the end of 1918, did not read first-hand statements of the German case; they read English interpretations of those statements. In London is the clearing house and transformer station. There the latest notions from the mainland are sifted out, carefully diluted with English water, and put into neat packages for the Yankee trade. The English not only get a chance to ameliorate or embellish; they also determine very largely what ideas Americans are to hear of at all. Whatever fails to interest them, or is in any way obnoxious to them, is not likely to cross the ocean. This explains why it is that most literate Americans are so densely ignorant of many Continentals who have been celebrated at home for years, for example, Huysmans,

Hartleben, Vaihinger, Merezhkovsky, Keyserling, Snoil-
sky, Mauthner, Altenberg, Heidenstam, Alfred Kerr. It
also explains why they so grossly overestimate various
third-raters, laughed at at home, for example, Brieux.
These fellows simply happen to interest the English *intelligentsia,* and are thus palmed off upon the gaping
colonists of Yankeedom. In the case of Brieux the hocus-
pocus was achieved by one man, George Bernard Shaw,
a Scotch blue-nose disguised as an Irish patriot and English soothsayer. Shaw, at bottom, has the ideas of a Presbyterian elder, and so the moral frenzy of Brieux en-
chanted him. . . .

This wholesale import and export business in Continental fancies is of no little benefit, of course, to the
generality of Americans. If it did not exist they would
probably never hear of many of the salient Continentals
at all, for the obvious incompetence of most of the native
and resident introducers of intellectual ambassadors
makes them suspicious even of those who, like Boyd and
Nathan, are thoroughly competent. To this day there is
no American translation of the plays of Ibsen; we use the
William Archer Scotch-English translations, most of
them atrociously bad, out still better than nothing. So
with the works of Nietzsche, Anatole France, Georg
Brandes, Turgeniev, Dostoyevsky, Tolstoi, and other
moderns after their kind. I can think of but one important exception: the work of Gerhart Hauptmann,
done into English by and under the supervision of
Ludwig Lewisohn. But even here Lewisohn used a number of English translations of single plays: the English
were still ahead of him, though they stopped half way.
He is, in any case, a very extraordinary American, and
the Department of Justice kept an eye on him during the
war. The average American professor is far too dull a
fellow to undertake so difficult an enterprise. Even when
he sports a German Ph.D. one usually finds on examination that all he knows about modern German literature
is that a *Mass* of Hofbräu in Munich used to cost 27
Pfennig downstairs and 32 *Pfennig* upstairs. The German

universities were formerly very tolerant of foreigners. Many an American, in preparation for professing at Harvard, spent a couple of years roaming from one to the other of them without picking up enough German to read the *Berliner Tageblatt*. Such frauds swarm in all our lesser universities, and many of them, during the war, became eminent authorities upon the crimes of Nietzsche and the errors of Treitschke.

3

In rainy weather, when my old wounds ache and the four humors do battle in my spleen, I often find myself speculating sourly as to the future of the Republic. Native opinion, of course, is to the effect that it will be secure and glorious; the superstition that progress must always be upward and onward will not down; in virulence and popularity it matches the superstition that money can accomplish anything. But this view is not shared by most reflective foreigners, as any one may find out by looking into such a book as Ferdinand Kürnberger's "Der Amerikamüde," Sholom Asch's "America," Ernest von Wolzogen's "Ein Dichter in Dollarica," W. L. George's "Hail, Columbia!", Annalise Schmidt's "Der Amerikanische Mensch" or Sienkiewicz's "After Bread," or by hearkening unto the confidences, if obtainable, of such returned immigrants as Georges Clemenceau, Knut Hamsun, George Santayana, Clemens von Pirquet, John Masefield and Maxim Gorky, and, via the ouija board, Antonin Dvořák, Frank Wedekind and Edwin Klebs. The American Republic, as nations go, has led a safe and easy life, with no serious enemies to menace it, either within or without, and no grim struggle with want. Getting a living here has always been easier than anywhere else in Christendom; getting a secure foothold has been possible to whole classes of men who would have remained submerged in Europe, as the character of our plutocracy, and no less of our *intelligentsia* so brilliantly shows. The American people have never had to face such titanic assaults as those suffered by the people of

Holland, Poland and half a dozen other little countries; they have not lived with a ring of powerful and unconscionable enemies about them, as the Germans have lived since the Middle Ages; they have not been torn by class wars, as the French, the Spaniards and the Russians have been torn; they have not thrown their strength into far-flung and exhausting colonial enterprises, like the English. All their foreign wars have been fought with foes either too weak to resist them or too heavily engaged elsewhere to make more than a half-hearted attempt. The combats with Mexico and Spain were not wars; they were simply lynchings. Even the Civil War, compared to the larger European conflicts since the invention of gunpowder, was trivial in its character and transient in its effects. The population of the United States, when it began, was about 31,500,000—say 10 per cent. under the population of France in 1914. But after four years of struggle, the number of men killed in action or dead of wounds, in the two armies, came to but 200,000—probably little more than a sixth of the total losses of France between 1914 and 1918. Nor was there any very extensive destruction of property. In all save a small area in the North there was none at all, and even in the South only a few towns of any importance were destroyed. The average Northerner passed through the four years scarcely aware, save by report, that a war was going on. In the South the breath of Mars blew more hotly, but even there large numbers of men escaped service, and the general hardship everywhere fell a great deal short of the hardships suffered by the Belgians, the French of the North, the Germans of East Prussia, and the Serbians and Rumanians in the World War. The agonies of the South have been much exaggerated in popular romance; they were probably more severe during Reconstruction, when they were chiefly psychical, than they were during the actual war. Certainly General Robert E. Lee was in a favorable position to estimate the military achievement of the Confederacy. Well, Lee was of the opinion that his army was very badly supported by the civil population, and that its final disaster was largely due to that ineffective support.

Coming down to the time of the World War, one finds precious few signs that the American people, facing an antagonist of equal strength and with both hands free, could be relied upon to give a creditable account of themselves. The American share in that great struggle, in fact, was marked by poltroonery almost as conspicuously as it was marked by knavery. Let us consider briefly what the nation did. For a few months it viewed the struggle idly and unintelligently, as a yokel might stare at a sword-swallower at a county fair. Then, seeing a chance to profit, it undertook with sudden alacrity the ghoulish office of *Kriegslieferant*. One of the contestants being debarred, by the chances of war, from buying, it devoted its whole energies, for two years, to purveying to the other. Meanwhile, it made every effort to aid its customer by lending him the cloak of its neutrality—that is, by demanding all the privileges of a neutral and yet carrying on a stupendous wholesale effort to promote the war. On the official side, this neutrality was fraudulent from the start, as the revelations of Mr. Tumulty have since demonstrated; popularly it became more and more fraudulent as the debts of the customer contestant piled up, and it became more and more apparent—a fact diligently made known by his partisans—that they would be worthless if he failed to win. Then, in the end, covert aid was transformed into overt aid. And under what gallant conditions! In brief, there stood a nation of 65,-000,000 people, which, without effective allies, had just closed two and a half years of homeric conflict by completely defeating an enemy state of 135,000,000 and two lesser ones of more than 10,000,000 together, and now stood at bay before a combination of at least 140,000,000. Upon this battle-scarred and war-weary foe the Republic of 100,000,000 freemen now flung itself, so lifting the odds to 4 to 1. And after a year and a half more of struggle it emerged triumphant—a knightly victor surely!

There is no need to rehearse the astounding and unprecedented swinishness that accompanied this glorious business—the colossal waste of public money, the savage persecution of all opponents and critics of the war, the open bribery of labor, the half-insane reviling of the enemy, the manufacture of false news, the knavish robbery of enemy civilians, the incessant spy hunts, the floating of public loans by a process of blackmail, the degradation of the Red Cross to partisan uses, the complete abandonment of all decency, decorum and self-respect. The facts must be remembered with shame by every civilized American; lest they be forgotten by the generations of the future I am even now engaged with collaborators upon an exhaustive record of them, in twenty volumes folio. More important to the present purpose are two things that are apt to be overlooked, the first of which is the capital fact that the war was "sold" to the American people, as the phrase has it, not by appealing to their courage, but by appealing to their cowardice—in brief, by adopting the assumption that they were not warlike at all, and certainly not gallant and chivalrous, but merely craven and fearful. The first selling point of the proponents of American participation was the contention that the Germans, with gigantic wars still raging on both fronts, were preparing to invade the United States, burn down all the towns, murder all the men, and carry off all the women—that their victory would bring staggering and irresistible reprisals for the American violation of the duties of a neutral. The second selling point was that the entrance of the United States would end the war almost instantly—that the Germans would be so overwhelmingly outnumbered, in men and guns, that it would be impossible for them to make any effective defense—above all, that it would be impossible for them to inflict any serious damage upon their new foes. Neither argument, it must be plain, showed the slightest belief in the warlike skill and courage of the American people. Both were grounded upon the frank theory that the only way to make the mob fight was to scare it half to death, and then show it a way to fight without risk, to stab a helpless antagonist in the back. And both were mellowed and reënforced by the hint that such a noble assault, beside being safe, would also be extremely profitable—that it would convert very dubious debts into very good debts, and dispose forever of a diligent and dangerous competitor for trade, especially in Latin America. All the idealist nonsense emitted by Dr. Wilson and company was simply icing on the cake. Most of it was abandoned as soon as the bullets began to fly, and the rest consisted simply of meaningless words—the idiotic babbling of a Presbyterian evangelist turned prophet and seer.

The other thing that needs to be remembered is the permanent effect of so dishonest and cowardly a business upon the national character, already far too much inclined toward easy ventures and long odds. Somewhere in his diaries Wilfrid Scawen Blunt speaks of the marked debasement that showed itself in the English spirit after the brutal robbery and assassination of the South African Republics. The heroes that the mob followed after Mafeking Day were far inferior to the heroes that it had followed in the days before the war. The English gentleman began to disappear from public life, and in his place appeared a rabble-rousing bounder obviously almost identical with the American professional politician—the Lloyd-George, Chamberlain, F. E. Smith, Isaacs-Reading, Churchill, Bottomley, Northcliffe type. Worse, old ideals went with old heroes. Personal freedom and strict legality, says Blunt, vanished from the English tables of the law, and there was a shift of the social and political center of gravity to a lower plane. Precisely the same effect is now visible in the United States. The overwhelming majority of conscripts went into the army unwillingly, and once there they were debauched by the twin forces of the official propaganda that I have mentioned and a harsh, unintelligent discipline. The first made them almost incapable of soldierly thought and conduct; the second converted them into cringing goose-steppers. The consequences display themselves in the amazing activities of

the American Legion, and in the rise of such correlative
organizations as the Ku Klux Klan. It is impossible to fit
any reasonable concept of the soldierly into the familiar
proceedings of the Legion. Its members conduct themselves like a gang of Methodist vice-crusaders on the
loose, or a Southern lynching party. They are forever
discovering preposterous burglars under the national
bed, and they advance to the attack, not gallantly and at
fair odds, but cravenly and in overwhelming force. Some
of their enterprises, to be set forth at length in the record
I have mentioned, have been of almost unbelievable baseness—the mobbing of harmless Socialists, the prohibition
of concerts by musicians of enemy nationality, the mutila-
tion of cows designed for shipment abroad to feed starving children, the roughing of women, service as strike-
breakers, the persecution of helpless foreigners, regardless
of nationality.

During the last few months of the war, when stories
of the tyrannical ill-usage of conscripts began to filter
back to the United States, it was predicted that they
would demand the punishment of the guilty when they
got home, and that if it was not promptly forthcoming
they would take it into their own hands. It was predicted,
too, that they would array themselves against the excesses
of Palmer, Burleson and company, and insist upon a
restoration of that democratic freedom for which they
had theoretically fought. But they actually did none of
these things. So far as I know, not a single martinet of a
lieutenant or captain has been manhandled by his late
victims; the most they have done has been to appeal to
Congress for revenge and damages. Nor have they
thrown their influence against the mediæval despotism
which grew up at home during the war; on the contrary,
they have supported it actively, and if it has lessened
since 1919 the change has been wrought without their
aid and in spite of their opposition. In sum, they show all
the stigmata of inferior men whose natural inferiority has
been made worse by oppression. Their chief organization
is dominated by shrewd ex-officers who operate it to their

own ends—politicians in search of jobs, Chamber of Commerce witch-hunters, and other such vermin. It seems to be wholly devoid of patriotism, courage, or sense. Nothing quite resembling it existed in the country before the war, not even in the South. There is nothing like it anywhere else on earth. It is a typical product of two years of heroic effort to arouse and capitalize the worst instincts of the mob, and it symbolizes very dramatically the ill effects of that effort upon the general American character.

Would men so degraded in gallantry and honor, so completely purged of all the military virtues, so submerged in baseness of spirit—would such pitiful caricatures of soldiers offer the necessary resistance to a public enemy who was equal, or perhaps superior in men and resources, and who came on with confidence, daring and resolution—say England supported by Germany as *Kriegslieferant* and with her inevitable swarms of Continental allies, or Japan with the Asiatic hordes behind her? Against the best opinion of the chatauquas, of Congress and of the patriotic press I presume to doubt it. It seems to me quite certain, indeed, that an American army fairly representing the American people, if it ever meets another army of anything remotely resembling like strength, will be defeated, and that defeat will be indistinguishable from rout. I believe that, at any odds less than two to one, even the exhausted German army of 1918 would have defeated it, and in this view, I think, I am joined by many men whose military judgment is far better than mine—particularly by many French officers. The changes in the American character since the Civil War, due partly to the wearing out of the old Anglo-Saxon stock, inferior to begin with, and partly to the infusion of the worst elements of other stocks, have surely not made for the fostering of the military virtues. The old cool head is gone, and the old dogged way with difficulties. The typical American of to-day has lost all the love of liberty that his forefathers had, and all their distrust of emotion, and pride in self-reliance. He is led no longer by Davy Crocketts; he is led by cheer leaders, press agents, word-mongers, up-lifters. I do not believe that such a faint-hearted and in-flammatory fellow, shoved into a war demanding every resource of courage, ingenuity and pertinacity, would give a good account of himself. He is fit for lynching-bees and heretic-hunts, but he is not fit for tight corners and desperate odds.

Nevertheless, his docility and pusillanimity may be overestimated, and sometimes I think that they *are* over-estimated by his present masters. They assume that there is absolutely no limit to his capacity for being put on and knocked about—that he will submit to any invasion of his freedom and dignity, however outrageous, so long as it is depicted in melodious terms. He permitted the late war to be "sold" to him by the methods of the grind-shop auctioneer. He submitted to conscription without any of the resistance shown by his brother democrats of Canada and Australia. He got no further than academic protests against the brutal usage he had to face in the army. He came home and found Prohibition foisted on him, and contented himself with a few feeble objurgations. He is a pliant slave of capitalism, and ever ready to help it put down fellow-slaves who venture to revolt. But this very weakness, this very credulity and poverty of spirit, on some easily conceivable to-morrow, may convert him into a rebel of a peculiarly insane kind, and so beset the Re-public from within with difficulties quite as formidable as those which threaten to afflict it from without. What Mr. James N. Wood calls the corsair of democracy—that is, the professional mob-master, the merchant of delusions, the pumper-up of popular fears and rages—is still content to work for capitalism, and capitalism knows how to re-ward him to his taste. He is the eloquent statesman, the patriotic editor, the fount of inspiration, the prancing milch-cow of optimism. He becomes public leader, Gov-ernor, Senator, President. He is Billy Sunday, Cyrus K. Curtis, Dr. Frank Crane, Charles E. Hughes, Taft, Wil-son, Cal Coolidge, General Wood, Harding. His, perhaps, is the best of trades under democracy—but it has its temptations! Let us try to picture a master corsair, thoroughly adept at pulling the mob nose, who suddenly bethought himself of that Pepin the Short who found himself mayor of the palace and made himself King of the Franks. There were lightnings along that horizon in the days of Roosevelt; there were thunder growls when Bryan emerged from the Nebraska steppes. On some great day of fate, as yet unrevealed by the gods, such a professor of the central democratic science may throw off his employers and set up a business for himself. When that day comes there will be plenty of excuse for black type on the front pages of the newspapers.

I incline to think that military disaster will give him his inspiration and his opportunity—that he will take the form, so dear to democracies, of a man on horseback. The chances are bad to-day simply because the mob is relatively comfortable—because capitalism has been able to give it relative ease and plenty of food in return for its docility. Genuine poverty is very rare in the United States, and actual hardship is almost unknown. There are times when the proletariat is short of phonograph records, silk shirts and movie tickets, but there are very few times when it is short of nourishment. Even during the most severe business depression, with hundreds of thousands out of work, most of these apparent sufferers, if they are willing, are able to get livings outside their trades. The cities may be choked with idle men, but the country is nearly always short of labor. And if all other resources fail, there are always public agencies to feed the hungry: capitalism is careful to keep them from despair. No American knows what it means to live as millions of Europeans lived during the war and have lived, in some places, since: with the loaves of the baker reduced to half size and no meat at all in the meatshop. But the time may come and it may not be far off. A national military disaster would disorganize all industry in the United States, already sufficiently wasteful and chaotic, and introduce the American people, for the first time in their history, to genuine want—and capital would be unable to relieve them. The day of such disaster will bring the savior foreordained. The slaves will follow him, their eyes fixed ecstatically upon the newest New Jerusalem. Men bred to respond automatically to shibboleths will respond to this worst and most insane one. Bolshevism, said General Foch, is a disease of defeated nations.

But do not misunderstand me: I predict no revolution in the grand manner, no melodramatic collapse of capitalism, no repetition of what has gone on in Russia. The American proletarian is not brave and romantic enough for that; to do him simple justice, he is not silly enough. Capitalism, in the long run, will win in the United States, if only for the reason that every American hopes to be a capitalist before he dies. Its roots go down to the deepest, darkest levels of the national soil; in all its characters, and particularly in its antipathy to the dreams of man, it is thoroughly American. To-day it seems to be immovably secure, given continued peace and plenty, and not all the demagogues in the land, consecrating themselves desperately to the one holy purpose, could shake it. Only a cataclysm will ever do that. But is a cataclysm conceivable? Isn't the United States the richest nation ever heard of in history, and isn't it a fact that modern wars are won by money? It is not a fact. Wars are won to-day, as in Napoleon's day, by the largest battalions, and the largest battalions, in the next great struggle, may not be on the side of the Republic. The usurious profits it wrung from the last war are as tempting as negotiable securities hung on the wash-line, as pre-Prohibition Scotch stored in open cellars. Its knavish ways with friends and foes alike have left it only foes. It is plunging ill-equipped into a competition for a living in the world that will be to the death. And the late Disarmament Conference left it almost ham-strung. Before the conference it had the Pacific in its grip, and with the Pacific in its grip it might have parleyed for a fair half of the Atlantic. But when the Japs and the English had finished their operations upon the Feather Duster, Popinjay Lodge, Master-Mind Root, Vacuum Underwood, young Teddy Roosevelt and the rest of their so-willing dupes there was apparent a baleful change. The Republic is extremely insecure to-day on both fronts, and it will be more insecure to-morrow. And it has no friends.

However, as I say, I do not fear for capitalism. It will weather the storm, and no doubt it will be the stronger for it afterward. The inferior man hates it, but there is too much envy mixed with his hatred, in the land of the theoretically free, for him to want to destroy it utterly, or even to wound it incurably. He struggles against it now, but always wistfully, always with a sneaking respect. On the day of Armageddon he may attempt a more violent onslaught. But in the long run he will be beaten. In the long run the corsairs will sell him out, and hand him over to his enemy. Perhaps—who knows?—the combat may raise that enemy to genuine strength and dignity. Out of it may come the superman.

4

All the while I have been forgetting the third of my reasons for remaining so faithful a citizen of the Federation, despite all the lascivious inducements from expatriates to follow them beyond the seas, and all the surly suggestions from patriots that I succumb. It is the reason which grows out of my mediæval but unashamed taste for the bizarre and indelicate, my congenital weakness for comedy of the grosser varieties. The United States, to my eye, is incomparably the greatest show on earth. It is a show which avoids diligently all the kinds of clowning which tire me most quickly—for example, royal ceremonials, the tedious hocus-pocus of *haut politique,* the taking of politics seriously—and lays chief stress upon the kinds which delight me unceasingly—for example, the ribald combats of demagogues, the exquisitely ingenious operations of master rogues, the pursuit of witches and heretics, the desperate struggles of inferior men to claw their way into Heaven. We have clowns in constant practice among us who are as far above the clowns of any other great state as a Jack Dempsey is above a paralytic—and not a few dozen or score of them, but whole droves and herds. Human enterprises which, in all other Christian countries, are resigned despairingly to an incurable dullness—things that seem devoid of exhilarating amusement by their very nature—are here lifted to such vast heights of buffoonery that contemplating them strains the midriff almost to breaking. I cite an example: the worship of God. Everywhere else on earth it is carried on in a solemn and dispiriting manner; in England, of course, the bishops are obscene, but the average man seldom gets a fair chance to laugh at them and enjoy them. Now come home. Here we not only have bishops who are enormously more obscene than even the most gifted of the English bishops; we have also a huge force of lesser specialists in ecclesiastical mountebankery —tin-horn Loyolas, Savonarolas and Xaviers of a hundred fantastic rites, each performing untiringly and each full of a grotesque and illimitable whimsicality. Every American town, however small, has one of its own: a holy clerk with so fine a talent for introducing the arts of jazz into the salvation of the damned that his performance takes on all the gaudiness of a four-ring circus, and the bald announcement that he will raid Hell on such and such a night is enough to empty all the town blind-pigs and bordellos and pack his sanctuary to the doors. And to aid him and inspire him there are traveling experts to whom he stands in the relation of a wart to the Matterhorn— stupendous masters of theological imbecility, contrivers of doctrines utterly preposterous, heirs to the Joseph Smith, Mother Eddy and John Alexander Dowie tradition—Bryan, Sunday, and their like. These are the eminences of the American Sacred College. I delight in them. Their proceedings make me a happier American.

Turn, now, to politics. Consider, for example, a campaign for the Presidency. Would it be possible to imagine anything more uproariously idiotic—a deafening, nerve-wracking battle to the death between Tweedledum and Tweedledee, Harlequin and Sganarelle, Gobbo and Dr. Cook—the unspeakable, with fearful snorts, gradually swallowing the inconceivable? I defy any one to match it elsewhere on this earth. In other lands, at worst, there are at least intelligible issues, coherent ideas, salient personalities. Somebody says something, and somebody replies. But what did Harding say in 1920, and what did Cox reply? Who was Harding, anyhow, and who was Cox? Here, having perfected democracy, we lift the whole combat to symbolism, to transcendentalism, to metaphysics. Here we load a pair of palpably tin cannon with blank cartridges charged with talcum powder, and so let fly. Here one may howl over the show without any uneasy reminder that it is serious, and that some one may be hurt. I hold that this elevation of politics to the plane of undiluted comedy is peculiarly American, that nowhere else on this disreputable ball has the art of the sham-battle been developed to such fineness. Two experiences are in point. During the Harding-Cox combat of bladders an article of mine, dealing with some of its more melodramatic phases, was translated into German and reprinted by a Berlin paper. At the head of it the editor was careful to insert a preface explaining to his readers, but recently delivered to democracy, that such contests were not taken seriously by intelligent Americans, and warning them solemnly against getting into sweats over politics. At about the same time I had dinner with an Englishman. From cocktails to bromo seltzer he bewailed the political lassitude of the English populace—its growing indifference to the whole partisan harlequinade. Here were two typical foreign attitudes: the Germans were in danger of making politics too harsh and implacable, and the English were in danger of forgetting politics altogether. Both attitudes, it must be plain, make for bad shows. Observing a German campaign, one is uncomfortably harassed and stirred up; observing an English campaign (at least in times of peace), one falls asleep. In the United States the thing is done better. Here politics is purged of all menace, all sinister quality, all genuine significance, and stuffed with such gorgeous humors, such inordinate farce that one comes to the end of a campaign with one's ribs loose, and ready for "King Lear," or a hanging, or a course of medical journals.

But feeling better for the laugh. *Ridi si sapis,* said Martial. Mirth is necessary to wisdom, to comfort, above all, to happiness. Well, here is the land of mirth, as Germany is the land of metaphysics and France is the land of fornication. Here the buffoonery never stops. What could be more delightful than the endless struggle of the Puritan to make the joy of the minority unlawful and impossible? The effort is itself a greater joy to one standing on the side-lines than any or all of the carnal joys that it combats. Always, when I contemplate an up-lifter at his hopeless business, I recall a scene in an old-time burlesque show, witnessed for hire in my days as a dramatic critic. A chorus girl executed a fall upon the stage, and Rudolph Krausemeyer, the Swiss comedian, rushed to her aid. As he stooped painfully to succor her, Irving Rabinovitz, the Zionist comedian, fetched him a fearful clout across the cofferdam with a slap-stick. So the uplifter, the soul-saver, the Americanizer, striving to make the Republic fit for Y. M. C. A. secretaries. He is the eternal American, ever moved by the best of inten-tions, ever running *a la* Krausemeyer to the rescue of virtue, and ever getting his pantaloons fanned by the Devil. I am naturally sinful, and such spectacles caress me. If the slap-stick were a sash-weight the show would be cruel, and I'd probably complain to the *Polizei.* As it is, I know that the uplifter is not really hurt, but simply shocked. The blow, in fact, does him good, for it helps to get him into Heaven, as exegetes prove from Matthew v, 11: *Heureux serez-vous, lorsqu'on vous outragera, qu'on vous persécutera,* and so on. As for me, it makes me a more contented man, and hence a better citizen. One man prefers the Republic because it pays better wages than Bulgaria. Another because it has laws to keep him sober and his daughter chaste. Another because the Woolworth Building is higher than the cathedral at Chartres. An-other because, living here, he can read the New York *Evening Journal.* Another because there is a warrant out for him somewhere else. Me, I like it because it amuses me to my taste. I never get tired of the show. It is worth every cent it costs.

That cost, it seems to me is very moderate. Taxes in the United States are not actually high. I figure, for example, that my private share of the expense of maintaining the Hon. Mr. Harding in the White House this year will work out to less than 80 cents. Try to think of better sport for the money: in New York it has been estimated that it costs $8 to get comfortably tight, and $17.50, on an average, to pinch a girl's arm. The United States Senate will cost me perhaps $11 for the year, but against that expense set the subscription price of the *Congressional Record,* about $15, which, as a journalist, I receive for nothing. For $4 less than nothing I am thus entertained as Solomon never was by his hooch dancers. Col. George Brinton McClellan Harvey costs me but 25 cents a year; I get Nicholas Murray Butler free. Finally, there is young Teddy Roosevelt, the naval expert. Teddy costs me, as I work it out, about 11 cents a year, or less than a cent a month. More, he entertains me doubly for the money, first as naval expert, and secondly as a walking *attentat* upon democracy, a devastating proof that there is nothing, after all, in that superstition. We Americans subscribe to the doctrine of human equality—and the Rooseveltii reduce it to an absurdity as brilliantly as the sons of Veit Bach. Where is your equal opportunity now? Here in this Eden of clowns, with the highest rewards of clowning theoretically open to every poor boy— here in the very citadel of democracy we found and cherish a clown *dynasty!*

HUNEKER: A MEMORY

There was a stimulating aliveness about him always, an air of living eagerly and a bit recklessly, a sort of defiant resiliency. In his very frame and form something provocative showed itself—an insolent singularity, obvious to even the most careless glance. That Caligulan profile of his was more than simply unusual in a free republic, consecrated to good works; to a respectable American, encountering it in the lobby of the Metropolitan or in the smoke-room of a *Doppelschraubenschnellpostdampfer,* it must have suggested inevitably the dark enterprises and illicit metaphysics of a Heliogabalus. More, there was always something rakish and defiant about his hat—it was too white, or it curled in the wrong way, or a feather peeped from the band—and a hint of antinomianism in his cravat. Yet more, he ran to exotic tastes in eating and drinking, preferring occult goulashes and risi-bisis to honest American steaks, and great floods of Pilsner to the harsh beverages of God-fearing men. Finally, there was his talk, that cataract of sublime trivialities: gossip lifted to the plane of the gods, the unmentionable bedizened with an astounding importance, and even profundity.

In his early days, when he performed the tonal and carnal prodigies that he liked to talk of afterward, I was at nurse, and too young to have any traffic with him. When I encountered him at last he was in the high flush of the middle years, and had already become a tradition in the little world that critics inhabit. We sat down to luncheon at one o'clock; I think it must have been at Lüchow's, his favorite refuge and rostrum to the end. At six, when I had to go, the waiter was hauling in his tenth (or was it twentieth?) *Seidel* of Pilsner, and he was bringing to a close *prestissimo* the most amazing monologue that these ears (up to that time) had ever funnelled into this consciousness. What a stew, indeed! Berlioz and the question of the clang-tint of the viola, the psychopathological causes of the suicide of Tschaikowsky, why Nietzsche had to leave Sils Maria between days in 1887, the echoes of Flaubert in Joseph Conrad (then but newly dawned), the precise topography of the warts of Liszt, George Bernard Shaw's heroic but vain struggles to throw off Presbyterianism, how Frau Cosima saved Wagner from the libidinous Swedish baroness, what to drink when playing Chopin, what Cézanne thought of his disciples, the defects in the structure of "Sister Carrie," Anton Seidl and the musical union, the complex love affairs of Gounod, the early days of David Belasco, the varying talents and idiosyncrasies of Lillian Russell's earlier husbands, whether a girl educated at Vassar could ever really learn to love, the exact composition of chicken paprika, the correct tempo of the Vienna waltz, the style of William Dean Howells, what George Moore said about German bathrooms, the true inwardness of the affair between D'Annunzio and Duse, the origin of the theory that all oboe players are crazy, why Löwenbräu survived exportation better than Hofbräu, Ibsen's loathing of Norwegians, the best remedy for Rhine wine *Katzenjammer,* how to play Brahms, the degeneration of the Bal Bullier, the sheer physical impossibility of getting Dvořák drunk, the genuine last words of Walt Whitman. . . .

I left in a sort of fever, and it was a couple of days later before I began to sort out my impressions, and formulate a coherent image. Was the man allusive in his books—so allusive that popular report credited him with the actual manufacture of authorities? Then he was ten times as allusive in his discourse—a veritable geyser of unfamiliar names, shocking epigrams in strange tongues, unearthly philosophies out of the backwaters of Scandinavia, Transylvania, Bulgaria, the Basque country, the Ukraine. And did he, in his criticism, pass facilely from the author to the man, and from the man to his wife, and to the wives of his friends? Then at the *Biertisch* he began long beyond the point where the last honest wife gives up the ghost, and so, full tilt, ran into such complexities of adultery that a plain sinner could scarcely follow him. I try to give you, ineptly and grotesquely, some notion of the talk of the man, but I must fail inevitably. It was, in brief, chaos, and chaos cannot be described. But it was chaos made to gleam and coruscate with every device of the seven arts—chaos drenched in all the colors imaginable, chaos scored for an orchestra which made the great band of Berlioz seem like a fife and drum corps. One night a few months before the war, I sat in the Paris Opera House listening to the first performance of Richard Strauss's "Josef's Legend," with Strauss himself conducting. On the stage there was a riot of hues that swung the eyes 'round and 'round in a crazy mazurka; in the orchestra there were such volleys and explosions of tone that the ears (I fall into a Hunekeran trope) began to go pale and clammy with surgical shock. Suddenly, above all the uproar, a piccolo launched into a new and saucy tune—in an unrelated key! . . . Instantly and quite naturally, I thought of the incomparable James. When he gave a show at Lüchow's he never forgot that anarchistic passage for the piccolo.

I observe a tendency since his death to estimate him in terms of the content of his books. Even Frank Harris, who certainly should know better, goes there for the facts about him. Nothing could do him worse injustice. In those books, of course, there is a great deal of perfectly sound stuff; the wonder is, in truth, that so much of it holds up so well to-day—for example, the essays on Strauss, on Brahms and on Nietzsche, and the whole volume on Chopin. But the real Huneker never got himself formally between covers, if one forgets "Old Fogy" and parts of "Painted Veils." The volumes of his regular canon are made up, in the main, of articles

written for the more intellectual magazines and newspapers of their era, and they are full of a conscious
striving to qualify for respectable company. Huneker,
always curiously modest, never got over the notion
that it was a singular honor for a man such as he—a
mere diurnal scribbler, innocent of academic robes—to
be published by so austere a publisher as Scribner.
More than once, anchored at the beer-table, we discussed
the matter at length, I always arguing that all the
honor was enjoyed by Scribner. But Huneker, I believe
in all sincerity, would not have it so, any more than
he would have it that he was a better music critic than
his two colleagues, the pedantic Krehbiel and the nonsensical Finck. This illogical modesty, of course, had its
limits; it made him cautious about expressing himself,
but it seldom led him into downright assumptions of
false personality. Nowhere in all his books will you find
him doing the things that every right-thinking Anglo-
Saxon critic is supposed to do—the Middleton Murry,
Paul Elmer More, Clutton-Brock sort of puerility—
solemn essays on Coleridge and Addison, abysmal discussions of the relative merits of Schumann and Mendelssohn, horrible treatises upon the relations of Goethe to
the Romantic Movement, dull scratchings in a hundred
such exhausted and sterile fields. Such enterprises were
not for Huneker; he kept himself out of that black
coat. But I am convinced that he always had his own
raiment pressed carefully before he left Lüchow's for
the temple of Athene—and maybe changed cravats, and
put on a boiled shirt, and took the feather out of his
hat. The simon-pure Huneker, the Huneker who was
the true essence and prime motor of the more courtly
Huneker—remained behind. This real Huneker survives
in conversations that still haunt the rafters of the beer-
halls of two continents, and in a vast mass of newspaper impromptus, thrown off too hastily to be reduced
to complete decorum, and in two books that stand outside the official canon, and yet contain the man himself
as not even "Iconoclasts" or the Chopin book contains

him, to wit, the "Old Fogy" aforesaid and the "Painted
Veils" of his last year. Both were published, so to
speak, out of the back door—the former by a music
publisher in Philadelphia and the latter in a small and
expensive edition for the admittedly damned. There is
a chapter in "Painted Veils" that is Huneker to every
last hitch of the shoulders and twinkle of the eye—the
chapter in which the hero soliloquizes on art, life, im-
mortality, and women—especially women. And there
are half a dozen chapters in "Old Fogy"—superficially
buffoonery, but how penetrating! how gorgeously
flavored! how learned!—that come completely up to the
same high specification. If I had to choose one Huneker
book and give up all the others, I'd choose "Old Fogy"
instantly. In it Huneker is utterly himself. In it the last
trace of the pedagogue vanishes. Art is no longer, even
by implication, a device for improving the mind. It
is wholly a magnificent adventure.

The notion of it is what Huneker brought into
American criticism, and it is for that bringing that he
will be remembered. No other critic of his generation
had a tenth of his influence. Almost singlehanded he
overthrew the æsthetic theory that had flourished in the
United States since the death of Poe, and set up an
utterly contrary æsthetic theory in its place. If the
younger men of to-day have emancipated themselves
from the Puritan æsthetic, if the schoolmaster is now
palpably on the defensive, and no longer the unchallenged assassin of the fine arts that he once was, if he
has already begun to compromise somewhat absurdly
with new and sounder ideas, and even to lift his voice
in artificial hosannahs, then Huneker certainly deserves
all the credit for the change. What he brought back
from Paris was precisely the thing that was most
suspected in the America of those days: the capacity for
gusto. Huneker had that capacity in a degree unmatched
by any other critic. When his soul went adventuring
among masterpieces it did not go in Sunday broadcloth;
it went with vine leaves in its hair. The rest of the

appraisers and criers-up—even Howells, with all his humor—could never quite rid themselves of the professorial manner. When they praised it was always with some hint of ethical, or, at all events, of cultural purpose; when they condemned that purpose was even plainer. The arts, to them, constituted a sort of school for the psyche; their aim was to discipline and mellow the spirit. But to Huneker their one aim was always to make the spirit glad—to set it, in Nietzsche's phrase, to dancing with arms and legs. He had absolutely no feeling for extra-æsthetic valuations. If a work of art that stood before him was honest, if it was original, if it was beautiful and thoroughly alive, then he was for it to his last corpuscle. What if it violated all the accepted canons? Then let the accepted canons go hang! What if it lacked all purpose to improve and lift up? Then so much the better! What if it shocked all right-feeling men, and made them blush and tremble? Then damn all men of right feeling forevermore.

With this ethical atheism, so strange in the United States and so abhorrent to most Americans, there went something that was probably also part of the loot of Paris: an insatiable curiosity about the artist as man. This curiosity was responsible for two of Huneker's salient characters: his habit of mixing even the most serious criticism with cynical and often scandalous gossip, and his pervasive foreignness. I believe that it is almost literally true to say that he could never quite make up his mind about a new symphony until he had seen the composer's mistress, or at all events a good photograph of her. He thought of Wagner, not alone in terms of melody and harmony, but also in terms of the Triebschen idyl and the Bayreuth tragicomedy. Go through his books and you will see how often he was fascinated by mere eccentricity of personality. I doubt that even Huysmans, had he been a respectable French Huguenot, would have interested him; certainly his enthusiasm for Verlaine, Villiers de l'Isle Adam and other such fantastic fish was centered upon the men quite as much as upon the artists. His foreignness, so often urged against him by defenders of the national tradition, was grounded largely on the fact that such eccentric personalities were rare in the Republic—rare, and well watched by the *Polizei*. When one bobbed up, he was alert at once—even though the newcomer was only a Roosevelt. The rest of the American people he dismissed as a horde of slaves, goose-steppers, cads, Methodists; he could not imagine one of them becoming a first-rate artist, save by a miracle. Even the American executant was under his suspicion, for he knew very well that playing the fiddle was a great deal more than scraping four strings of copper and catgut with a switch from a horse's tail. What he asked himself was how a man could play Bach decently, and then, after playing, go from the hall to a soda-fountain, or a political meeting, or a lecture at the Harvard Club. Overseas there was a better air for artists, and overseas Huneker looked for them.

These fundamental theories of his, of course, had their defects. They were a bit too simple, and often very much too hospitable. Huneker, clinging to them, certainly did his share of whooping for the sort of revolutionist who is here to-day and gone to-morrow; he was fugelman, in his time, for more than one cause that was lost almost as soon as it was stated. More, his prejudices made him somewhat anæsthetic, at times, to the new men who were not brilliant in color but respectably drab, and who tried to do their work within the law. Particularly in his later years, when the old gusto began to die out and all that remained of it was habit, he was apt to go chasing after strange birds and so miss seeing the elephants go by. I could put together a very pretty list of frauds that he praised. I could concoct another list of genuine *arrivés* that he overlooked. But all that is merely saying that there were human limits to him; the professors, on their side, have sinned far worse, and in both directions. Looking back over the whole of his work, one must needs be amazed by the general soundness of his judgments. He discerned, in the main, what was good and he described it in terms that were seldom bettered afterward. His successive heroes, always under fire when he first championed them, almost invariably moved to secure ground and became solid men, challenged by no one save fools— Ibsen, Nietzsche, Brahms, Strauss, Cézanne, Stirner, Synge, the Russian composers, the Russian novelists. He did for this Western world what Georg Brandes was doing for Continental Europe—sorting out the new-comers with sharp eyes, and giving mighty lifts to those who deserved it. Brandes did it in terms of the old academic bombast; he was never more the professor than when he was arguing for some hobgoblin of the professors. But Huneker did it with verve and grace; he made it, not schoolmastering, but a glorious deliverance from schoolmastering. As I say, his influence was enormous. The fine arts, at his touch, shed all their Anglo-American lugubriousness, and became provocative and joyous. The spirit of senility got out of them and the spirit of youth got into them. His criticism, for all its French basis, was thoroughly American—vastly more American, in fact, than the New England ponderosity that it displaced. Though he was an Easterner and a cockney of the cockneys, he picked up some of the Western spaciousness that showed itself in Mark Twain. And all the young men followed him.

A good many of them, I daresay, followed him so ardently that they got a good distance ahead of him, and often, perhaps, embarrassed him by taking his name in vain. For all his enterprise and iconoclasm, indeed, there was not much of the Berserker in him, and his floutings of the national æsthetic tradition seldom took the form of forthright challenges. Here the strange modesty that I have mentioned always stayed him as a like weakness stayed Mark Twain. He could never quite rid himself of the feeling that he was no more than an amateur among the gaudy doctors who roared in the reviews, and that it would be unseemly for him

133

to forget their authority. I have a notion that this feeling was born in the days when he stood almost alone, with the whole faculty grouped in a pained circle around him. He was then too miserable a worm to be noticed at all. Later on, gaining importance, he was lectured somewhat severely for his violation of decorum; in England even Max Beerbohm made an idiotic assault upon him. It was the Germans and the French, in fact, who first praised him intelligently—and these friends were too far away to help a timorous man in a row at home. This sensation of isolation and littleness, I suppose, explains his fidelity to the newspapers, and the otherwise inexplicable joy that he always took in his forgotten work for the *Musical Courier,* in his day a very dubious journal. In such waters he felt at ease. There he could disport without thought of the dignity of publishers and the eagle eyes of campus reviewers. Some of the connections that he formed were full of an ironical inappropriateness. His discomforts in his *Puck* days showed themselves in the feebleness of his work; when he served the *Times* he was as well placed as a Cabell at a colored ball. Perhaps the *Sun,* in the years before it was munseyized, offered him the best berth that he ever had, save it were his old one on *Mlle. New York.* But whatever the flag, he served it loyally, and got a lot of fun out of the business. He liked the pressure of newspaper work; he liked the associations that it involved, the gabble in the press-room of the Opera House, the exchanges of news and gossip; above all, he liked the relative ease of the intellectual harness. In a newspaper article he could say whatever happened to pop into his mind, and if it looked thin the next day, then there was, after all, no harm done. But when he sat down to write a book—or rather to compile it, for all of his volumes were reworked magazine (and sometimes newspaper) articles—he became self-conscious, and so knew uneasiness. The tightness of his style, its one salient defect, was probably the result of this weakness. The corrected clippings that constituted most of his

manuscripts are so beladen with revisions and rerevisions
that they are almost indecipherable.

Thus the growth of Huneker's celebrity in his later
years filled him with wonder, and never quite convinced him. He was certainly wholly free from any
desire to gather disciples about him and found a school.
There was, of course, some pride of authorship in him,
and he liked to know that his books were read and
admired; in particular, he was pleased by their translation into German and Czech. But it seemed to me that
he shrank from the bellicosity that so often got into
praise of them—that he disliked being set up as the opponent and superior of the professors whom he always
vaguely respected and the rival newspaper critics whose
friendship he esteemed far above their professional
admiration, or even respect. I could never draw him
into a discussion of these rivals, save perhaps a discussion of their historic feats at beer-guzzling. He wrote
vastly better than any of them and knew far more
about the arts than most of them, and he was undoubtedly aware of it in his heart, but it embarrassed
him to hear this superiority put into plain terms. His
intense gregariousness probably accounted for part of
this reluctance to pit himself against them; he could
not imagine a world without a great deal of easy
comradeship in it, and much casual slapping of backs.
But under it all was the chronic underestimation of
himself that I have discussed—his fear that he had
spread himself over too many arts, and that his equip-
ment was thus defective in every one of them. "Steeple-
jack" is full of this apologetic timidity. In its very title,
as he explains it, there is a confession of inferiority
that is almost maudlin: "Life has been the Barmecide's
feast to me," and so on. In the book itself he constantly
takes refuge in triviality from the harsh challenges of
critical parties, and as constantly avoids facts that would
shock the Philistines. One might reasonably assume,
reading it from end to end, that his early days in Paris
were spent in the fashion of a Y. M. C. A. secretary. A

few drinking bouts, of course, and a love affair in the manner of Dubuque, Iowa—but where are the wenches?

More than once, indeed, the book sinks to downright equivocation—for example, in the Roosevelt episodes. Certainly no one who knew Huneker in life will ever argue seriously that he was deceived by the Roosevelt buncombe, or that his view of life was at all comparable to that of the great demagogue. He stood, in fact, at the opposite pole. He saw the world, not as a moral show, but as a sort of glorified Follies. He was absolutely devoid of that obsession with the problem of conduct which was Roosevelt's main virtue in the eyes of a stupid and superstitious people. More, he was wholly against Roosevelt on many concrete issues—the race suicide banality, the Panama swindle, the war. He was far too much the realist to believe in the American case, either before or after 1917, and the manner in which it was urged, by Roosevelt and others, violated his notions of truth, honor and decency. I assume nothing here; I simply record what he told me himself. Nevertheless, the sheer notoriety of the Rough Rider— his picturesque personality and talent as a mountebank—had its effect on Huneker, and so he was a bit flattered when he was summoned to Oyster Bay, and there accepted gravely the nonsense that was poured into his ear, and even repeated some of it without a cackle in his book. To say that he actually believed in it would be to libel him. It was precisely such hollow tosh that he stood against in his rôle of critic of art and life; it was by exposing its hollowness that he lifted himself above the general. The same weakness induced him to accept membership in the National Institute of Arts and Letters. The offer of it to a man of his age and attainments, after he had been passed over year after year in favor of all sorts of cheapjack novelists and tenth-rate compilers of college textbooks, was intrinsically insulting; it was almost as if the Musical Union had offered to admit a Brahms. But with the insult went a certain gage of respectability, a certain

formal forgiveness for old frivolities, a certain abatement
of old doubts and self-questionings and so Huneker accepted. Later on, reviewing the episode in his own mind,
he found it the spring of doubts that were even more
uncomfortable. His last letter to me was devoted to the
matter. He was by then eager to maintain that he
had got in by a process only partly under his control,
and that, being in, he could discover no decorous way
of getting out.

But perhaps I devote too much space to the elements
in the man that worked against his own free development. They were, after all, grounded upon qualities
that are certainly not to be deprecated—modesty, good-
will to his fellow-men, a fine sense of team-work, a
distaste for acrimonious and useless strife. These qualities
gave him great charm. He was not only humorous; he
was also good-humored; even when the crushing discomforts of his last illness were upon him his amiability
never faltered. And in addition to humor there was
wit, a far rarer thing. His most casual talk was full of
this wit, and it bathed everything that he discussed in
a new and brilliant light. I have never encountered a
man who was further removed from dullness; it seemed
a literal impossibility for him to open his mouth without discharging some word or phrase that arrested the
attention and stuck in the memory. And under it all,
giving an extraordinary quality to the verbal fireworks,
there was a solid and apparently illimitable learning.
The man knew as much as forty average men, and his
knowledge was well-ordered and instantly available. He
had read everything and had seen everything and heard
everything, and nothing that he had ever read or seen
or heard quite passed out of his mind.

Here, in three words, was the main virtue of his
criticism—its gigantic richness. It had the dazzling charm
of an ornate and intricate design, a blazing fabric of
fine silks. It was no mere pontifical statement of one
man's reactions to a set of ideas; it was a sort of essence
of the reactions of many men—of all the men, in fact,

worth hearing. Huneker discarded their scaffolding, their ifs and whereases, and presented only what was important and arresting in their conclusions. It was never a mere *pastiche;* the selection was made delicately, discreetly, with almost unerring taste and judgment. And in the summing up there was always the clearest possible statement of the whole matter. What finally emerged was a body of doctrine that came, I believe, very close to the truth. Into an assembly of national critics who had long wallowed in dogmatic puerilities, Huneker entered with a taste infinitely surer and more civilized, a learning infinitely greater, and an address infinitely more engaging. No man was less the reformer by inclination, and yet he became a reformer beyond compare. He emancipated criticism in America from its old slavery to stupidity, and with it he emancipated all the arts themselves.

THE NATURE OF LIBERTY

Every time an officer of the constabulary, in the execution of his just and awful powers under American law, produces a compound fracture of the occiput of some citizen in his custody, with hemorrhage, shock, coma and death, there comes a feeble, falsetto protest from specialists in human liberty. Is it a fact without significance that this protest is never supported by the great body of American freemen, setting aside the actual heirs and creditors of the victim? I think not. Here, as usual, public opinion is very realistic. It does not rise against the policeman for the plain and simple reason that it does not question his right to do what he has done. Policemen are not given night-sticks for ornament. They are given them for the purpose of cracking the skulls of the recalcitrant plain people, Democrats and Republicans alike. When they execute that high duty they are palpably within their rights.

The specialists aforesaid are the same fanatics who shake the air with sobs every time the Postmaster-General of the United States bars a periodical from the mails because its ideas do not please him, and every time some poor Russian is deported for reading Karl Marx, and every time a Prohibition enforcement officer murders a bootlegger who resists his levies, and every time agents of the Department of Justice throw an Italian out of the window, and every time the Ku Klux Klan or the American Legion tars and feathers a Socialist evangelist. In brief, they are Radicals, and to scratch one with a pitchfork is to expose a Bolshevik. They are men standing in contempt of American institutions and in enmity to American idealism. And their evil principles are no less offensive to right-thinking and red-blooded Americans when they are United States Senators or editors of wealthy newspapers than when they are degraded I. W. W.'s throwing dead cats and infernal machines into meetings of the Rotary Club.

What ails them primarily is the ignorant and uncritical monomania that afflicts every sort of fanatic, at all times and everywhere. Having mastered with their limited faculties the theoretical principles set forth in the Bill of Rights, they work themselves into a passionate conviction that those principles are identical with the rules of law and justice, and ought to be enforced literally, and without the slightest regard for circumstance and expediency. It is precisely as if a High Church rector, accidentally looking into the Book of Chronicles, and especially Chapter II, should suddenly issue a mandate from his pulpit ordering his parishioners, on penalty of excommunication and the fires of hell, to follow exactly the example set forth, to wit: "And Jesse begat his first born Eliab, and Abinadab the second, and Shimma the third, Netheneel the fouth, Raddai the fifth, Ozen the sixth, David the seventh," and so on. It might be very sound theoretical theology, but it would surely be out of harmony with modern ideas, and the rev. gentleman would be extremely lucky if the bishop did not give him 10 days in the diocesan hoosegow.

So with the Bill of Rights. As adopted by the Fathers of the Republic, it was gross, crude, inelastic, a bit fanciful and transcendental. It specified the rights of a citizen, but it said nothing whatever about his duties. Since then, by the orderly processes of legislative science and by the even more subtle and beautiful devices of juridic art, it has been kneaded and mellowed into a far greater pliability and reasonableness. On the one hand, the citizen still retains the great privilege of membership in the most superb free nation ever witnessed on this earth. On the other hand, as a result of countless shrewd enactments and sagacious decisions, his natural lusts and appetites are held in laudable check, and he is thus kept in order and decorum. No artificial impediment stands in the way of his highest aspiration. He may become anything, including even a policeman. But once a policeman, he is protected by the legislative and judicial arms in the peculiar rights and prerogatives that go with his high office, including especially the right to jug the laity at his will, to sweat and mug them, to subject them to the third degree, and to subdue their resistance by beating out their brains. Those who are unaware of this are simply ignorant of the basic principles of American jurisprudence, as they have been exposed times without number by the courts of first instance and ratified in lofty terms by the Supreme Court of the United States. The one aim of the controlling decisions, magnificently attained, is to safeguard public order and the public security, and to substitute a judicial process for the inchoate and dangerous interaction of discordant egos.

Let us imagine an example. You are, say, a peaceable citizen on your way home from your place of employment. A police sergeant, detecting you in the crowd, approaches you, lays his hand on your collar, and informs you that you are under arrest for killing a trolley conductor in Altoona, Pa., in 1917. Amazed by the accusation, you decide hastily that the officer has lost his wits, and take to your heels. He pursues you. You continue to run. He draws his revolver and fires at you. He misses you. He fires again and fetches you in the leg. You fall and he is upon you. You prepare to resist his apparently maniacal assault. He beats you into insensibility with his espantoon, and drags you to the patrol box.

Arrived at the watch house you are locked in a room with five detectives, and for six hours they question you with subtle art. You grow angry—perhaps robbed of your customary politeness by the throbbing in your head and leg—and answer tartly. They knock you down. Having failed to wring a confession. from you, they lock you in a cell, and leave you there all night. The next day you are taken to police headquarters, your photograph is made for the Rogues' Gallery, and a print is duly deposited in the section labeled "Murderers." You are then carted to jail and locked up again. There you remain until the trolley conductor's wife comes down from Altoona to identify you. She astonishes the police by saying that you are not the man. The actual murderer, it appears, was an Italian. After holding you a day or two longer, to search your house for stills, audit your income tax returns, and investigate the premarital chastity of your wife, they let you go.

You are naturally somewhat irritated by your experience and perhaps your wife urges you to seek redress. Well, what are your remedies? If you are a firebrand, you reach out absurdly for those of a preposterous nature: the instant jailing of the sergeant, the dismissal of the Police Commissioner, the release of Mooney, a fair trial for Sacco and Vanzetti, free trade with Russia, One Big Union. But if you are a 100 per cent. American and respect the laws and institutions of your country, you send for your solicitor—and at once he shows you just how far your rights go, and where they end.

141

You cannot cause the arrest of the sergeant, for you resisted him when he attempted to arrest you, and when you resisted him he acquired an instant right to take you by force. You cannot proceed against him for accusing you falsely, for he has a right to make summary arrests for felony, and the courts have many times decided that a public officer, so long as he cannot be charged with corruption or malice, is not liable for errors of judgment made in the execution of his sworn duty. You cannot get the detectives on the mat, for when they questioned you you were a prisoner accused of murder, and it was their duty and their right to do so. You cannot sue the turnkey at the watch house or the warden at the jail for locking you up, for they received your body, as the law says, in a lawful and regular manner, and would have been liable to penalty if they had turned you loose.

But have you no redress whatever, no rights at all? Certainly you have a right, and the courts have jealously guarded it. You have a clear right, guaranteed to you under the Constitution, to go into a court of equity and apply for a mandamus requiring the *Polizei* to cease forthwith to expose your portrait in the Rogues' Gallery among the murderers. This is your inalienable right, and no man or men on earth can take it away from you. You cannot prevent them cherishing your portrait in their secret files, but you can get an order commanding them to refrain forever from exposing it to the gaze of idle visitors, and if you can introduce yourself unseen into their studio and prove that they disregard that order, you can have them haled into court for contempt and fined by the learned judge.

Thus the law, statute, common and case, protects the free American against injustice. It is ignorance of that subtle and perfect process and not any special love of liberty *per se* that causes radicals of anti-American kidney to rage every time an officer of the *gendarmerie,* in the simple execution of his duty, knocks a citizen in the head. The *gendarme* plainly has an inherent and inalienable right to knock him in the head: it is an essential part of his general prerogative as a sworn officer of the public peace and a representative of the sovereign power of the state. He may, true enough, exercise that prerogative in a manner liable to challenge on the ground that it is imprudent and lacking in sound judgment. On such questions reasonable men may differ. But it must be obvious that the sane and decorous way to settle differences of opinion of that sort is not by public outcry and florid appeals to sentimentality, not by ill-disguised playing to class consciousness and antisocial prejudice, but by an orderly resort to the checks and remedies superimposed upon the Bill of Rights by the calm deliberation and austere logic of the courts of equity.

The law protects the citizen. But to get its protection he must show due respect for its wise and delicate processes.

MEMORIAL SERVICE

Where is the grave-yard of dead gods? What lingering mourner waters their mounds? There was a day when Jupiter was the king of the gods, and any man who doubted his puissance was *ipso facto* a barbarian and an ignoramus. But where in all the world is there a man who worships Jupiter to-day? And what of Huitzilopochtli? In one year—and it is no more than five hundred years ago—50,000 youths and maidens were slain in sacrifice to him. To-day, if he is remembered at all, it is only by some vagrant savage in the depths of the Mexican forest. Huitzilopochtli, like many other gods, had no human father; his mother was a virtuous widow; he was born of an apparently innocent flirtation

143

that she carried on with the sun. When he frowned, his father, the sun, stood still. When he roared with rage, earthquakes engulfed whole cities. When he thirsted he was watered with 10,000 gallons of human blood. But to-day Huitzilopochtli is as magnificently forgotten as Allen G. Thurman. Once the peer of Allah, Buddha and Wotan, he is now the peer of General Coxey, Richmond P. Hobson, Nan Patterson, Alton G. Parker, Adelina Patti, General Weyler and Tom Sharkey.

Speaking of Huitzilopochtli recalls his brother, Tezcatilpoca. Tezcatilpoca was almost as powerful: he consumed 25,000 virgins a year. Lead me to his tomb: I would weep, and hang a *couronne des perles*. But who knows where it is? Or where the grave of Quitzalcoatl is? Or Tialoc? Or Chalchihuitlicue? Or Xiehtecutli? Or Centeotl, that sweet one? Or Tlazolteotl, the goddess of love? Or Mictlan? Or Ixtlilton? Or Omacatl? Or Yacatecutli? Or Mixcoatl? Or Xipe? Or all the host of Tzitzimitles? Where are their bones? Where is the willow on which they hung their harps? In what forlorn and unheard-of hell do they await the resurrection morn? Who enjoys their residuary estates? Or that of Dis, whom Cæsar found to be the chief god of the Celts? Or that of Tarves, the bull? Or that of Moccos, the pig? Or that of Epona, the mare? Or that of Mullo, the celestial jack-ass? There was a time when the Irish revered all these gods as violently as they now hate the English. But to-day even the drunkest Irishman laughs at them.

But they have company in oblivion: the hell of dead gods is as crowded as the Presbyterian hell for babies. Damona is there, and Esus, and Drunemeton, and Silvana, and Dervones, and Adsalluta, and Deva, and Belisama, and Axona, and Vintios, and Taranuous, and Sulis, and Cocidius, and Adsmerius, and Dumiatis, and Caletos, and Moccus, and Ollovidius, and Albiorix, and Leucitius, and Vitucadrus, and Ogmios, and Uxellimus, and Borvo, and Grannos, and Mogons. All mighty gods in their day, worshiped by millions, full of demands and impositions, able to bind and loose—all gods of the first class, not dilettanti. Men labored for generations to build vast temples to them—temples with stones as large as hay-wagons. The business of interpreting their whims occupied thousands of priests, wizards, archdeacons, evangelists, haruspices, bishops, archbishops. To doubt them was to die, usually at the stake. Armies took to the field to defend them against infidels: villages were burned, women and children were butchered, cattle were driven off. Yet in the end they all withered and died, and to-day there is none so poor to do them reverence. Worse, the very tombs in which they lie are lost, and so even a respectful stranger is debarred from paying them the slightest and politest homage.

What has become of Sutekh, once the high god of the whole Nile Valley? What has become of:

Resheph	Isis
Anath	Ptah
Ashtoreth	Anubis
Baal	Addu
Astarte	Shalem
Hadad	Dagon
El	Sharrab
Nergal	Yau
Nebo	Amon-Re
Ninib	Osiris
Melek	Sebek
Ahijah	Molech?

All these were once gods of the highest eminence. Many of them are mentioned with fear and trembling in the Old Testament. They ranked, five or six thousand years ago, with Jahveh himself; the worst of them stood far higher than Thor. Yet they have all gone down the chute, and with them the following:

Bilé	Gunfled
Lêr	Sokk-mimi
Arianrod	Memetona
Morrigu	Dagda
Govannon	Kerridwen

Pwyll	Beltis
Ogyrvan	Nusku
Dea Dia	Ni-zu
Gwydion	Sahi
Manawyddan	Aa
Nuada Argetlam	Allatu
Tagd	Jupiter
Goibniu	Cunina
Odin	Potina
Llaw Gyffes	Statilinus
Lleu	Diana of Ephesus
Ogma	Robigus
Mider	Pluto
Rigantona	Ops
Marzin	Meditrina
Mars	Vesta
Ceros	Tilmun
Vaticanus	Zer-panitu
Edulia	Merodach
Adeona	U-ki
Iuno Lucina	Dauke
Saturn	Gasan-abzu
Furrina	Elum
Vediovis	U-Tin-dir-ki
Consus	Marduk
Cronos	Nin-lil-la
Enki	Nin
Engurra	Persephone
Belus	Istar
Dimmer	Lagas
Mu-ul-lil	U-urugal
Ubargisi	Sirtumu
Ubilulu	Ea
Gasan-lil	Nirig
U-dimmer-an-kia	Nebo
Enurestu	Samas
U-sab-sib	Ma-banba anna
U-Mersi	En-Mersi
Tammuz	Amurru
Venus	Sin
Bau	AbilAddu
Mulu-hursang	Apsu
Anu	Dagan

Elali	Beltu
Isum	Dumu-zi-abzu
Mami	Kuski-banda
Nin-man	Kaawanu
Zaraqu	Nin-azu
Suqamunu	Lugal-Amarada
Zagaga	Qarradu
Assur	Ura-gala
Aku	Ueras

You may think I spoof. That I invent the names. I do not. Ask the rector to lend you any good treatise on comparative religion: you will find them all listed. They were gods of the highest standing and dignity—gods of civilized peoples—worshiped and believed in by millions. All were theoretically omnipotent, omniscient and immortal. And all are dead.

THE KING

Perhaps the most valuable asset that any man can have in this world is a naturally superior air, a talent for sniffishness and reserve. The generality of men are always greatly impressed by it, and accept it freely as a proof of genuine merit. One need but disdain them to gain their respect. Their congenital stupidity and timorousness make them turn to any leader who offers, and the sign of leadership that they recognize most readily is that which shows itself in external manner. This is the true explanation of the survival of monarchism, which invariably lives through its perennial deaths. It is the popular theory, at least in America, that monarchism is a curse fastened upon the common people from above—that the monarch saddles it upon them without their consent and against their will. The theory is without support in the facts. Kings are created, not by kings, but by the people. They visualize one of the ineradicable needs of all third-rate men, which means of nine men out of ten, and that is the need of something to venerate, to bow down to, to follow and obey.

The king business begins to grow precarious, not when kings reach out for greater powers, but when they begin to resign and renounce their powers. The czars of Russia were quite secure upon the throne so long as they ran Russia like a reformatory, but the moment they began to yield to liberal ideas, *i.e.,* by emancipating the serfs and setting up constitutionalism, their doom was sounded. The people saw this yielding as a sign of weakness; they began to suspect that the czars, after all, were not actually superior to other men. And so they turned to other and antagonistic leaders, all as cock-sure as the czars had once been, and in the course of time they were stimulated to rebellion. These leaders, or, at all events, the two or three most resolute and daring of them, then undertook to run the country in the precise way that it had been run in the palmy days of the monarchy. That is to say, they seized and exerted irresistible power and laid claim to infallible wisdom. History will date their downfall from the day they began to ease their pretensions. Once they confessed, even by implication, that they were merely human, the common people began to turn against them.

THE DISMAL SCIENCE

Every man, as the Psalmist says, to his own poison, or poisons, as the case may be. One of mine, following hard after theology, is political economy. What! Political economy, that dismal science? Well, why not? Its dismalness is largely a delusion, due to the fact that its chief ornaments, at least in our own day, are university professors. The professor must be an obscurantist or he is nothing; he has a special and unmatchable talent for dullness; his central aim is not to expose the truth clearly, but to exhibit his profundity, his esotericity—in brief, to stagger sophomores and other professors. The notion that German is a gnarled and unintelligible language arises out of the circumstance that it is so much written by professors. It took a rebel member of the clan, swinging to the antipodes in his unearthly treason, to prove its explicitness, its resiliency, its downright beauty. But Nietzsches are few, and so German remains soggy, and political economy continues to be swathed in dullness. As I say, however, that dullness is only superficial. There is no more engrossing book in the English language than Adam Smith's "The Wealth of Nations"; surely the eighteenth century produced nothing that can be read with greater ease to-day. Nor is there any inherent reason why even the most technical divisions of its subject should have gathered cobwebs with the passing of the years. Taxation, for example, is eternally lively; it concerns nine-tenths of us more directly than either smallpox or golf, and has just as much drama in it; moreover, it has been mellowed and made gay by as many gaudy, preposterous theories. As for foreign exchange, it is almost as romantic as young love, and quite as resistant to formulæ. Do the professors make an autopsy of it? Then read the occasional treatises of some professor of it who is not a professor, say, Garet Garrett or John Moody.

Unluckily, Garretts and Moodys are almost as rare as Nietzsches, and so the amateur of such things must be content to wrestle with the professors, seeking the violet of human interest beneath the avalanche of their graceless parts of speech. A hard business, I daresay, to one not practiced, and to its hardness there is added the disquiet of a doubt. That doubt does not concern itself with the doctrine preached, at least not directly.

There may be in it nothing intrinsically dubious; on the contrary, it may appear as sound as the binomial theorem, as well supported as the dogma of infant damnation. But all the time a troubling question keeps afloat in the air, and that is briefly this: What would happen to the learned professors if they took the other side? In other words, to what extent is political economy, as professors expound and practice it, a free science, in the sense that mathematics and physiology are free sciences? At what place, if any, is speculation pulled up by a rule that beyond lies treason, anarchy and disaster? These questions, I hope I need not add, are not inspired by any heterodoxy in my own black heart. I am, in many fields, a flouter of the accepted revelation and hence immoral, but the field of economics is not one of them. Here, indeed, I know of no man who is more orthodox than I am. I believe that the present organization of society, as bad as it is, is better than any other that has ever been proposed. I reject all the sure cures in current agitation, from government ownership to the single tax. I am in favor of free competition in all human enterprises, and to the utmost limit. I admire successful scoundrels, and shrink from Socialists as I shrink from Methodists. But all the same, the aforesaid doubt pursues me when I plow through the solemn disproofs and expositions of the learned professors of economics, and that doubt will not down. It is not logical or evidential, but purely psychological. And what it is grounded on is an unshakable belief that no man's opinion is worth a hoot, however well supported and maintained, so long as he is not absolutely free, if the spirit moves him, to support and maintain the exactly contrary opinion. In brief, human reason is a weak and paltry thing so long as it is not wholly free reason. The fact lies in its very nature, and is revealed by its entire history. A man may be perfectly honest in a contention, and he may be astute and persuasive in maintaining it, but the moment the slightest compulsion to maintain it is laid upon him, the moment the slightest external reward goes with his partisanship or the slightest penalty with its abandonment, then there appears a defect in his ratiocination that is more deep-seated than any error in fact and more destructive than any conscious and deliberate bias. He may seek the truth and the truth only, and bring up his highest talents and diligence to the business, but always there is a specter behind his chair, a warning in his ear. Always it is safer and more hygienic for him to think one way than to think another way, and in that bald fact there is excuse enough to hold his whole chain of syllogisms in suspicion. He may be earnest, he may be honest, but he is not free, and if he is not free, he is not anything.

Well, are the reverend professors of economics free? With the highest respect, I presume to question it. Their colleagues of archeology may be reasonably called free, and their colleagues of bacteriology, and those of Latin grammar and sidereal astronomy, and those of many another science and mystery, but when one comes to the faculty of political economy one finds that freedom as plainly conditioned, though perhaps not as openly, as in the faculty of theology. And for a plain reason. Political economy, so to speak, hits the employers of the professors where they live. It deals, not with ideas that affect those employers only occasionally or only indirectly or only as ideas, but with ideas that have an imminent and continuous influence upon their personal welfare and security, and that affect profoundly the very foundations of that social and economic structure upon which their whole existence is based. It is, in brief, the science of the ways and means whereby they have come to such estate, and maintain themselves in such estate, that they are able to hire and boss professors. It is the boat in which they sail down perilous waters— and they must needs yell, or be more or less than human, when it is rocked. Now and then that yell duly resounds in the groves of learning. One remembers, for example, the trial, condemnation and execution of Prof. Dr. Scott Nearing at the University of Pennsylvania, a seminary that is highly typical, both in its staff and in its control. Nearing, I have no doubt, was wrong in his notions—honestly, perhaps, but still wrong. In so far as I heard them stated at the time, they seemed to me to be hollow and of no validity. He has since discharged them from the chautauquan stump; and at the usual hinds. They have been chiefly accepted and celebrated by men I regard as asses. But Nearing was not thrown out of the University of Pennsylvania, angrily and ignominiously, because he was honestly wrong, or because his errors made him incompetent to prepare sophomores for their examinations; he was thrown out because his efforts to get at the truth disturbed the security and equanimity of the rich ignoranti who happened to control the university, and because the academic slaves and satellites of these shopmen were restive under his competition for the attention of the student-body. In three words, he was thrown out because he was not safe and sane and orthodox. Had his aberration gone in the other direction, had he defended child labor as ardently as he denounced it and denounced the minimum wage as ardently as he defended it, then he would have been quite as secure in his post, for all his cavorting in the newspapers, as Chancellor Day was at Syracuse.

Now consider the case of the professors of economics, near and far, who have *not* been thrown out. Who will say that the lesson of the Nearing *débâcle* has been lost upon them? Who will say that the potency of the wealthy men who command our universities—or most of them—has not stuck in their minds? And who will say that, with this sticking remembered, their arguments against Nearing's so-called ideas are as worthy of confidence and respect as they would be if they were quite free to go over to Nearing's side without damage? Who, indeed, will give them full credit, even when they are right, so long as they are hamstrung, nose-ringed and tied up in gilded pens? It seems to me that these considerations are enough to cast a glow of suspicion over the whole of American political economy, at least in so far as it comes from college economists. And, in the main, it has that source, for, barring a few brilliant journalists, all our economists of any repute are professors. Many of them are able men, and most of them are undoubtedly honest men, as honesty goes in the world, but over practically every one of them there stands a board of trustees with its legs in the stock-market and its eyes on the established order, and that board is ever alert for heresy in the science of its being, and has ready means of punishing it, and a hearty enthusiasm for the business. Not every professor, perhaps, may be sent straight to the block, as Nearing was, but there are plenty of pillories and guardhouses on the way, and every last pedagogue must be well aware of it.

Political economy, in so far as it is a science at all, was not pumped up and embellished by any such academic clients and ticket-of-leave men. It was put on its legs by inquirers who were not only safe from all dousing in the campus pump, but who were also free from the mental timorousness and conformity which go inevitably with school-teaching—in brief, by men of the world, accustomed to its free air, its hospitality to originality and plain speaking. Adam Smith, true enough, was once a professor, but he threw up his chair to go to Paris, and there he met, not more professors, but all the current enemies of professors—the Nearings and Henry Georges and Karl Marxes of the time. And the book that he wrote was not orthodox, but revolutionary. Consider the others of that bulk and beam: Bentham, Ricardo, Mill and their like. Bentham held no post at the mercy of bankers and tripesellers; he was a man of independent means, a lawyer and politician, and a heretic in general practice. It is impossible to imagine such a man occupying a chair at Harvard or Princeton. He had a hand in too many pies: he was too rebellious and contumacious: he had too little respect for authority, either academic or worldly. Moreover, his mind was too wide for a professor; he could never remain safely in a groove; the whole field of social organization invited his inquiries and experiments. Ricardo? Another man of easy means and great worldly experience—by academic standards, not even educated. To-day, I daresay, such meager diplomas as he could show would not suffice to get him an instructor's berth in a fresh-water seminary in Iowa. As for Mill, he was so well grounded by his father that he knew more, at eighteen, than any of the universities could teach him, and his life thereafter was the exact antithesis of that of a cloistered pedagogue. Moreover, he was a heretic in religion and probably violated the Mann Act of those days—an offense almost as heinous, in a college professor of economics, as giving three cheers for Prince Kropotkin.

I might lengthen the list, but humanely refrain. The point is that these early English economists were all perfectly free men, with complete liberty to tell the truth as they saw it, regardless of its orthodoxy or lack of orthodoxy. I do not say that the typical American economist of to-day is not as honest, nor even that he is not as diligent and competent, but I do say that he is not as free —that penalties would come upon him for stating ideas that Smith or Ricardo or Bentham or Mill, had he so desired, would have been free to state without damage. And in that menace there is an ineradicable criticism of the ideas that he does state, and it lingers even when they are plausible and are accepted. In France and Germany, where the universities and colleges are controlled by the state, the practical effect of such pressure has been frequently demonstrated. In the former country the violent debate over social and economic problems during the quarter century before the war produced a long list of professors cashiered for heterodoxy, headed by the names of Jean Jaures and Gustave Herve. In Germany it needed no Nietzsche to point out the deadening produced by this state control. Germany, in fact, got out of it an entirely new species of economist—the state Socialist who flirted with radicalism with one eye and kept the other upon his chair, his salary and his pension.

The Nearing case and the rebellions of various pedagogues elsewhere show that we in America stand within the shadow of a somewhat similar danger. In economics, as in the other sciences, we are probably producing men who are as good as those on view in any other country. They are not to be surpassed for learning and originality, and there is no reason to believe that they lack honesty and courage. But honesty and courage, as men go in the world, are after all merely relative values. There comes a point at which even the most honest man considers consequences, and even the most courageous looks before he leaps. The difficulty lies in establishing the position of that point. So long as it is in doubt, there will remain, too, the other doubt that I have described. I rise in meeting, I repeat, not as a radical, but as one of the most hunkerous of the orthodox. I can imagine nothing more dubious in fact and wobbly in logic than some of the doctrines that amateur economists, chiefly Socialists, have set afloat in this country during the past dozen years. I have even gone to the trouble of writing a book against them; my convictions and instincts are all on the other side. But I should be a great deal more comfortable in those convictions and instincts if I were convinced that the learned professors were really in full and absolute possession of academic freedom—if I could imagine them taking the other tack now and then without damnation to their jobs, their lecture dates, their book sales and their hides.

PATRIOTISM

Patriotism is conceivable to a civilized man in times of stress and storm, when his country is wobbling and sore beset. His country then appeals to him as any victim of misfortune appeals to him—say, a street-walker pursued by the police. But when it is safe, happy and prosperous it can only excite his loathing. The things that make countries safe, happy and prosperous—a secure peace, an active trade, political serenity at home—are all intrinsically corrupting and disgusting. It is as impossible for a civilized man to love his country in good times as it would be for him to respect a politician.

VIRTUE

Pale druggists in remote towns of the Epworth League and flannel nightgown belts, endlessly wrapping up bottles of Peruna. . . . Women hidden away in the damp kitchens of unpainted houses along the railroad tracks, frying tough beefsteaks. . . . Lime and cement dealers being initiated into the Knights of Pythias, the Red Men or the Woodmen of the World. . . . Watchmen at lonely railroad crossings in Iowa, hoping that they'll be able to get off to hear the United Brethren evangelist preach. . . . Ticket-choppers in the subway, breathing sweat in its gaseous form. . . . Family doctors in poor neighborhoods, faithfully relying upon the therapeutics taught in their Eclectic Medical College in 1884. . . . Farmers plowing sterile fields behind sad meditative horses, both suffering from the bites of insects. . . . Greeks tending all-night coffee-joints in the suburban wildernesses where the trolley-cars stop. . . . Grocery-clerks stealing prunes and ginger-snaps, and trying to make assignations with soapy servant-girls. . . . Women confined for the ninth or tenth time, wondering helplessly what it is all about. . . . Methodist preachers retired after forty years of service in the trenches of God, upon pensions of $600 a year. . . . Wives and daughters of Middle Western country bankers, marooned in Los Angeles, going tremblingly to swami séances in dark, smelly rooms. . . . Chauffeurs in huge fur coats waiting outside theaters filled with folks applauding Robert Edeson and Jane Cowl. . . . Decayed and hopeless men writing editorials at midnight for leading papers in Mississippi, Arkansas and Alabama. . . . Owners of the principal candy-stores in Green River, Neb., and Tyrone, Pa. . . . Presidents of one-building universities in the rural fastnesses of Kentucky and Tennessee. . . . Women with babies in their arms weeping over moving-pictures in the Elks' Hall at Schmidtsville, Mo. . . . Babies just born to the wives of milk-wagon drivers. . . . Judges on the benches of petty county courts in Virginia, Vermont and Idaho. . . . Conductors of accommodation trains running between Kokomo, Ind., and Logansport. . . .

THE HUSBANDMAN

A reader for years of the *Congressional Record*, I have encountered in its dense and pregnant columns denunciations of almost every human act or idea that is imaginable to political pathology, from adultery to Zionism, and of all classes of men whose crimes the legislative mind can grasp, from atheists to Zoroastrians, but never once, so far as I can recall, has that great journal shown the slightest insolence, direct or indirect, to the humble husbandman, the lonely companion of *Bos taurus,* the sweating and persecuted farmer. He is, on the contrary, the pet above all other pets, the enchantment and delight, the saint and archangel of all the unearthly Sganarelles and Scaramouches who roar in the two houses of Congress. He is more to them, day in and day out, than whole herds of Honest Workingmen, Gallant Jack Tars and Heroic Miners; he is more, even, than a platoon of Unknown Soldiers. There are days when one or another of these totems of the statesman is bathed with such devotion that it would make the Gracchi blush, but there is never a day that the farmer, too, doesn't get his share, and there is many a day when he gets ten times his share —when, indeed, he is completely submerged in rhetorical vaseline, so that it is hard to tell which end of him is made in the image of God and which is mere hoof. No session ever begins without a grand assault at all arms upon his hereditary foes, from the boll-weevil and the San José scale to Wall Street and the Interstate Commerce Commission. And no session comes to an end without a huge grist of new laws to save him from them—laws embodying the most subtle statecraft of the most daring and ingenious body of lawmakers ever assembled under one roof on the habitable globe. One might almost argue that the chief, and perhaps even only aim of legislation in These States is to succor and secure the farmer. If, while the bombs of goose-grease and rockets of pomade are going off in the two Chambers, certain evil men meet in the basement and hook *banderillas* into him—say, by inserting jokers into the chemical schedule of a new tariff bill, or by getting the long-haul rules changed, or by manipulating the loans of the Federal Reserve Banks —then the crime is not against him alone; it is against the whole American people, the common decency of Christendom, and the Holy Ghost. Horn a farmer, and you stand in contumacy to the platforms of all known parties, to the devout faith of all known statesmen, and to God. *Laborantem agricolam oportet primum de fructibus percipere.*

Paul wrote to the Bishop of Ephesus, at the latest, in the year 65 A.D.; the doctrine that I have thus ascribed to the Mesmers and Grimaldis of our politics is therefore not a novelty of their contrivance. Nor is it, indeed, their monopoly, for it seems to be shared by all Americans who are articulate and devote themselves to political metaphysics and good works. The farmer is praised by all who mention him at all, from archbishops to zoölogists, day in and day out. He is praised for his industry, his frugality, his patriotism, his altruistic passion. He is praised for staying on the farm, for laboriously wringing our bread and meat from the reluctant soil, for renouncing Babylon to guard the horned cattle on the hills. He is praised for his patient fidelity to the oldest of learned professions, and the most honorable, and the most necessary to all of us. He takes on, in political speeches and newspaper editorials, a sort of mystical character. He is no longer a mundane laborer, scratching for the dollar, full of staphylococci, smelling heavily of sweat and dung; he is a high priest in a rustic temple, pouring out his heart's blood upon the altar of Ceres. The farmer, thus depicted, grows heroic, lyrical, pathetic, affecting. To murmur against him becomes a sort of sacrilege, like murmuring against the Constitution, Human Freedom, the Cause of Democracy. . . . Nevertheless, being already doomed, I herewith and hereby presume to do it. More, my murmur is scored in the manner of Berlioz, for ten thousand trombones *fortissimo,* with harsh, cacophonous chords for bombardons and ophicleides in the bass clef. Let the farmer, so far as I am concerned, be damned forevermore! To hell with him, and bad luck to him! He is, unless I err, no hero at all, and no priest, and no altruist, but simply a tedious fraud and ignoramus, a cheap rogue and hypocrite, the eternal Jack of the human pack. He deserves all that he suffers under our economic system, and more. Any city man, not insane, who sheds tears for him is shedding tears of the crocodile.

No more grasping, selfish and dishonest mammal, indeed, is known to students of the Anthropoidea. When the going is good for him he robs the rest of us up to the extreme limit of our endurance; when the going is bad he comes bawling for help out of the public till. Has anyone ever heard of a farmer making any sacrifice of his own interests, however slight, to the common good? Has anyone ever heard of a farmer practising or advocating any political idea that was not absolutely self-seeking— that was not, in fact, deliberately designed to loot the rest of us to his gain? Greenbackism, free silver, government guarantee of prices, all the complex fiscal imbecilities of the cow State John Baptists—these are the contributions of the virtuous husbandmen to American political theory. There has never been a time, in good seasons or bad, when his hands were not itching for more; there has never been a time when he was not ready to support any charlatan, however grotesque, who promised to get it for him. Why, indeed, are politicians so polite to him—before election, so romantically amorous? For the plain and simple reason that only one issue ever interests or fetches him, and that is the issue of his own profit. He must be promised something definite and valuable, to be paid to him alone, or he is off after some other mountebank. He simply cannot imagine himself as a citizen of a commonwealth, in duty bound to give as well as take; he can imagine himself only as getting all and giving nothing.

Yet we are asked to venerate this prehensile moron as the *Ur*-burgher, the citizen *par excellence,* the foundation-stone of the state! And why? Because he produces something that all of us must have—that we must get somehow on penalty of death. And how do we get it from him? By submitting helplessly to his unconscionable blackmailing—by paying him, not under any rule of reason, but in proportion to his roguery and incompetence, and hence to the direness of our need. I doubt that the human race, as a whole, would submit to that sort of high-jacking, year in and year out, from any other necessary class of men. When the American railroad workman attempted it, in 1916, there was instant indignation; when a certain small squad of the *Polizei* tried it, a few years later, there was such universal horror that a politician who denounced the crime became President of the United States. But the farmers do it over and over again, without challenge or reprisal, and the only thing that keeps them from reducing us, at intervals, to actual famine is their own imbecile knavery. They are all willing and eager to pillage us by starving us, but they can't do it because they can't resist attempts to swindle each other. Recall, for example, the case of the cotton-growers in the South. They agreed among themselves to cut down the cotton acreage in order to inflate the price—and instantly every party to the agreement began planting *more* cotton in order to profit by the abstinence of his neighbors. That abstinence being wholly imaginary, the price of cotton fell instead of going up—and then the entire pack of scoundrels began demanding assistance from the national treasury—in brief, began demanding that the rest of us indemnify them for the failure of their plot to blackmail us!

The same demand is made almost annually by the wheat farmers of the Middle West. It is the theory of the zanies who perform at Washington that a grower of wheat devotes himself to that banal art in a philanthropic and patriotic spirit—that he plants and harvests his crop in order that the folks of the cities may not go without bread. It is the plain fact that he raises wheat because it takes less labor than any other crop—because it enables him, after working sixty days a year, to loaf the rest of the twelve months. If wheat-raising could be taken out of the hands of such lazy *fellahin* and organized as the production of iron or cement is organized, the price might be reduced by a half, and still leave a large profit for *entrepreneurs*. It vacillates dangerously to-day, not because speculators manipulate it, but because the crop is irregular and undependable—that is to say, because those who make it are incompetent. The worst speculators, as everyone knows, are the farmers themselves. They hold their wheat as long as they can, borrowing our money from the country banks and hoping prayerfully for a rise. If it goes up, then we pay them an extra and unearned profit. If it goes down, then they demand legislation to prevent it going down next time. Sixty days a year they work; the rest of the time they gamble with our bellies. It is probably the safest gambling ever heard of. Now and then, true enough, a yokel who plunges too heavily comes to grief, and is ingested by the county-town mortgage-shark; now and then a whole county, or State or even larger area goes bankrupt, and the financial dominoes begin falling down all along the line from Saleratus Center to New York. But such catastrophes are rare, and they leave no scars. When a speculator goes broke in Wall Street it is a scandalous matter, and if he happens to have rooked anybody of importance he is railroaded to jail. But when a speculator goes broke in the great open spaces, there is a great rush of political leucocytes to the scene, and presently it is made known that the sin was not the speculator's at all, but his projected victims', and that it is the prime duty of the latter, by lawful order upon the Treasurer of the United States, to reimburse him his losses and set him up for a new trial.

The notion that wheat would be much cheaper and the supply far more dependable if it were grown, not by a motley horde of such puerile loafers and gamblers, but by competent men intelligently organized is not mine; I borrow it from Henry Ford, a busted seer. Since he betrayed them to Dr. Coolidge for a mess of pottage, the poor Liberals, once so enamored of his sagacity, denounce Ford as an idiot and a villain; nevertheless, the fact remains that his discussion of the wastefulness of our present system of wheat-growing, in the autobiography which he didn't write, is full of a powerful plausibility. Ford was born and brought up on a farm—and it was a farm, as farms go, that was very competently managed. But he knows very well that even the most competent farmer is but seldom more adept than a chimpanzee playing the violin. The Liberals, indeed, cannot controvert his judgment; they have been thrown back upon belaboring his political morals. What he proposes, they argue, is simply the enslavement of the present farmer, now so gloriously free. With capitalism gradually absorbing his fields, he would have to go to work as a wage-slave. Well, why not? For one, I surely offer no objection. All the rubber we use to-day is raised by slave labor; so is all the morphine consumed at Hollywood. Our children are taught in school by slaves; our newspapers are edited by slaves.

Wheat raised by slave labor would be just as nutritious as wheat raised by men earning $10,000 a year, and a great deal cheaper. If the business showed a good profit, the political clowns at Washington would launch schemes to confiscate it, as they now launch schemes to make good the losses of the farmers. In any case, why bother about the fate of the farmer? If wheat went to $10 a bushel to-morrow, and all the workmen of the cities became slaves in name as well as in fact, no farmer in this grand land of freedom would consent voluntarily to a reduction of as much as ⅛ of a cent a bushel. "The greatest wolves," says E. W. Howe, another graduate of the farm, "are the farmers who bring produce to town to sell." Wolves? Let us not insult *Canis lupus*. I move the substitution of *Hyæna hyæna*.

Meanwhile, how much truth is in the common theory that the husbandman is harassed and looted by our economic system, that the men of the cities prey upon him—specifically, that he is the chronic victim of such devices as the tariff, railroad regulation, and the banking system? So far as I can make out, there is none whatever. The net effect of our present banking system, as I have already said, is that the money accumulated by the cities is used to finance the farmers, and that they employ it to blackmail the cities. As for the tariff, is it a fact that it damages the farmer, or benefits him? Let us turn for light to the worst Tariff Act ever heard of in human history: that of 1922. It put a duty of 30 cents a bushel on wheat, and so barred out Canadian wheat, and gave the American farmer a vast and unfair advantage. For months running the difference in the price of wheat on the two sides of the American-Canadian border—wheat raised on farms not a mile apart—ran from 25 to 30 cents a bushel. Danish butter was barred out by a duty of 8 cents a pound—and the American farmer pocketed the 8 cents. Potatoes carried a duty of 50 cents a hundredweight—and the potato growers of Maine, eager, as the phrase has it, to mop up, raised such an enormous crop that the market was glutted, and they went bankrupt, and began bawling for government aid. High duties were put, too, upon meats, upon cheese, upon wool—in brief, upon practically everything that the farmer produced. But his profits were taken from him by even higher duties upon manufactured goods, and by high freight rates? Were they, indeed? There was, in fact, no duty at all upon many of the things he consumed. There was no duty, for example, upon shoes. The duty upon woolen goods gave a smaller advantage to the manufacturer than the duty on wool gave to the farmer. So with the duty on cotton goods. Automobiles were cheaper in the United States than anywhere else on earth. So were all agricultural implements. So were groceries. So were fertilizers.

But here I come to the brink of an abyss of statistics, and had better haul up. The enlightened reader is invited to investigate them for himself; they will bring him, I believe, some surprises, particularly if he has been reading the *Congressional Record* and accepting it gravely. They by no means exhaust the case against the consecrated husbandman. I have said that the only political idea he can grasp is one which promises him a direct profit. It is, alas, not quite true: he can also grasp one which has the sole effect of annoying and damaging his enemy, the city man. The same mountebanks who get to Washington by promising to augment his gains and make good his losses devote whatever time is left over from that enterprise to saddling the rest of us with oppressive and idiotic laws, all hatched on the farm. There, where the cows low through the still night, and the jug of peruna stands behind the stove, and bathing begins, as at Biarritz, with the vernal equinox—there is the reservoir of all the nonsensical legislation which now makes the United States a buffoon among the great nations. It was among country Methodists, practitioners of a theology degraded almost to the level of voodooism, that Prohibition was invented, and it was by country Methodists, nine-tenths of them actual followers of the plow, that it was fastened upon the rest of us, to the damage of our bank accounts, our dignity and our ease. What lies under it, and under all the other crazy enactments of its category, is no more and no less than the yokel's congenital and incurable hatred of the city man—his simian rage against everyone who, as he sees it, is having a better time than he is.

That this malice is at the bottom of Prohibition, and not any altruistic yearning to put down the evils of drink, is shown clearly by the fact that most of the State enforcement acts—and even the Volstead Act, as it is interpreted at Washington—permit the farmer himself to make cider as in the past, and that every effort to deprive him of that astounding immunity has met with the opposition of his representatives. In other words, the thing he is against is not the use of alcohol *per se,* but simply the use of alcohol in its more charming and romantic forms. Prohibition, as everyone knows, has not materially diminished the consumption of alcohol in the cities, but it has obviously forced the city man to drink decoctions that he would have spurned in the old days—that is, it has forced him to drink such dreadful stuff as the farmer has always drunk. The farmer is thus content with it: it brings his enemy down to his own level. The same animus is visible in innumerable other moral statutes, all ardently supported by the peasantry. For example, the Mann Act. The aim of this amazing law, of course, is not to put down adultery; it is simply to put down that variety of adultery which is most agreeable. What got it upon the books was simply the constant gabble in the rural newspapers about the byzantine debaucheries of urban Antinomians—rich stockbrokers who frequented Atlantic City from Friday to Monday, vaudeville actors who traveled about the country with beautiful mistresses, and so on. Such aphrodisiacal tales, read beside the kitchen-stove by hinds condemned to monogamous misery with stupid, unclean and ill-natured wives, naturally aroused in them a vast detestation of errant cockneys, and this detestation eventually rolled up enough force to attract the attention of the quacks who make laws at Washington. The result was the Mann Act. Since then a number of the cow States have passed Mann Acts of their own, usually forbidding the use of automobiles "for immoral purposes." But there is nowhere a law forbidding the use of barns, cow-stables, hay-ricks and other such familiar rustic ateliers of sin. That is to say, there is nowhere a law forbidding yokels to drag virgins into infamy by the technic practised since Tertiary times on the farms; there are only laws forbidding city youths to do it according to the technic of the great municipalities.

Here we come to the limits of bucolic moral endeavor. It never prohibits acts that are common on the farms; it only prohibits acts that are common in the cities. In many of the Middle Western States there are statutes forbidding the smoking of cigarettes, for cigarette-smoking, to the louts of those wastes, bears the aspect of a citified and levantine vice, and if they attempted it themselves they would be derided by their fellows and perhaps divorced by their wives, just as they would be derided and divorced if they bathed every day, or dressed for dinner, or attempted to play the piano. But chewing tobacco, whether in public or in private, is nowhere forbidden by law, for the plain reason that nine-tenths of all husbandmen practise it, as they practise the drinking of raw corn liquor. The act not only lies within their tastes; it also lies within their means, and hence within their *mores*. As a consequence the inhabitants of the towns in those remote marches are free to chew tobacco all they please, even at divine service, but are clapped into jail the instant they light cigarettes. The same consideration gets into comstockery, which is chiefly supported, like Prohibition, by farmers and chiefly aimed at city men. The Comstock Act is very seldom invoked against newspapers, for the matter printed in newspapers lies within the comprehension of the peasantry, and hence within their sphere of enjoyment. Nor is it often invoked against cheap books of a frankly pornographic character—such things as "Night Life in Chicago," "Adventures on a Pullman Sleeper" and "The Confessions of an ex-Nun"—for when yokels read at all, it is commonly such garbage that they prefer. But they are hot against the infinitely less gross naughtiness of serious books, including the so-called classics, for these books they simply cannot read. In consequence the force of comstockery is chiefly directed against such literature. For one actually vile book that it suppresses it attempts to suppress at least a dozen good ones.

Now the pious husbandman shows signs of an itch to proceed further. Not content with assaulting us with his degraded and abominable ethics, he begins trying to force upon us his still worse theology. On the steppes Methodism has got itself all the estate and dignity of a State religion; it becomes a criminal offense to teach any doctrine in contempt of it. No civilized man, to be sure, is yet actually in jail for the crime; civilized men simply keep out of such bleak parking spaces for human Fords, as they keep out of Congress and Franz Josef Land. But the long arm of the Wesleyan revelation now begins to stretch forth toward Nineveh. The mountebank, Bryan, after years of preying upon the rustics on the promise that he would show them how to loot the cities by wholesale and *à outrance,* now reverses his collar and proposes to lead them in a *jehad* against what remains of American intelligence, already beleaguered in a few walled towns. We are not only to abandon the social customs of civilization at the behest of a rabble of peasants who sleep in their underclothes; we are now to give up all the basic ideas of civilization and adopt the gross superstitions of the same mob. Is this fanciful? Is the menace remote, and to be disregarded? My apologies for suggesting that perhaps you are one of the multitude who thought that way about Prohibition, and only half a dozen years ago. Bryan is a protean harlequin, and more favored by God than is commonly assumed. He lost with free silver but he won with Prohibition. The chances, if my mathematics do not fail, are thus 1 to 1 that he will win, if he keeps his health, with Fundamentalism—in his own phrase, that God will be put into the Constitution. If he does, then *Eoanthrophus* will triumph finally over *Homo sapiens*. If he does, then the humble swineherd will drive us all into his pen.

Not much gift for Vision is needed to imagine the main outlines of the ensuing *Kultur*. The city man, as now, will bear nine-tenths of the tax burden; the rural total immersionist will make all the laws. With Genesis firmly lodged in the Testament of the Fathers he will be ten times as potent as he is now and a hundred times as assiduous. No constitutional impediment will remain to cripple his moral fancy. The Wesleyan code of Kansas and Mississippi, Vermont and Minnesota will be forced upon all of us by the full military and naval power of the United States. Civilization will gradually become felonious everywhere in the Republic, as it already is in Arkansas. What I sing, I suppose, is a sort of Utopia. But it is not the Utopia of bawdy poets and metaphysicians; it is not the familiar Utopia of the books. It is a Utopia dreamed by simpler and more virtuous men—by seven millions of Christian bumpkins, far-flung in forty-eight sovereign States. They dream it on their long journeys down the twelve billion furrows of their seven million farms, up hill and down dale in the heat of the day. They dream it behind the egg-stove on winter nights, their boots off and their socks scorching, Holy Writ in their hands. They dream it as they commune with *Bos taurus, Sus scrofa, Mephitis mephitis,* the Methodist pastor, the Ford agent. It floats before their eyes as they scan the Sears-Roebuck catalogue for horse liniment, porous plasters and Bordeaux mixture; it rises before them when they assemble in their Little Bethels to be instructed in the word of God, the plots of the Pope, the crimes of the atheists and Jews; it transfigures the chautauquan who looms before them with his Great Message. This Utopia haunts and tortures them; they long to make it real. They have tried prayer, and it has failed; now they turn to the secular arm. The dung-fork glitters in the sun as the host prepares to march. . . .

Well, these are the sweet-smelling and altruistic agronomists whose sorrows are the *leit-motif* of our politics, whose votes keep us supplied with Bryans and Bleases, whose welfare is alleged to be the chief end of democratic statecraft, whose patriotism is the so-called bulwark of this so-called Republic!

THE POLITICIAN

Half the sorrows of the world, I suppose, are caused by making false assumptions. If the truth were only easier to ascertain the remedy for them would consist simply of ascertaining it and accepting it. This business, alas, is usually impossible, but fortunately not always: now and then, by some occult process, half rational and half instinctive, the truth gets itself found out and an ancient false assumption goes overboard. I point, in the field of the social relations, to one which afflicted the human race for millenniums: that one, to wit, which credited the rev. clergy with a mysterious wisdom and awful powers. Obviously, it has ceased to trouble all the superior varieties of men. It may survive in those remote marches where human beings go to bed with the cows, but certainly it has vanished from the cities. Asphalt and the apostolic succession, indeed, seem to be irreconcilable enemies. I can think of no clergyman in any great American city today whose public dignity and influence are much above those of an ordinary Class I Babbitt. It is hard for even the most diligent and passionate of the ancient order to get upon the first pages of the newspapers; he must make a clown-show, discreditable to his fraying cloth, or he must blush unseen. When bishops begin launching thunderbolts against heretics, the towns do not tremble; they laugh. When elders denounce sin, sin only grows more popular. Imagine a city man getting a notice from the ordinary of his diocese that he had been excommunicated. It would trouble him far less, I venture, than his morning *Katzenjammer*.

The reason for all this is not hard to find. All the superior varieties of men—and even the lowest varieties of city workmen are at least superior to peasants—have simply rid themselves of their old belief in devils. Hell no longer affrights and palsies them, and so the magic of those who profess to save them from it no longer impresses them. That profession, I believe, was bogus, and its acceptance was therefore a false assumption. Being so, it made men unhappy; getting rid of it has delivered them. They are no longer susceptible to ecclesiastical alarms and extortions; *ergo,* they sleep and eat better. Think of what life must have been under such princes of damnation as Cotton Mather and Jonathan Edwards, with even bartenders and metaphysicians believing in them! And then compare it to life under Bishop Manning and the Rev. Dr. John Roach Straton, with only a few half-wits believing in them! Or turn to the backwoods of the Republic, where the devil is still feared, and with him his professional exterminators. In the country towns the clergy are still almost as influential as they were in Mather's day, and there, as everyone knows, they remain public nuisances, and civilized life is almost impossible. In such Neolithic regions nothing can go on without their consent, on penalty of anathema and hell-fire; as a result, nothing goes on that is worth recording. It is this survival of sacerdotal authority, I begin to believe, and not hookworm, malaria or the event of April 9, 1865, that is chiefly responsible for the cultural paralysis of the late Confederate States. The South lacks big cities; it is run by its country towns—and in every country town there is some Baptist *mullah* who rules by scaring the peasantry. The false assumption that his pretensions are sound, that he can actually bind and loose, that contumacy to him is a variety of cursing God—this false assumption is what makes the yokels so uneasy, so nervous, and hence so unhappy. If they could throw it off they would burn fewer Aframericans and sing more songs. If they could be purged of it they would be purged of Ku Kluxry too.

The cities got rid of that false assumption half a century ago, and have been making cultural progress ever since. Somewhat later they got rid of its brother, to wit, respect for government, and, in particular, respect for its visible agents, the police. That respect—traditional, and hence irrational—had been, for years, in increasingly unpleasant collision with a great body of obvious facts. The police, by assumption austere and almost sacrosanct, were gradually discovered to be, in reality, a pack of rogues and but little removed, save by superior impudence and enterprise, from the cut-throats and purse-snatchers they were set to catch. When, a few decades ago, the American people, at least in the big cities, began to accept them frankly for what they were—when the old false assumption of their integrity and public usefulness was quietly abandoned and a new and more accurate assumption of their roguery was adopted in its place—when this change was effected there was a measurable increase, I believe, in the public happiness. It no longer astonished anyone when policemen were taken in evildoing; indignation therefore abated, and with it its pains. If, before that time, the corps of Prohibition enforcement officers—*i.e.,* a corps of undisguised scoundrels with badges—had been launched upon the populace, there would have been a great roar of wrath, and much anguished gnashing of teeth. People would have felt themselves put upon, injured, insulted. But with the old false assumption about policemen removed from their minds, they met the new onslaught calmly and even smilingly. Today no one is indignant over the fact that the extortions of these new *Polizei* increase the cost of potable alcohol. The false assumption that the police are altruistic agents of a benevolent state has been replaced by the sound assumption that they are gentlemen engaged assiduously, like the rest of us, in finding meat and raiment for their families and in laying up funds to buy Liberty Bonds in the next war to end war. This is human progress, for it increases human happiness.

So much for the evidence. The deduction I propose to make from it is simply this: that a like increase would follow if the American people could only rid themselves of another and worse false assumption that still rides them—one that corrupts all their thinking about the great business of politics, and vastly augments their discontent and unhappiness—the assumption, that is, that politicians are divided into two classes, and that one of those classes is made up of good ones. I need not argue, I hope, that this assumption is almost universally held among us. Our whole politics, indeed, is based upon it, and has been based upon it since the earliest days. What is any political campaign save a concerted effort to turn out a set of politicians who are admittedly bad and put in a set who are thought to be better? The former assumption, I believe, is always sound; the latter is just as certainly false. For if experience teaches us anything at all it teaches us this: that a good politician, under democracy, is quite as unthinkable as an honest burglar. His very existence, indeed, is a standing subversion of the public good in every rational sense. He is not one who serves the common weal; he is simply one who preys upon the commonwealth. It is to the interest of all the rest of us to hold down his powers to an irreducible minimum, and to reduce his compensation to nothing; it is to his interest to augment his powers at all hazards, and to make his compensation all the traffic will bear. To argue that these aims are identical is to argue palpable nonsense. The politician, at his ideal best, never even remotely approximated in practice, is a necessary evil; at his worst he is an almost intolerable nuisance.

What I contend is simply that he would be measurably less a nuisance if we got rid of our old false assumption about him, and regarded him in the cold light of fact. At once, I believe, two-thirds of his obnoxiousness would vanish. He would remain a nuisance, but he would cease to be a swindler; the injury of having to pay freight on him would cease to be complicated by the insult of being rooked. It is the insult and not the injury that makes the deeper wounds, and causes the greater permanent damage to the national psyche. All of us have been trained, since infancy, in putting up with necessary evils, plainly recognized *as* evils. We know, for example, that the young of the human species commonly smell badly; that garbage men, bootblacks and messenger boys commonly smell worse. These facts are not agreeable, but they remain tolerable because they are universally assumed—because there is no sense of having been tricked and cozened in their perennial discovery. But try to imagine how distressing fatherhood would become if prospective fathers were all taught that the human infant radiates an aroma like the rose—if the truth came constantly as a surprise! Each fresh victim of the deception would feel that he had been basely swindled—that his own child was somehow bogus. Not infrequently, I suppose, he would be tempted to make away with it in some quiet manner, and have another—only to be shocked again. That procedure would be idiotic, admittedly, yet it is exactly the one we follow in politics. At each election we vote in a new set of politicians, insanely assuming that they are better than the set turned out. And at each election we are, as they say in the Motherland, done in.

Of late the fraud has become so gross that the plain people begin to show a great restlessness under it. Like animals in a cage, they trot from one corner to another, endlessly seeking a way out. If the Democrats win one year, it is a pretty sure sign that they will lose the next year. State after State becomes doubtful, pivotal, skittish; even the solid South begins to break. In the cities it is still worse. An evil circle is formed. First the poor taxpayers, robbed by the politicians of one great party and then by those of the other, turn to a group of free-lance rogues in the middle ground—non-partisan candidates, Liberals, reformers or what not: the name is unimportant. Then, flayed and pillaged by these gentry as they never were by the old-time professionals, they go back in despair to the latter, and are flayed and pillaged again. Back to Bach! Back to Tammany! Tammany reigns in New York because the Mitchel outfit was found to be intolerable—in other words, because the reformers were found to be even worse than the professionals. Is the fact surprising? Why should it be? Reformers and professionals are alike politicians in search of jobs; both are trying to bilk the taxpayers. Neither ever has any other motive. If any genuinely honest and altruistic politician had come to the surface in America in my time I'd have heard of him, for I have always frequented newspaper offices, and in a newspaper office the news of such a marvel would cause a dreadful tumult. I can recall no such tumult. The unanimous opinion of all the journalists that I know, excluding a few Liberals who are obviously somewhat balmy—they all believed, for example, that the late war would end war—is that, since the days of the national Thors and Wotans, no politician who was not out for himself, and for himself alone, has ever drawn the breath of life in the United States.

The gradual disintegration of Liberalism among us, in fact, offers an excellent proof of the truth of my thesis. The Liberals have come to grief by fooling their customers, not merely once too often, but a hundred times too often. Over and over again they have trotted out some new hero, usually from the great open spaces, only to see him taken in the immemorial malpractices within ten days. Their graveyard, indeed, is filled with cracked and upset headstones, many covered with ribald pencilings. Every time there is a scandal in the grand manner the Liberals lose almost as many general officers as either the Democrats or Republicans. Of late, racked beyond endurance by such catastrophes at home, they have gone abroad for their principal heroes; losing humor as well as hope, they now ask us to venerate such astounding paladins as the Hon. Bela Kun, a gentleman who, in any American State, would not only be in the calaboose, but actually in the death-house. But this absurdity is only an offshoot of a deeper one. Their primary error lies in making the false assumption that some politicians are better than others. This error they share with the whole American people.

I propose that it be renounced, and contend that its renunciation would greatly rationalize and improve our politics. I do not argue that there would be any improvement in our politicians; on the contrary, I believe that they would remain substantially as they are today, and perhaps grow even worse. But what I do argue is that recognizing them frankly for what they are would instantly and automatically dissipate the indignation caused by their present abominations, and that the disappearance of this indignation would promote the public contentment and happiness. Under my scheme there would be no more false assumptions and no more false hopes, and hence no more painful surprises, no more bitter resentment of fraud, no more despair. Politicians, in so far as they remained necessary, would be kept at work—but not with any insane notion that they were archangels. Their rascality would be assumed and discounted, as the rascality of the police is now assumed and discounted. Machinery would be gradually developed to limit it and counteract it. In the end, it might be utilized in some publicly profitable manner, as the insensitiveness to filth of garbage men is now utilized, as the reverence of the clergy for capitalism is now utilized. The result, perhaps, would be a world no better than the present one, but it would at least be a world more intelligent.

In all this I sincerely hope that no one will mistake me for one who shares the indignation I have spoken of—that is, for one who believes that politicians can be made good, and cherishes a fond scheme for making them so. I believe nothing of the sort. On the contrary, I am convinced that the art and mystery they practise is essentially and incurably anti-social—that they must remain irreconcilable enemies of the common weal until the end of time. But I maintain that this fact, in itself, is not a bar to their employment. There are, under Christian civilization, many necessary offices that demand the possession

175

of anti-social talents. A professional soldier, regarded realistically, is much worse than a professional politician, for he is a professional murderer and kidnaper, whereas the politician is only a professional sharper and sneak-thief. A clergyman, too, begins to shrink and shrivel on analysis; the work he does in the world is basically almost indistinguishable from that of an astrologer, a witch-doctor or a fortune-teller. He pretends falsely that he can get sinners out of hell, and collects money from them on that promise, tacit or express. If he had to go before a jury with that pretension it would probably go hard with him. But we do not send him before a jury; we grant him his hocus-pocus on the ground that it is necessary to his office, and that his office is necessary to civilization, so-called. I pass over the journalist delicately; the time has not come to turn State's evidence. Suffice it to say that he, too, would probably wither under a stiff cross-examination. If he is no murderer, like the soldier, then he is at least a sharper and swindler, like the politician.

What I plead for, if I may borrow a term in disrepute, is simply *Realpolitik, i.e.,* realism in politics. I can imagine a political campaign purged of all the current false assumptions and false pretenses—a campaign in which, on election day, the voters went to the polls clearly informed that the choice between them was not between an angel and a devil, a good man and a bad man, an altruist and a go-getter, but between two frank go-getters, the one, perhaps, excelling at beautiful and nonsensical words and the other at silent and prehensile deeds—the one a chautauqua orator and the other a porch-climber. There would be, in that choice, something candid, free and exhilarating. Buncombe would be adjourned. The voter would make his selection in the full knowledge of all the facts, as he makes his selection between two heads of cabbage, or two evening papers, or two brands of chewing tobacco. Today he chooses his rulers as he buys bootleg whiskey, never knowing precisely what he is getting, only certain that it is not what it pretends to be. The Scotch may turn out to be wood alcohol or it may turn out to be gasoline; in either case it is not Scotch. How much better if it were plainly labelled, for wood alcohol and gasoline both have their uses—higher uses, indeed, than Scotch. The danger is that the swindled and poisoned consumer, despairing of ever avoiding them when he doesn't want them, may prohibit them even when he does want them, and actually enforce his own prohibition. The danger is that the hopeless voter, forever victimized by his false assumption about politicians, may in the end gather such ferocious indignation that he will abolish them teetotally and at one insane swoop, and so cause government by the people, for the people and with the people to perish from this earth.

ON GOVERNMENT

1

"Government," said William Godwin in that "Enquiry Concerning Political Justice" which got Shelley two wives and lost him £6000 a year, "can have no more than two legitimate purposes: the suppression of injustice against individuals within the community, and the common defense against external invasion." The dictum, after a hundred and thirty-one years, remains unimproved and perhaps unimprovable. Today, to be sure, with Darwin behind us, we'd make some change in its terms: what Godwin was trying to say, obviously, was that the central aim of government was to ameliorate the struggle for existence—to cherish and protect the dignity of man in the midst of the brutal strife of *Homo neanderthalensis*. But that change would be simply substituting a *cliché* of the Nineteenth Century for one of the Eighteenth. All the furious discussion of the subject that has gone on in the intervening time has not changed the basic idea in the slightest. To the plain man of today, as to the most fanatical Liberal or Socialist, government appears primarily as a device for compensating his weakness, a machine for protecting him in rights that he could not make secure with his own arm. Even the Tory holds the same view of it: its essential function, to him, is to safeguard his property against the lascivious desires of those who, if they were not policed, would be tempted to grab it. "Government," said George Washington, "is not reason, it is not eloquence—it is force." Bad government is that which is weak, irresolute and lacking in constabulary enterprise; when one has defined it, one has also defined a bad bishop, cavalry captain or policeman. Good government is that which delivers the citizen from the risk of being done out of his life and property too arbitrarily and violently—one that relieves him sufficiently from the barbaric business of guarding them to enable him to engage in gentler, more dignified and more agreeable undertakings, to his own content and profit, and the advantage, it may be, of the commonwealth.

Unfortunately, this function is performed only imperfectly by any of the forms of government now visible in Christendom, and Dr. Johnson was perhaps justified in dismissing them all as but various aspects of the same fraud. The citizen of today, even in the most civilized states, is not only secured but defectively against other citizens who aspire to exploit and injure him—for example, highwaymen, bankers, quack doctors, clergymen, sellers of oil stock and contaminated liquor, and so-called reformers of all sorts—and against external foes, military, commercial and philosophical; he is also exploited and injured almost without measure by the government itself—in other words, by the very agency which professes to protect him. That agency becomes, indeed, one of the most dangerous and insatiable of the inimical forces present in his everyday environment. He finds it more difficult and costly to survive in the face of it than it is to survive in the face of any other enemy. He may, if he has prudence, guard himself effectively against all the known varieties of private criminals, from stockbrokers to pickpockets and from lawyers to kidnapers, and he may, if he has been burnt enough, learn to guard himself also against the rogues who seek to rob him by the subtler device of playing upon his sentimentalities and superstitions: charity mongers, idealists, soul-savers, and others after their kind. But he can no more escape the taxgatherer and the policemen, in all their protean and multitudinous guises, than he can escape the ultimate mortician. They beset him constantly, day in and day out, in ever-increasing numbers and in ever more disarming masks and attitudes. They invade his liberty, affront his dignity and greatly incommode his search for happiness, and every year they demand and wrest from him a larger and larger share of his worldly goods. The average American of today works more than a full day in every week to support his government. It already costs him more than his pleasures and almost as much as his vices, and in another half century, no doubt, it will begin to cost as much as his necessities.

These gross extortions and tyrannies, of course, are all practised on the theory that they are not only unavoidable, but also laudable—that government oppresses its victims in order to confer upon them the great boons mentioned by Godwin. But that theory, I believe, begins to be quite as dishonest as the chiropractor's pretense that he pummels his patient's spine in order to cure his cancer: the actual object, obviously, is simply to cure his solvency. What keeps such notions in full credit, and safeguards them against destructive analysis, is chiefly the survival into our enlightened age of a concept hatched in the black days of absolutism—the concept, to wit, that government is something that is superior to and quite distinct from all other human institutions—that it is, in its essence, not a mere organization of ordinary men, like the Ku Klux Klan, the United States Steel Corporation or Columbia University, but a transcendental organism composed of aloof and impersonal powers, devoid wholly of self-interest and not to be measured by merely human standards. One hears it spoken of, not uncommonly, as one hears the law of gravitation and the grace of God spoken of—as if its acts had no human motive in them and stood clearly above human fallibility. This concept, I need not argue, is full of error. The government at Washington is no more impersonal than the cloak and suit business is impersonal. It is operated by precisely the same sort of men, and to almost the same ends. When we say that it has decided to do this or that, that it proposes or aspires to do this or that—usually to the great cost and inconvenience of nine-tenths of us—we simply say that a definite man or group of men has decided to do it, or proposes or aspires to do it; and when we examine this group of men realistically we almost invariably find that it is composed of individuals who are not only not superior to the general, but plainly and depressingly inferior, both in common sense and in common decency— that the act of government we are called upon to ratify and submit to is, in its essence, no more than an act of self-interest by men who, if no mythical authority stood behind them, would have a hard time of it surviving in the struggle for existence.

2

These men, in point of fact, are seldom if ever moved by anything rationally describable as public spirit; there is actually no more public spirit among them than among so many burglars or street-walkers. Their purpose, first, last and all the time, is to promote their private advantage, and to that end, and that end alone, they exercise all the vast powers that are in their hands. Sometimes the thing they want is mere security in their jobs; sometimes they want gaudier and more lucrative jobs; sometimes they are content with their jobs and their pay but yearn for more power. Whatever it is they seek, whether security, greater ease, more money or more power, it has to come out of the common stock, and so it diminishes the shares of all other men. Putting a new job-holder to work decreases the wages of every wage-earner in the land—not enough to be noticed, perhaps, but enough to leave its mark. Giving a job-holder more power takes something away from the liberty of all of us: we are less free than we were in proportion as he has more authority. Theoretically, we get something for what we thus give up, but actually we usually get absolutely nothing. Suppose two-thirds of the members of the national House of Representatives were dumped into the Washington garbage incinerator tomorrow, what would we lose to offset our gain of their salaries and the salaries of their parasites? It may be plausibly argued, of course, that the House itself is necessary to our happiness and salvation —that we need it as we need trolley conductors, chiropodists and the men who bite off puppies' tails. But even if that be granted—and I, for one, am by no means disposed to grant it—the plain fact remains that all the useful work the House does might be done just as well by fifty men, and that the rest are of no more utility to the commonwealth, in any rational sense, than so many tightrope walkers or teachers of mah jong.

The Fathers, when they launched the Republic, were under no illusions as to the nature of government. Washington's view of its inner nature I have already quoted; Jefferson it was who said sagely that "the government is best which governs least." The Constitution in its first form, perhaps, was designed chiefly to check the rising pretensions of the lower orders, drunk with the democratic fustian of the Revolutionary era, but when the Bill of Rights was added to it its guns began to point more especially at the government itself, *i.e.,* at the class of job-holders, ever bent upon oppressing the citizen to the limit of his endurance. It is, perhaps, a fact provocative of sour mirth that the Bill of Rights was designed trustfully to prohibit forever two of the favorite crimes of all known governments: the seizure of private property without adequate compensation and the invasion of the citizen's liberty without justifiable cause and due process of law. It is a fact provocative of mirth yet more sour that the execution of these prohibitions was put into the hands of courts, which is to say, into the hands of lawyers, which is to say, into the hands of men specifically educated to discover legal excuses for dishonest, dishonorable and anti-social acts. The actual history of the Constitution, as everyone knows, has been a history of the gradual abandonment of all such impediments to governmental tyranny. Today we live frankly under a government of men, not of laws. What is the Bill of Rights to a Roosevelt, a Wilson, a Palmer, a Daugherty, a Burns? Under such tin-horn Cæsars the essential enmity between government and citizen becomes only too plain, and one gets all the proof that is needed of the eternal impossibility of protecting the latter against the former. The government can not only evoke fear in its victims; it can also evoke a sort of superstitious reverence. It is thus both an army and a church, and with sharp weapons in both hands it is virtually irresistible. Its personnel, true enough, may be changed, and so may the external forms of the fraud it practises, but its inner nature is immutable.

Politics, as hopeful men practise it in the world, consists mainly of the delusion that a change in form is a change in substance. The American colonists, when they got rid of the Potsdam tyrant, believed fondly that they were getting rid of oppressive taxes forever and setting up complete liberty. They found almost instantly that taxes were higher than ever, and before many years they were writhing under the Alien and Sedition Acts. The French, when they threw off the monarchy at last, looked forward to a Golden Age of peace, plenty and freedom. They are now wrecked by war, bankrupted beyond any chance of recovery, and hag-ridden by an apparently unbreakable combination of the most corrupt and cynical politicians ever seen in the world. The experience of the Russians and Germans is even more eloquent. The former have been ruined by their

saviors, and in so far as they have any power of reflection left, long for the restoration of the tyranny
they once ascribed to the devil. The latter, delivered
from the Hohenzollerns, now find the Schmidts and
Krauses ten times as expensive and oppressive. Six
months after the republic was set up a German cabinet
minister, for the first time in the history of the nation,
was in flight over the border, his loot under his arm.
In the first flush of surprise and indignation the people
took to assassinating politicians, but before long they
gave it up as hopeless: Schmidt fell but Kraus still lived,
and so government kept its vitality and its character.
Many Germans, reduced to despair, now advocate a
complete abolition of political government; if Stinnes
had lived they would have tried to make him dictator
of the country. But political government, *i.e.,* government by professional job-holders, would have remained
in fact, despite its theoretical abolition, and its nature
would have been unchanged.

If downright revolution is thus incapable of curing
the disease, the ordinary reforms that men believe in
sink to the level of bald quackeries. Consider, for
example, the history of so-called Civil Service Reform
in the United States. It came in on a wave of intense
public indignation against the whole governmental
imposture; it represented a violent and romantic effort
to substitute an ideal of public service for the familiar
harsh reality of public exploitation. For fifty years the
American people had sweated and suffered under the
spoils system, that lovely legacy of the "reforms" of the
Jackson era. By the opening of the eighties they were
ready to dispose of it by fair means or foul. The job-
holder, once theoretically a freeman discharging a lofty
and necessary duty, was seen clearly to be no more than
a rat devouring the communal corn; his public position
was indistinguishable from that of a child-stealer, a
well-poisoner or a Sunday-school superintendent; and
that of his brother, the government contractor and
purveyor, was even lower. Many men of both classes,

including some very important ones, were clapped into
jail, and many others had to depart for Canada between
days, along with the nightly squad of clerical seducers
and absconding bank cashiers. Thereupon seers and
prophets arose to lead the people out of the wilderness.
A few wild ones proposed, in effect, that government
be abolished altogether, but the notion outraged democratic sentiment, and so most of them followed the
job-holders into jail; some, in fact, were put to death
by more or less due process of law. The majority of
soothsayers were less revolutionary: they proposed only
that the race of job-holders be reformed by force, that
government be purged and denaturized.

This was undertaken by what came to be called Civil
Service Reform. The essence of Civil Service Reform
was the notion that the job-holder, in return for his
high prerogatives and immunities, should be compelled
to do an honest day's work—that he should fit himself
for it by hard effort, as a barber fits himself for cutting
hair. Led by such men of Vision as E. L. Godkin,
Charles J. Bonaparte and Theodore Roosevelt (that, of
course, was before Roosevelt deserted the flag and became himself the archetypical job-holder), the reformers
proceeded grimly toward the dreadful purpose of making the job-holder a mere slave, like a bookkeeper in a
wholesale house. His pay and emoluments were cut
down and his labors were increased. Once the proudest
and most envied citizen of the Republic, free to oppress
all other citizens to the limit of their endurance, he
became at one stroke a serf groaning in a pen, with
a pistol pointed at his head. If, despite the bars and
artillery surrounding him, his thrift enabled him to
make a show of decent prosperity, he was clapped into
prison *ipso facto,* and almost without a trial. A few
short years saw his fall from the dizziest height of ease
to the lowest abyss of misery.

This, of course, could not go on, else politics would
have tumbled into chaos and government would have
lost its basic character; nay, its very life. What is

more, it did *not* go on, for human ingenuity, despite the troubles of the time, was still functioning, and presently it found a remedy for the disease—a remedy so perfect, indeed, that the patient did not know he was taking it. That remedy was achieved by the simple process of making two slight changes in the ideal of Civil Service Reform itself. First the word Reform was lopped off, and then the word Civil. There remained, then, only Service. This Service saved the day for the job-holder; it gave him a new lease upon his job; it diverted public suspicion from him; it converted him from a criminal into a sort of philanthropist. It remains with us today, the heir and assign of the old spoils system, as the bootlegger is the heir and assign of the saloon-keeper.

3

The chief achievement of Service is that it has sucked reform into the governmental orbit, and so made it official and impeccable—more, highly profitable. The old-time reformer was one who got nothing for his psychic corn-cures and shin-plasters—who gave them away freely to all comers, seeking only righteousness himself—who often, indeed, took a beating into the bargain. The new reformer, safe in a government job, with a drastic and complex law behind him, is one who is paid in legal tender, unfailingly proffered, for his passionate but usually unintelligible services to humanity —a prophet of the new enlightenment, a priest at a glittering and immense shrine. He is the fellow who enforces the Volstead Act, the Mann Act, all the endless laws for putting down sin. He is the bright evangelist who tours the country teaching mothers how to have babies, spreading the latest inventions in pedagogy, road-making, the export trade, hog-raising and vegetable-canning, waging an eternal war upon illiteracy, hook-worm, the white slave trade, patent medicines, the foot and mouth disease, cholera infantum, adultery, rum. He is, quite as often as not, female; he is a lady Ph.D., cocksure, bellicose, very well paid. Male or female, he represents the new governmental tyranny; he is Vision, vice the spoils system, retired. The old-time job-holder, penned in the cage of the Civil Service, is now only a peon, a brother to the ox. He has to work quite as hard as if he labored for Judge Gary or Henry Ford, and he is very much worse paid. The high prerogatives and usufructs of government have slipped out of his hands. They are exercised and enjoyed today by the apostles of Service, a horde growing daily, vastly and irresistibly, in numbers, impudence, power and pay.

Few of the groaning taxpayers of These States, indeed, realize how far this public merchandizing of buncombe has displaced the old spoils system, or how much it is costing them every year. During the Civil War an army contractor who went to Washington looking for loot announced frankly what he was after; as a result, he was constantly under suspicion, and was lucky if he got away with as much as $100,000; only a few Vanderbilts and Morgans actually stole more. During the late war he called himself a dollar-a-year-man, put on a major's uniform, took oath to die if need be for the cause of democracy—and went home with a million, at least. The job-holder has undergone a similar metamorphosis; maybe apotheosis would be a better aimed word. In the days of the spoils system he was, at best, an amateurish and inept performer. The only reason he ever offered for demanding a place at the public trough was that he deserved it—that he had done his share to elect the ticket. The easy answer to him was that he was an obvious loafer and scoundrel, and deserved nothing. But what answer is to be made to his heir and assign, the evangelist of Service, the prophet of Vision? He doesn't start off with a bald demand for a job; he starts off with a Message. He has discovered the long-sought sure cure for all the sorrows of the world; he has the infallible scheme for putting down justice, misery, ignorance, suffering, sin; his appeal is not to the rules of a sinister and discreditable game, but to the bursting heart of humanity, the noblest and loftiest sentiments of man. His job is never in the foreground; it is concealed in his Vision. To get at the former one must first dispose of the latter. Well, who is to do it? What true-born American will volunteer for the cynical office? Half are too idiotic and the rest are too cowardly. It takes courage to flaunt and make a mock of Vision—and where is courage?

Certainly not in this imperial commonwealth of natural kneebenders and marchers in parades. Nowhere else in Christendom, save only in France, is government more extravagant, nonsensical, unintelligent and corrupt than here, and nowhere else is it so secure. It becomes a sort of crime even to protest against its villainies; all the late investigations of waste and corruption in Washington were attacked and brought to wreck in the name of duty, decorum, patriotism. The citizen objecting to felony by the agents of the sovereign state, acting in its name, found himself posted as an anarchist! There was, of course, some logic in this imbecility, as there is in everything insane. It was felt that too violent an onslaught upon the disease might do gross damage to the patient, that the attempt to extirpate what was foul and excrescent might imperil what was useful and necessary. Is government, then, useful and necessary? So is a doctor. But suppose the dear fellow claimed the right, every time he was called in to prescribe for a bellyache or a ringing in the ears, to raid the family silver, use the family tooth-brushes, and execute the *droit de seigneur* upon the house-maid? Is it simply a coincidence that the only necessary functionaries who actually perform any comparable brigandage are the lawyers—the very men who, under democracy, chiefly determined the form, policies and acts of the government?

This great pox of civilization, alas, I believe to be incurable, and so I propose no new quackery for its treatment. I am against dosing it, and I am against killing it. All I presume to argue is that something

would be accomplished by viewing it more realistically
—by ceasing to let its necessary and perhaps useful
functions blind us to its ever-increasing crimes against
the ordinary rights of the free citizen and the common
decencies of the world. The fact that it is generally
respected—that it possesses effective machinery for prop-
agating and safeguarding that respect—is the main
shield of the rogues and vagabonds who use it to
exploit the great masses of diligent and credulous men.
Whenever you hear anyone bawling for more respect for
the laws, whether it be a Coolidge on his imperial
throne or an humble county judge in his hedge court,
you have before you one who is trying to use them to
his private advantage; whenever you hear of new legislation for putting down dissent and rebellion you may
be sure that it is promoted by scoundrels. The extortions
and oppressions of government will go on so long as
such bare fraudulence deceives and disarms the victims
—so long as they are ready to swallow the immemorial
official theory that protesting against the stealings of
the archbishop's secretary's nephew's mistress' illegitimate son is a sin against the Holy Ghost. They will
come to an end when the victims begin to differentiate
clearly between government as a necessary device for
maintaining order in the world and government as a
device for maintaining the authority and prosperity of
predatory rascals and swindlers. In other words, they
will come to an end on the Tuesday following the
first Monday of November preceding the Resurrection
Morn.

THE CAPITAL OF A GREAT REPUBLIC

The fourth secretary of the Paraguayan legation. . . . The chief clerk to the House committee on industrial arts and expositions. . . . The secretary to the secretary to the Secretary of Labor. . . . The brother to the former Congressman from the third Idaho district. . . . The messenger to the chief of the Senate folding-room. . . . The doorkeeper outside the committee-room of the House committee on the disposition of useless executive papers. . . . The chief correspondent of the Toomsboro, Ga., *Banner* in the Senate press-gallery. . . . The stenographer to the assistant chief entomologist of the Bureau of Animal Industry. . . . The third assistant chief computor in the office of the Naval Almanac. . . . The assistant Attorney-General in charge of the investigation of postal frauds in the South Central States. . . . The former wife of the former secretary to the former member of the Interstate Commerce Commission. . . . The brother to the wife of the *chargé d'affaires* of Czecho-Slovakia. . . . The bootlegger to the ranking Democratic member of the committee on the election of President, Vice-President and representatives in Congress. . . . The acting assistant doorkeeper of the House visitors' gallery. . . . The junior Senator from Delaware. . . . The assistant to the secretary to the chief clerk of the Division of Audits and Disbursements, Bureau of Stationary and Supplies, Postoffice Department. . . . The press-agent to the chaplain of the House. . . . The commercial attaché to the American legation at Quito. . . . The chauffeur to the fourth assistant Post-

master-General. . . . The acting substitute elevator-man
in the Washington monument. . . . The brother to the
wife of the brother-in-law of the Vice-President. . . .
The aunt to the sister of the wife of the officer in charge
of ceremonials, State Department. . . . The neighbor of
the cousin of the step-father of the sister-in-law of the
President's pastor. . . . The superintendent of char-
women in Temporary Storehouse B7, Bureau of Navy
Yards and Docks. . . . The assistant confidential clerk
to the acting chief examiner of the Patent Office. . . .
The valet to the Chief Justice.

BILDER AUS SCHÖNER ZEIT

The excellent lunch that the illustrious Crispi
used to serve at Delmonico's at five o'clock in the afternoon. . . . The incomparable orange blossom cocktails
at Sherry's, and the plates of salted nuts. . . . The
tavern cocktails at the Beaux Arts, each with its
dash of absinthe. . . . The Franziskaner Mai-Bock at
Lüchow's. . . . Dear old Sieg's noble Rhine wines at
the Kaiserhof. . . . The long-tailed clams and Spring
onions at Rogers', with Pilsner to wash them down. . . .
The amazingly good American quasi-Pilsner, made by
Herr Abner, on the Raleigh roof in Washington. . . .
The Castel del Remy at the Brevoort, cheap but
perfect. . . . The very dark Kulmbacher at the Pabst
place in 125th street in the last days of civilization. . . .
The burgundy from the Cresta Blanca vineyards in
California. . . . Michelob on warm Summer evenings,
with the crowd singing "Throw Out the Lifeline!" . . .
The oldtime Florestan cocktails—50 per cent. London
gin, 25 per cent. French vermouth and 25 per cent.
Martini-Rossi, with a dash of Angostura bitters—drink

half, then drink a glass of beer, and then drink the other half. . . . That Hoboken red wine, so strangely smooth and lovely. . . . The bad red wine (but capital cooking) at the Frenchman's in Lexington avenue. . . . Del Pezzo's superb Chianti. . . . The ale at Keen's. . . . Obst's herrings, with Löwenbraü to slack them. . . . The astounding cocktail made by the head waiter at Henri's. . . . Drinking Faust all night in St. Louis in 1904. . . . The musty ale at Losekam's in Washington. . . . The draft *Helles* at Krüger's in Philadelphia. . . . A Pilsner luncheon at the old Grand Union, from one to six. . . . A stray bottle of perfect sauterne found in Rahway, New Jersey. . . . A wild night drinking Swedish punch and hot water. . . . Two or three hot Scotch nights. . . . Twenty or thirty Bass' ale nights. . . . Five or six hundred Pilsner nights. . . .

CONRAD

Some time ago I put in a blue afternoon re-reading Joseph Conrad's "Youth." A *blue* afternoon? What nonsense! The touch of the man is like the touch of Schubert. One approaches him in various and unhappy moods: depressed, dubious, despairing; one leaves him in the clear, yellow sunshine that Nietzsche found in Bizet's music. But here again the phrase is inept. Sunshine suggests the imbecile, barnyard joy of the human kohlrabi—the official optimism of a steadily delighted and increasingly insane Republic. What the enigmatical Pole has to offer is something quite different. If its parallel is to be found in music, it is not in Schubert, but in Beethoven—perhaps even more accurately in Johann Sebastian Bach. It is the joy, not of mere satisfaction, but of understanding—the profound

191

but surely not merry delight which goes with the comprehension of a fundamental fact—above all, of a fact that has been coy and elusive. Certainly the order of the world that Conrad sets forth with such diabolical eloquence and plausibility is no banal moral order, no childish sequence of virtuous causes and edifying effects. Rather it has an atheistic and even demoniacal smack: to the earnest Bible student it must be more than a little disconcerting. The God he visualizes is no loving papa in a house-coat and carpet-slippers, inculcating the great principles of Christian ethics by applying occasional strokes *a posteriori*. What he sees is something quite different: an extremely ingenious and humorous Improvisatore and Comedian, with a dab of red on His nose and maybe somewhat the worse for drink—a furious and far from amiable banjoist upon the human spine, and rattler of human bones. Kurtz, in "Youth," makes a capital banjo for that exalted and cynical talent. And the music that issues forth—what a superb *Hexentanz* it is!

One of the curiosities of critical stupidity is the doctrine that Conrad is without humor. No doubt it flows out of a more general error; to wit, the assumption that tragedy is always pathetic, that death itself is inevitably a gloomy business. That error, I suppose, will persist in the world until some extraordinary astute mime conceives the plan of playing "King Lear" as a farce—I mean deliberately. That it *is* a farce seems to me quite as obvious as the fact that "Romeo and Juliet" is another, this time lamentably coarse. To adopt the contrary theory—to view it as a great moral and spiritual spectacle, capable of purging and uplifting the psyche like marriage to a red-haired widow or a month in the trenches—to toy with such notions is to borrow the critical standards of a party of old ladies weeping over the damnation of the heathen. In point of fact, death, like love, is intrinsically farcical—a solemn kicking of a brick under a plug-hat—and most other human agonies, once they transcend the physical—*i.e.,* the unescapably real—have far more of irony in them than of pathos. Looking back upon them after they have eased one seldom shivers: one smiles—perhaps sourly but nevertheless spontaneously. This, at all events, is the notion that seems to me implicit in every line of Conrad. I give you "Heart of Darkness" as the archetype of his whole work and the keystone of his metaphysical system. Here we have all imaginable human hopes and aspirations reduced to one common denominator of folly and failure, and here we have a play of humor that is infinitely mordant and searching. Turn to pages 136 and 137 of the American edition—the story is in the volume called "Youth"—: the burial of the helmsman. Turn then to 178-184: Marlow's last interview with Kurtz's intended. The farce mounts by slow stages to dizzy and breath-taking heights. One hears harsh roars of cosmic laughter, vast splutterings of transcendental mirth, echoing and reëchoing down the black corridors of empty space. The curtain descends at last upon a wild dance in a dissecting-room. The mutilated dead rise up and jig. . . .

It is curious, re-reading a thrice-familiar story, how often one finds surprises in it. I have been amazed, toward the close of "The End of the Tether," to discover that the *Fair Maid* was wrecked, not by the deliberate act of Captain Whalley, but by the machination of the unspeakable Massy. How is one to account for so preposterous an error? Certainly I thought I knew "The End of the Tether" as well as I knew anything in this world—and yet there was that incredible misunderstanding of it, lodged firmly in my mind. Perhaps there is criticism of a sort in my blunder: it may be a fact that the old skipper willed the thing himself—that his willing it is visible in all that goes before—that Conrad, in introducing Massy's puerile infamy at the end, made some sacrifice of inner veracity to the exigencies of what, at bottom, is somewhat too neat and well-made a tale. The story, in fact, belongs to the author's earlier manner; I guess that it was written before "Youth" and surely before "Heart of Darkness." But for all that, its proportions remain truly colossal. It is one of the most magnificent narratives, long or short, old or new, in the English language, and with "Youth" and "Heart of Darkness" it makes up what is probably the best book of imaginative writing that the English literature of the Twentieth Century can yet show. Conrad learned a great deal after he wrote it, true enough. In "Lord Jim," in "Victory," and, above all, in a "A Personal Record," there are momentary illuminations, blinding flashes of brilliance that he was incapable of in those days of experiment; but no other book of his seems to me to hold so steadily to so high a general level—none other, as a whole, is more satisfying and more marvelous. There is in "Heart of Darkness" a perfection of design which one encounters only rarely and miraculously in prose fiction: it belongs rather to music. I can't imagine taking a single sentence out of that stupendous tale without leaving a visible gap; it is as thoroughly *durch componiert* as a fugue. And I can't imagine adding anything to it, even so little as a word, without doing it damage. As it stands it is austerely and beautifully perfect, just as the slow movement of the Unfinished Symphony is perfect.

I observe of late a tendency to examine the English of Conrad rather biliously. This folly is cultivated chiefly in England, where, I suppose, chauvinistic motives enter into the matter. It is the just boast of great empires that they draw in talents from near and far, exhausting the little nations to augment their own puissance; it is their misfortune that these talents often remain defectively assimilated. Conrad remained the Slav to the end. The people of his tales, whatever he calls them, are always as much Slavs as he is; the language in which he describes them retains a sharp, exotic flavor. But to say that this flavor constitutes a blemish is to say something so preposterous that only schoolmasters and their dupes may be thought of as giving it credit.

The truly first-rate writer is not one who uses the language as such dolts demand that it be used; he is one who reworks it in spite of their prohibitions. It is his distinction that he thinks in a manner different from the thinking of ordinary men; that he is free from that slavery to embalmed ideas which makes them so respectable and so dull. Obviously, he cannot translate his notions into terms of everyday without doing violence to their inner integrity; as well ask a Richard Strauss to funnel all his music into the chaste jugs of Prof. Dr. Jadassohn. What Conrad brought into English literature was a new concept of the relations between fact and fact, idea and idea, and what he contributed to the complex and difficult art of writing English was a new way of putting words together. His style now amazes and irritates pedants because it does not roll along in the old ruts. Well, it is precisely that rolling along in the old ruts that he tried to avoid—and it was precisely that avoidance which made him what he is. What lies under most of his alleged sins seems to me to be simple enough: he views English logically and analytically, and not through a haze of senseless traditions and arbitrary taboos. No Oxford mincing is in him. If he cannot find his phrase above the salt, he seeks it below. His English, in a word, is innocent. And if, at times, there gets into it a color that is strange and even bizarre, then the fact is something to rejoice over, for a living language is like a man suffering incessantly from small internal hemorrhages, and what it needs above all else is constant transfusions of new blood from other tongues. The day the gates go up, that day it begins to die.

A very great man, this Mr. Conrad. As yet, I believe decidedly underestimated, even by many of his post-mortem advocates. Most of his first acclaimers mistook him for a mere romantic—a talented but somewhat uncouth follower of the Stevenson tradition, with the orthodox cutlass exchanged for a Malay *kris*. Later on he began to be heard of as a linguistic and vocational marvel: it was astonishing that any men bred to Polish should write English at all, and more astonishing that a country gentleman from the Ukraine should hold a master's certificate in the British merchant marine. Such banal attitudes are now archaic, but I suspect that they have been largely responsible for the slowness with which his fame has spread in the world. At all events, he is vastly less read and esteemed in foreign parts than he ought to be, and very few Continental Europeans have risen to any genuine comprehension of his stature. When one reflects that the Nobel Prize was given to such third-raters as Benavente, Heidenstam, Gjellerup and Tagore, with Conrad passed over, one begins to grasp the depth and density of the ignorance prevailing in the world, even among the relatively enlightened. One "Lord Jim," as human document and as work of art, is worth all the works produced by all the Benaventes and Gjellerups since the time of Rameses II. It is, indeed, an indecency of criticism to speak of such unlike things in the same breath: as well talk of Brahms in terms of Mendelssohn. Nor is "Lord Jim" a chance masterpiece, an isolated peak. On the contrary, it is but one unit in a long series of extraordinary and almost incomparable works—a series sprung suddenly and overwhelmingly into full dignity with "Almayer's Folly." I challenge the nobility and gentry of Christendom to point to another Opus 1 as magnificently planned and turned out as "Almayer's Folly." The more one studies it, the more it seems miraculous. If it is not a work of absolute genius then no work of absolute genius exists on this earth.

LARDNER

A few years ago a young college professor, eager to make a name for himself, brought out a laborious "critical" edition of "Sam Slick," by judge Thomas C. Haliburton, eighty-seven years after its first publication. It turned out to be quite unreadable—a dreadful series of archaic jocosities about varieties of *Homo americanus* long perished and forgotten, in a dialect now intelligible only to paleophilologists. Sometimes I have a fear that the same fate awaits Ring Lardner. The professors of his own day, of course, are quite unaware of him, save perhaps as a low zany to be enjoyed behind the door. They would no more venture to whoop him up publicly and officially than their predecessors of 1880 would have ventured to whoop up Mark Twain, or their remoter predecessors of 1837 would have dared to say anything for Haliburton. In such matters the academic mind, being chiefly animated by a fear of sneers, works very slowly. So slowly, indeed, does it work that it usually works too late. By the time Mark Twain got into the text-books for sophomores two-thirds of his compositions, as the Young Intellectuals say, had already begun to date; by the time Haliburton was served up as a sandwich between introduction and notes he was already dead. As I say, I suspect sadly that Lardner is doomed to go the same route. His stories, it seems to me, are superbly adroit and amusing; no other contemporary American, sober or gay, writes better. But I doubt that they last: our grandchildren will wonder what they are about. It is not only, or even mainly, that the dialect that fills them will pass, though that fact is obviously a serious handicap in itself.

It is principally that the people they depict will pass, that Lardner's Low Down Americans—his incomparable baseball players, pugs, song-writers, Elks, small-town Rotarians and golf caddies—are flitting figures of a transient civilization, and doomed to be as puzzling and soporific, in the year 2000, as Haliburton's Yankee clock peddler is to-day.

The fact—if I may assume it to be a fact—is certain not to be set against Lardner's account; on the contrary, it is, in its way, highly complimentary to him. For he has deliberately applied himself, not to the anatomizing of the general human soul, but to the meticulous histological study of a few salient individuals of his time and nation, and he has done it with such subtle and penetrating skill that one must belong to his time and nation to follow him. I doubt that anyone who is not familiar with professional ball players, intimately and at first hand, will ever comprehend the full merit of the amazing sketches in "You Know Me, Al"; I doubt that anyone who has not given close and deliberate attention to the American vulgate will ever realize how magnificently Lardner handles it. He has had more imitators, I suppose, than any other living American writer, but has he any actual rivals? If so, I have yet to hear of them. They all try to write the speech of the streets as adeptly and as amusingly as he writes it, and they all fall short of him; the next best is miles and miles behind him. And they are all inferior in observation, in sense of character, in shrewdness and insight. His studies, to be sure, are never very profound; he makes no attempt to get at the primary springs of human motive; all his people share the same amiable stupidity, the same transparent vanity, the same shallow swinishness; they are all human Fords in bad repair, and alike at bottom. But if he thus confines himself to the surface, it yet remains a fact that his investigations on that surface are extraordinarily alert, ingenious and brilliant—that the character he finally sets before us, however roughly articulated as to bones, is so astoundingly realistic as to epidermis that the effort is indistinguishable from that of life itself. The old man in "The Golden Honeymoon" is not merely well done; he is perfect. And so is the girl in "Some Like Them Cold." And so, even, is the idiotic Frank X. Farrell in "Alibi Ike"—an extravagant grotesque and yet quite real from glabella to calcaneus.

Lardner knows more about the management of the short story than all of its professors. His stories are built very carefully, and yet they seem to be wholly spontaneous, and even formless. He has grasped the primary fact that no conceivable ingenuity can save a story that fails to show a recognizable and interesting character; he knows that a good character sketch is always a good story, no matter what its structure. Perhaps he gets less attention than he ought to get, even among the anti-academic critics, because his people are all lowly boors. For your reviewer of books, like every other sort of American, is always vastly impressed by fashionable pretensions. He belongs to the white collar class of labor, and shares its prejudices. He praises F. Scott Fitzgerald's stories of country-club flappers eloquently, and overlooks Fitzgerald's other stories, most of which are much better. He can't rid himself of the feeling that Edith Wharton, whose people have butlers, is a better novelist than Willa Cather, whose people, in the main, dine in their kitchens. He lingers under the spell of Henry James, whose most humble character, at any rate of the later years, was at least an Englishman, and hence superior. Lardner, so to speak, hits such critics under the belt. He not only fills his stories with people who read the tabloids, say "Shake hands with my friend," and buy diamond rings on the instalment plan; he also shows them having a good time in the world, and quite devoid of inferiority complexes. They amuse him sardonically, but he does not pity them. A fatal error! The moron, perhaps, has a place in fiction, as in life, but he is not to be treated too easily and casually. It must be shown that he suffers tragically because he cannot abandon the plow to write poetry, or the sample-case to study for opera. Lardner is more realistic. If his typical hero has a secret sorrow it is that he is too old to take up osteopathy and too much in dread of his wife to venture into bootlegging.

Of late a sharply acrid flavor has got into Lardner's buffoonery. His baseball players and fifth-rate pugilists, beginning in his first stories as harmless jackasses, gradually convert themselves into loathsome scoundrels. The same change shows itself in Sinclair Lewis; it is difficult, even for an American, to contemplate the American without yielding to something hard to distinguish from moral indignation. Turn, for example, to the sketches in the volume called "The Love Nest." The first tells the story of a cinema queen married to a magnate of the films. On the surface she seems to be nothing but a noodle, but underneath there is a sewer; the woman is such a pig that she makes one shudder. Again, he investigates another familiar type: the village practical joker. The fellow, in one form or other, has been laughed at since the days of Aristophanes. But here is a mercilessly realistic examination of his dunghill humor, and of its effects upon decent people. A third figure is a successful theatrical manager: he turns out to have the professional competence of a chiropractor and the honor of a Prohibition agent. A fourth is a writer of popular songs: stealing other men's ideas has become so fixed a habit with him that he comes to believe that he has an actual right to them. A fourth is a trained nurse—but I spare you this dreadful nurse. The rest are bores of the homicidal type. One gets the effect, communing with the whole gang, of visiting a museum of anatomy. They are as shocking as what one encounters there—but in every detail they are as unmistakably real.

Lardner conceals his new savagery, of course, beneath his old humor. It does not flag. No man writing among us has greater skill at the more extravagant varieties of jocosity. He sees startling and revelatory likeness between immensely disparate things, and he is full of pawky observations and bizarre comments. Two baseball players are palavering, and one of them, Young Jake, is boasting of his conquests during Spring practice below the Potomac. "Down South ain't here!" replies the other. "Those dames in some of those swamps, they lose their head when they see a man with shoes on!" The two proceed to the discussion of a third imbecile, guilty of some obscure tort. "Why," inquires Young Jake, "didn't you break his nose or bust him in the chin?" "His nose was already broke," replied the other, "and he didn't have no chin." Such wise cracks seem easy to devise. Broadway diverts itself by manufacturing them. They constitute the substance of half the town shows. But in those made by Lardner there is something far more than mere facile humor: they are all rigidly in character, and they illuminate that character. Few American novelists, great or small, have character more firmly in hand. Lardner does not see situations; he sees people. And what people! They are all as revolting as so many Methodist evangelists, and they are all as thoroughly American.

HERETICS

ALTGELD OF ILLINOIS, by Waldo R. Browne, New York: *B. W. Huebsch.* THE LAST OF THE HERETICS, by Algernon Sidney Crapsey. New York: *Alfred A. Knopf.* [The American Mercury, October, 1924.]

When I was a boy, in the early nineties of the last century, the reigning hobgoblin of the United States was John P. Altgeld, Governor of Illinois. From this distance the ill-fame that played about him seems

almost fabulous. He was a sort of horrendous combination of Trotsky and Raisuli, Darwin and the
German Crown Prince, Jesse James and Oscar Wilde,
with overtones of Wayne B. Wheeler and the McNamara
brothers. We have had, in these later years, no such
communal devil. The La Follette of 1917 was a popular
favorite compared to him; the Debs of the same time was
a spoiled darling. What I gathered from my elders, in
the awful years of adolescence, when my voice began
to break and vibrissæ sprouted on my lip, was that
Altgeld was a shameless advocate of rapine and assassination, an enemy alike to the Constitution and the
Ten Commandments—in short, a bloody and insatiable
anarchist. I was thus bred to fear him even more than
I feared the anonymous scoundrels who had stolen
Charlie Ross. When I dreamed, it was of catching him
in some public place and cutting off his head, to the
applause of the multitude.

The elders that I have mentioned were mainly business men, with a few *Gelehrte* thrown in. I learned
later on, by hard experience, that the opinions of such
gentlemen, particularly of public matters and public
men, were not always sound. Nevertheless, I continued
to have a bilious suspicion of the Hon. Mr. Altgeld,
and it survived even the discovery, made much later,
that men who had actually known him—for example, Theodore Dreiser—regarded him very highly. I
remember very well how shocked I was when Dreiser
made me privy to this fact. It made a dent, I suppose,
in my old view, but it surely did not dispose of it
altogether. I continued to believe that Altgeld, though
perhaps not an anarchist, as alleged, was at least a
blathering Socialist, and hence deserving of a few pro-
phylactic kicks in the pantaloons. I was far gone in my
forties before ever I got at the truth. Then I found it
in this modest book of Mr. Browne's—a volume that is
dreadfully written, but extremely illuminating. That
truth may be put very simply. Altgeld was not an
anarchist, nor was he a Socialist: he was simply a

sentimentalist. His error consisted in taking the college
yells of democracy seriously.

I do not go into the evidence, but refer you to the
book. It is very completely documented, and it leaves
little room for doubt, despite Mr. Browne's obvious
prejudice in favor of some of Altgeld's more dubious
ideas, especially the idea of government ownership. On
the main points his argument is quite beyond cavil.
Did Altgeld pardon the Chicago anarchists? Then it was
simply because they had been railroaded to jail on
evidence that should have made the very judge on the
bench guffaw—as men are still railroaded in California
to-day. Did he protest against Cleveland's invasion of
Chicago with Federal troops at the time of the Pullman
strike? Then it was because he knew only too well how
little they were needed—and what sinister influences had
cajoled poor old Grover into sending them. In brief,
Altgeld was one of the first public men in America to
protest by word and act against government by usurers
and their bashi-bazouks—the first open and avowed
advocate of the Bill of Rights since Jackson's time. A
romantic fellow, and a firm believer in the virtues of the
common people, he couldn't rid himself of the delusion
that they would follow him here—that after the yell of
rage there would come a resounding cheer. That belief
gradually degenerated into a hope, but I doubt that it
ever disappeared altogether. The common people met it
by turning Altgeld out of office, swiftly and ignominiously. After they had got rid of him as Governor of
Illinois, they even rejected him as mayor of Chicago. His
experience taught him a lesson, but like that of the
Aframerican on the gallows, it came too late.

What lesson is in his career for the rest of us? The
lesson, it seems to me, that any man who devotes himself to justice and common decency, under democracy,
is a very foolish fellow—that the generality of men have
no genuine respect for these things, and are always suspicious of the man who upholds them. Their public relations, like their private relations, are marked by the

qualities that mark the inferior man at all times and everywhere: cowardice, stupidity and cruelty. They are in favor of whoever is wielding the whip, even when their own hides must bear the blows. How easy it was to turn the morons of the American Legion upon their fellow-slaves! How heroically they voted for Harding, and then for Coolidge after him—and so helped to put down the Reds! Dog eats dog, world without end. In the Pullman strike at least half the labor unions of the United States were against the strikers, as they were against the more recent steel strikers, and helped to beat them. Altgeld battled for the under dog all his life—and the under dog bit him in the end. A pathetic career, but not without its touches of sardonic comedy. Altgeld, in error at bottom, was often also in error on the surface, and not infrequently somewhat grotesquely. He succumbed to the free silver mania. He supported Bryan— nay more, he may be said to have discovered and made Bryan. It is fortunate for him that he was dead and in hell by 1902, and so not forced to contemplate the later states of his handiwork. He was excessively romantic, but certainly no ignoramus. Imagine him listening to one of good Jennings' harangues against the elements of biology! Such men, indeed, are always happier dead. This world, and especially this Republic, is no place for idealists.

Another proof of it is offered by the career of Dr. Crapsey, whose trial for heresy entertained the damned in 1906. He is still alive as I write, and still full of steam. But I doubt that he is as sure as he used to be that common sense and common honesty pay. Many of the frauds who drove him out of the church, though they knew that he was right, are bishops to-day, and licensed to bind and loose. Others have been called by God, and sit upon His right hand. The church itself, as it has grown more sordid and swinish, has only grown more prosperous. In New York City its income approaches that of the bootleggers and it is almost as well regarded. Every new profiteer, even before he tries to horn into the Piping

Rock Club, subscribes to its articles. It is robbing the Church of Christ Scientist of all the rich Jews; they are having their sons baptized in its fonts and christened Llewellyn, Seymour and Murray. Certainly it would be difficult to imagine a more gloriously going concern. The rising spires of its steel and concrete cathedrals begin to bulge the floor of heaven; its clergy are sleek, fat and well-oiled; its bishops come next in precedence after movie stars and members of the firm of J. P. Morgan & Company. Lately it threw out another heretic—like Dr. Crapsey, one accused of putting the Sermon on the Mount above the conflicting genealogies of the Preacher. As for Crapsey himself, he has naught to console him in his old age save the thought that hell will at least be warm.

His book is extremely amusing and instructive. Like Altgeld, he confesses to foreign and poisonous blood. The *Stammvater* of the American Crapseii was a fellow named Kropps, apparently a Hessian. But his great-great grandson, the father of the heretic, married the daughter of a United States Senator, and so there is some amelioration of the horror. Like Altgeld again, Crapsey went to the Civil War as a boy scarcely out of knee breeches. Altgeld was so poor that he gladly took the $100 offered by a patriot who had been drafted and wanted a substitute; Crapsey volunteered. Both succumbed to camp fevers and were discharged. Both then took to Service among the downtrodden, Altgeld in politics and the law, and Crapsey in one of the outlying hereditaments of Trinity parish. Both were safe so long as they appeared to be fraudulent; the moment they began to show genuine belief in their doctrines they found themselves in difficulties. So Altgeld became the favorite hobgoblin of the Republic and Crapsey became its blackest heretic.

ON LIVING IN BALTIMORE

Some time ago, writing in an eminent Baltimore newspaper upon the Baltimore of my boyhood, I permitted myself an eloquent passage upon its charm, and let fall the doctrine that nearly all of that charm had vanished. Mere rhetoric, I greatly fear. The old charm, in truth, still survives in the town, despite the frantic efforts of the boosters and boomers who, in late years, have replaced all its ancient cobblestones with asphalt, and bedizened it with Great White Ways and suburban boulevards, and surrounded it with stinking steel plants and oil refineries, and increased its population from 400,-000 to 800,000. I am never more conscious of the fact than when I return to it from New York. Behind me lies the greatest city of the modern world, with more money in it than all Europe and more clowns and harlots than all Asia, and yet it has no more charm than a circus lot or a second-rate hotel. It can't show a single genuinely distinguished street. It hasn't a single park that is more lovely than a cemetery lot. It is without manner as it is without manners. Escaping from it to so ancient and solid a town as Baltimore is like coming out of a football crowd into quiet communion with a fair one who is also amiable, and has the gift of consolation for hard-beset and despairing men.

I have confessed to rhetoric, but I surely do not indulge in it here. For twenty-five years I have resisted a constant temptation to move to New York, and I resist it more easily to-day than I did when it began. I am, perhaps, the most arduous commuter ever heard of, even in that Babylon of commuters. My office is on Manhattan Island and has been there since 1914; yet I live, vote and have

my being in Baltimore, and go back there the instant my
job allows. If my desk bangs at 3 P.M. I leap for the 3.25
train. Four long hours in the Pullman follow, but the
first is the worst. My back, at all events, is toward New
York! Behind lies a place fit only for the gross business of
getting money; ahead is a place made for enjoying it.

What makes New York so dreadful, I believe, is
mainly the fact that the vast majority of its people have
been forced to rid themselves of one of the oldest and
most powerful of human instincts—the instinct to make
a permanent home. Crowded, shoved about and exploited
without mercy, they have lost the feeling that any part of
the earth belongs to them, and so they simply camp out
like tramps, waiting for the constables to rush in and
chase them away. I am not speaking here of the poor
(God knows how they exist in New York at all!); I am
speaking of the well-to-do, even of the rich. The very
richest man, in New York, is never quite sure that the
house he lives in now will be his next year—that he will
be able to resist the constant pressure of business expan-
sion and rising land values. I have known actual million-
aires to be chased out of their homes in this way, and
forced into apartments. In Baltimore too, the same pressure exists, to be sure, but it is not oppressive, for the
householder can meet it by yielding to it half way. It
may force him into the suburbs, even into the adjacent
country, but he is still in direct contact with the city,
sharing in its life, and wherever he lands he may make a
stand. But on Manhattan Island he is quickly brought up
by the rivers, and once he has crossed them he may as
well move to Syracuse or Trenton.

Nine times out of ten he tries to avoid crossing them.
That is, he moves into meaner quarters on the island
itself, and pays more for them. His house gives way to a
flat—one offering perhaps half the room for his goods
and chattels that his house offered. Next year he is in a
smaller flat, and three-fourths of his goods and chattels
have vanished. A few years more, and he is in two or
three rooms. Finally, he lands in an hotel. At this point

he ceases to exist as the head of a house. His quarters are precisely like the quarters of 50,000 other men. The front he presents to the world is simply an anonymous door on a gloomy corridor. Inside, he lives like a sardine in a can. Such a habitation, it must be plain, cannot be called a home. A home is not a mere transient shelter: its essence lies in its permanence, in its capacity for accretion and solidification, in its quality of representing, in all its details, the personalities of the people who live in it. In the course of years it becomes a sort of museum of these people; they give it its indefinable air, separating it from all other homes, as one human face is separated from all others. It is at once a refuge from the world, a treasure-house, a castle, and the shrine of a whole hierarchy of peculiarly private and potent gods.

This concept of the home cannot survive the mode of life that prevails in New York. I have seen it go to pieces under my eyes in the houses of my own friends. The intense crowding in the town, and the restlessness and unhappiness that go with it, make it almost impossible for anyone to accumulate the materials of a home—the trivial, fortuitous and often grotesque things that gather around a family, as glories and debts gather around a state. The New Yorker lacks the room to house them; he thus learns to live without them. In the end he is a stranger in the house he lives in. More and more, it tends to be no more than Job No. 16432b from this or that decorator's studio. I know one New Yorker, a man of considerable means, who moves every three years. Every time he moves his wife sells the entire contents of the apartment she is leaving, and employs a decorator to outfit the new one. To me, at all events, such a mode of living would be unendurable. The charm of getting home, as I see it, is the charm of getting back to what is inextricably my own—to things familiar and long loved, to things that belong to me alone and none other. I have lived in one house in Baltimore for nearly forty-five years. It has changed in that time, as I have—but somehow it still remains the same. No conceivable decorator's masterpiece could give me the same ease. It is as much a part of me as my two hands. If I had to leave it I'd be as certainly crippled as if I lost a leg.

I believe that this feeling for the hearth, for the immemorial lares and penates, is infinitely stronger in Baltimore than in New York—that it has better survived there, indeed, than in any other large city of America—and that its persistence accounts for the superior charm of the town. There are, of course, thousands of Baltimoreans in flats—but I know of none to whom a flat seems more than a make-shift, a substitute, a necessary and temporary evil. They are all planning to get out, to find house-room in one of the new suburbs, to resume living in a home. What they see about them is too painfully not theirs. The New Yorker has simply lost that discontent. He is a vagabond. His notions of the agreeable become those of a vaudeville actor. He takes on the shallowness and unpleasantness of any other homeless man. He is highly sophisticated, and inordinately trashy. The fact no doubt explains the lack of charm that one finds in his town; the fact that the normal man of Baltimore is almost his exact antithesis explains the charm that is there. Human relations, in such a place, tend to assume a solid permanence. A man's circle of friends becomes a sort of extension of his family circle. His contacts are with men and women who are rooted as he is. They are not moving all the time, and so they are not changing their friends all the time. Thus abiding relationships tend to be built up, and when fortune brings unexpected changes, they survive those changes. The men I know and esteem in Baltimore are, on the whole, men I have known and esteemed a long while; even those who have come into my ken relatively lately seem likely to last. But of the men I knew best when I first began going to New York, twenty-five years ago, not one is a friend to-day. Of those I knew best ten years ago, not six are friends. The rest have got lost in the riot, and the friends of to-day, I sometimes fear, will get lost in the same way.

In human relationships that are so casual there is seldom any satisfaction. It is our fellows who make life endurable to us, and give it a purpose and a meaning; if our contacts with them are light and frivolous there is something lacking, and it is something of the very first importance. What I contend is that in Baltimore, under a slow-moving and cautious social organization, touched by the Southern sun, such contacts are more enduring than elsewhere, and that life in consequence is more agreeable. Of the external embellishments of life there is a plenty there—as great a supply, indeed, to any rational taste, as in New York itself. But there is also something much better: a tradition of sound and comfortable living. A Baltimorean is not merely John Doe, an isolated individual of *Homo sapiens,* exactly like every other John Doe. He is John Doe *of* a certain place—of Baltimore, of a definite *house* in Baltimore. It is not by accident that all the peoples of Europe, very early in their history, distinguished their best men by adding *of* this or that place to their names.

THE CHAMPION

Of the forty-eight sovereign States of this imperial Federation, which is the worst? In what one of them is a civilized man most uncomfortable? Over half the votes, if the question were put to a vote, would probably be divided between California and Tennessee. Each, in its way, is almost unspeakable. Tennessee, of course, has never been civilized, save in a small area; even in the earliest days of the Republic it was regarded as barbaric by its neighbors. But California, at one time, promised to develop a charming and enlightened civilization. There was a touch of tropical balm in its air, and a touch of Latin and oriental color in its ideas. Like Louisiana, it seemed likely to resist Americanization for many years; perhaps forever. But now California, the old California, is simply extinct. What remains is an Alsatia of retired Ford agents and crazy fat women—a paradise of 100% Americanism and the New Thought. Its laws are the most extravagant and idiotic ever heard of in Christendom. Its public officers, and particularly its judges, are famous all over the world for their imbecilities. When one hears of it at all, one hears that some citizen has been jailed for reading the Constitution of the United States, or that some new swami in a yellow bedtick has got all the realtors' wives of Los Angeles by the ears. When one hears of it further, it is only to learn that some obscure movie lady in Hollywood has murdered another lover. The State is run by its Chambers of Commerce, which is to say, by the worst variety of resident shysters. No civilized man ever seems to take any part in its public life. Not an idea comes out of it—that is, not an idea beyond the grasp of a Kiwanis Club secretary, a Christian Science sorcerer, or a grand goblin of the American Legion. Twice, of late, it has offered the country candidates for the presidency. One was the Hon. Hiram Johnson and the other was the Hon. William Gibbs McAdoo! Only Vermont can beat that record.

The minority of civilized Californians—who lately, by the way, sent out a call from Los Angeles for succor, as if they were beset by wolves!—commonly lay the blame for this degeneration of a once-proud commonwealth upon the horde of morons that has flowed in from Iowa, Nebraska and the other cow States, seeking relief from the bitter climate of the steppes. The California realtors have been luring in these hinds for a generation past, and they now swarm in all the southern towns, especially Los Angeles. They come in with their savings, are swindled and sent home, and so make room for more. While they remain and have any part of their money left, they patronize the swamis, buy oil stock, gape at the movie folk, and pack the Methodist churches. Unques-

tionably, the influence of such vacuums has tended to
degrade the general tone of California life; what was
once a Spanish *fiesta* is now merely an upper Mississippi
valley street-carnival. But it is not to be forgotten that
the Native Sons have gone down the chute with the new-
comers—that there is no more sign of intellectual vigor in
the old stock than there is in the new stock. A few in-
transigeants hold out against the tide of 100% Americanism, but only a few. The rest bawl against the Reds
as loudly as any Iowa steer-stuffer.

The truth is that it is unjust to blame Iowa for the
decay of California, for Iowa itself is now moving up, not
down. And so is Nebraska. A few years ago both States
were as sterile, intellectually, as Spain, but both are showing signs of progress to-day, and in another generation
or two, as the Prohibition lunacy passes and the pall of
Methodism begins to lift, they will probably burst into
very vigorous activity. Some excellent stock is in them;
it is very little contaminated by what is called Anglo-
Saxon blood. Iowa, even to-day, is decidedly more civilized than California. It is producing more ideas, and,
more important still, it is carrying on a much less violent
war *against* ideas. I doubt that any man who read the
Constitution in Davenport or Des Moines would be
jailed for it, as Upton Sinclair (or one of his friends)
was in Pasadena. The American Legion would undoubtedly protest, but the police would probably do nothing,
for the learned judges of the State would not entertain
the charge.

Thus California remains something of a mystery. The
whole United States, of course, has been going down hill
since the beginning of the century, but why should one
State go so much faster than the others? Is the climate
to blame? Hardly. The climate of San Francisco is
thoroughly un-Californian, and yet San Francisco is almost as dead as Los Angeles. It was there, indeed, that
that California masterpiece, the Mooney case, was staged;
it was there that the cops made three efforts to convict
poor Fatty Arbuckle of murder in the first-degree; it was

there that the late Dr. Abrams launched a quackery that went Mother Eddy one better. San Francisco, once the home of Mark Twain and Bret Harte, is now ravaged by Prohibition enforcement officers. But if the climate is not to blame, then what is? Why should a great State, lovely physically and of romantic history, so violently renounce all sense and decency? What has got into it? God alone knows!

DEFINITION

Democracy is that system of government under which the people, having 35,717,342 native-born adult whites to choose from, including thousands who are handsome and many who are wise, pick out a Coolidge to be head of the State. It is as if a hungry man, set before a banquet prepared by master cooks and covering a table an acre in area, should turn his back upon the feast and stay his stomach by catching and eating flies.

JOURNALISM IN AMERICA

1

One of the agreeable spiritual phenomena of the great age in which we live is the soul-searching now going on among American journalists. Fifteen years ago, or even ten years ago, there was scarcely a sign of it. The working newspaper men of the Republic, of whom I have had the honor to be one since the last century, were then almost as complacent as so many Federal judges, movie magnates, or major-generals in the army. When they discussed their puissant craft at all, it was only to smack their chests proudly, boasting of their vast power in public matters, of their adamantine resistance to all the less tempting varieties of bribes, and of the fact that a politician of enlightened self-interest, giving them important but inaccurate news confidently, could rely upon them to mangle it beyond recognition before publishing it. I describe a sort of Golden Age, and confess frankly that I can't do so without a certain yielding to emotion. Salaries had been going up since the dawn of the new century, and the journalist, however humble, was beginning to feel his oats. For the first time in history he was paid as well as the human cranes and steam-shovels slinging rolls of paper in the cellar. He began to own two hats, two suits of clothes, two pairs of shoes, two walking-sticks, even two belts. He ceased to feed horribly in one-arm lunch-rooms and began to dine in places with fumigated waitresses, some of a considerable pulchritude and amiability, and red-shaped table lamps. He was, as such things are reckoned, happy. But at the heart of his happiness, alas, there yet gnawed a canker-worm. One enemy remained in his world, unscotched and apparently unscotchable, to wit, the business manager. The business manager, at will, could send up a blue slip and order him fired. In the face of that menace from below-stairs his literary superiors were helpless, up to and including the editor-in-chief. All of them were under the hoof of the business manager, and all the business manager ever thought of was advertising. Let an advertiser complain that his honor had been impugned or his *clavi* abraded, and off went a head.

It was the great war for human freedom, I suspect and allege, that brought the journalist deliverance from that last and most abominable hazard: he was, perhaps, one of the few real beneficiaries of all the carnage. As the struggle grew more savage on Flanders fields and business grew better and better at home, reporters of any capacity whatever got to be far too scarce to fire loosely.

Moreover, the business manager, with copy pouring over his desk almost unsolicited, began to lose his old dread of advertisers, and then even some of his natural respect for them. It was a sellers' market, in journalism as in the pants business. Customers were no longer kissed; the lesser among them actually began to stand in line. The new spirit, so strange and so exhilarating, spread like a benign pestilence, and presently it began to invade even the editorial rooms. In almost every American city, large or small, some flabbergasted advertiser, his money in his hand, sweat pouring from him as if he had seen a ghost, was kicked out with spectacular ceremonies. All the principal papers, suddenly grown rich, began also to grow independent, virtuous, touchy, sniffish. No — — — — could dictate to them, God damn! So the old free reading notices of the Bon Marché and the Palais Royal disappeared, salaries continued to climb, and the liberated journalist, taking huge breaths of thrilling air, began to think of himself as a professional man.

Upon that cogitation he is still engaged, and all the weeklies that print the news of the craft are full of its fruits. He elects representatives and they meet in lugubrious conclave to draw up codes of ethics. He begins to read books dealing with professional questions of other sorts—even books not dealing with professional questions. He changes his old cynical view of schools of journalism, and is lured, now and then, into lecturing in them himself. He no longer thinks of his calling as a business, like the haberdasher's or tallow chandler's, or as a game, like the stockbroker's or faro-dealer's, but as a profession, like the jurisconsult's or gynecologist's. His purpose is to set it on its legs as such—to inject plausible theories into its practice, and rid it of its old casualness and opportunism. He no longer sees it as a craft to be mastered in four days, and abandoned at the first sign of a better job. He begins to talk darkly of the long apprenticeship necessary to master its technic, of the wide information and sagacity needed to adorn it, of the high rewards that it offers—or may offer later on—to the man of true talent and devotion. Once he thought of himself, whenever he thought at all, as what Beethoven called a free artist—a gay adventurer careening down the charming highways of the world, the gutter ahead of him but ecstasy in his heart. Now he thinks of himself as a fellow of weight and responsibility, a beginning publicist and public man, sworn to the service of the born and unborn, heavy with duties to the Republic and to his profession.

In all this, I fear, there is some illusion, as there always is in human thinking. The journalist can no more see himself realistically than a bishop can see himself realistically. He gilds and engauds the picture, unconsciously and irresistibly. For one thing, and a most important one, he is probably somewhat in error about his professional status. He remains, for all his dreams, a hired man —the owner downstairs, or even the business manager, though he doesn't do it very often now, is still free to demand his head—and a hired man is not a professional man. The essence of a professional man is that he is answerable for his professional conduct only to his professional peers. A physician cannot be fired by any one, save when he has voluntarily converted himself into a jobholder; he is secure in his livelihood so long as he keeps his health, and can render service, or what they regard as service, to his patients. A lawyer is in the same boat. So is a dentist. So, even, is a horse-doctor. But a journalist still lingers in the twilight zone, along with the trained nurse, the embalmer, the rev. clergy and the great majority of engineers. He cannot sell his services directly to the consumer, but only to entrepreneurs, and so those entrepreneurs have the power of veto over all his soaring fancies. His codes of ethics are all right so long as they do not menace newspaper profits; the moment they do so the business manager, now quiescent, will begin to growl again. Nor has he the same freedom that the lawyers and the physicians have when it comes to fixing his own compensation; what he faces is not a client but a boss. Above all, he is unable, as yet, to control admission to his craft. It is constantly recruited, on its lowest levels, from men who have little professional training or none at all, and some of these men master its chief mysteries very quickly. Thus even the most competent journalist faces at all times a severe competition, easily expanded at need, and cannot afford to be too saucy. When a managing editor is fired there is always another one waiting to take his place, but there is seldom another place waiting for the managing editor.

All these things plainly diminish the autonomy of the journalist, and hamper his effort to lift his trade to professional rank and dignity. When he talks of codes of ethics, indeed, he only too often falls into mere tall talk, for he cannot enforce the rules he so solemnly draws up —that is, in the face of dissent from above. Nevertheless, his discussion of the subject is still not wholly absurd, for there remain plenty of rules that he *can* enforce, and I incline to think that there are more of them than of the other kind. Most of the evils that continue to beset American journalism to-day, in truth, are not due to the rascality of owners nor even to the Kiwanian bombast of business managers, but simply and solely to the stupidity, cowardice and Philistinism of working newspaper men. The majority of them, in almost every American city, are still ignoramuses, and proud of it. All the knowledge that they pack into their brains is, in every reasonable cultural sense, useless; it is the sort of knowledge that belongs, not to a professional man, but to a police captain, a railway mail-clerk, or a board-boy in a brokerage house. It is a mass of trivialities and puerilities; to recite it would be to make even a barber beg for mercy. What is missing from it, in brief, is everything worth knowing—everything that enters into the common knowledge of educated men. There are managing editors in the United States, and scores of them, who have never heard of Kant or Johannes Müller and never read the Constitution of the United States; there are city editors who do not know what a symphony is, or a streptococcus, or the Statute of Frauds; there are reporters by the thousand who could not pass the entrance examination for Harvard or Tuskegee, or even Yale. It is this vast and militant ignorance, this wide-spread and fathomless prejudice against intelligence, that makes American journalism so pathetically feeble and vulgar, and so generally disreputable. A man with so little intellectual enterprise that, dealing with news daily, he can go through life without taking in any news that is worth knowing—such a man, you may be sure, is lacking in professional dignity quite as much as he is lacking in curiosity. The delicate thing called honor can never be a function of stupidity. If it belongs to those men who are genuinely professional men, it belongs to them because they have lifted themselves to the plane of a true aristocracy, in learning as well as in liberty—because they have deliberately and successfully separated themselves from the great masses of men, to whom learning is an insult and liberty an agony. The journalists, in seeking to acquire that status, put the cart before the horse.

2

The facts that I here set forth are well known to every American newspaper man who rises above the ice-wagon driver level, and in those sad conferences which mark every gathering of the craft they do not go undiscussed. Even the American Society of Newspaper Editors, *i.e.,* of those journalists who have got into golf clubs and become minor Babbitts, has dealt with them at some of its annual pow-wows, albeit very gingerly and with many uneasy glances behind the door. But in general journalism suffers from a lack of alert and competent professional criticism; its slaves, afflicted by a natural inferiority complex, discountenance free speaking as a sort of treason; I have myself been damned as a public enemy for calling attention, ever and anon, to the intolerable incompetence and quackery of all save a small minority of the Washington correspondents. This struthion fear of the light is surely not to be noted in any of the actual professions. The medical men, in their trade journals, criticise one another frankly and sharply, and so do the lawyers in theirs: the latter, indeed, are not above taking occasional hacks at the very judges, their lawful fathers and patterns of grace. As for the clergy, every one knows that they devote a large part of their professional energy to refuting and damning their brethren, and that not a few of them do it on public stumps, with the laity invited. So, also, in the fine arts. It is impossible for an architect to affront humanity with a blotch without hearing from other architects, and it is impossible for a poet to print anything at all without tasting the clubs of other poets. Even dramatists, movie actors, chiropractors and politicians criticise one another, and so keep themselves on tiptoe. But not journalists. If a Heywood Broun is exasperated into telling the truth about the manhandling of a Snyder trial, or a Walter Lippmann exposes the imbecility of the Russian "news" in a New York *Times,* or an Oswald Garrison Villard turns his searchlight on a Boston *Herald* or a Washington *Star,* it is a rarity and an indecorum. The organs of the craft—and there are journals for journalists, just as there are doctors for doctors—are all filled with bilge borrowed from Rotary and Kiwanis. Reading them, one gathers the impression that every newspaper proprietor in the United States is a distinguished public figure, and every circulation manager a wizard. The editorial boys, it appears, never fall down on their jobs; they are not only geniuses, but also heroes. Some time ago, having read all such journals assiduously for years, I stopped my subscriptions to them. I found that I preferred the clipsheet of the Methodist Board of Temperance, Prohibition and Public Morals.

But if there is thus little or no frank and open discussion of the evils that beset journalism in the Republic, there is a great deal of private discontent and soul-searching, and it shows itself in all the fantastic codes of ethics that issue from embattled professors of journalism in the great rolling-mills of learning, and from editorial associations in the cow States. In such codes, I am sorry to have to repeat, I take no stock. Most of them are the handiwork of journalists of no professional importance what-

ever, and, what is worse, of no apparent sense. They run
the scale from metaphysical principia worthy of Rotary
to sets of rules fit only for the government of a
Y. M. C. A. lamasery or a State's prison. They concern
themselves furiously with abuses which are not peculiar
to journalism but run through the whole of American
life, and they are delicately silent about abuses that are
wholly journalistic, and could be remedied quickly and
without the slightest difficulty. Their purpose, I believe,
is largely rhetorical. They give a certain ease and comfort to the laboring patient without letting any of his
blood. Nevertheless, I am glad to see them multiply, for
though most of them may be hollow to-day, there is
always a chance that some solid substance may get into
them to-morrow. If they accomplish nothing else at the
moment, they at least accustom the journalist to the notion that his craft needs an overhauling. His old romantic optimism oozes out of him. He is no longer quite
happy. Out of his rising discomforts, I believe, there will
issue eventually a more realistic attitude toward the
problems that confront him, and on some bright day in
the future he may address himself rationally to the hard
business of solving them. Most of them, I believe, are
clearly soluble. More, most of them can be solved by
working newspaper men, without any help from experts
in ethics. What they call for is not any transcendental gift
for righteousness, but simply ordinary professional competence and common sense.

For example, the problem of false news. How does so
much of it get into the American newspapers, even the
good ones? Is it because journalists, as a class, are
habitual liars, and prefer what is not true to what is
true? I don't think it is. Rather, it is because journalists
are, in the main, extremely stupid, sentimental and
credulous fellows—because nothing is easier than to fool
them—because the majority of them lack the sharp intelligence that the proper discharge of their duties demands. The New York *Times* did not print all its
famous blather and balderdash about Russia because the

Hon. Mr. Ochs desired to deceive his customers, or because his slaves were in the pay of Russian reactionaries, but simply and solely because his slaves, facing the elemental professional problem of distinguishing between true news and false, turned out to be incompetent. All around the borders of Russia sat propagandists hired to fool them. In many cases, I have no doubt, they detected that purpose, and foiled it; we only know what they printed, not what they threw into their wastebaskets. But in many other cases they succumbed easily, and even ridiculously, and the result was the vast mass of puerile rubbish that Mr. Lippmann later made a show of. In other words, the editors of the American newspaper most brilliantly distinguished above its fellows for its news-gathering enterprise turned out to be unequal to a job of news-gathering presenting special but surely not insuperable difficulties. It was not an ethical failure, but a purely technical failure. And so was the same eminent newspaper's idiotic misreporting of the news from China in the early part of 1927, and the grotesque paralysis of the whole American press in the face of the Miami hurricane in 1926.

Obviously, the way to diminish such failures in future is not to adopt sonorous platitudes borrowed from the realtors, the morticians, the sanitary plumbers and Kiwanis, but to undertake an overhauling of the faulty technic, and of the incompetent personnel responsible for it. This overhauling, of course, will take some intelligence, but I don't think it will make demands that are impossible. The bootlegging, legal or delicatessen professions, confronted by like demands, would quickly furnish the talent necessary to meet them; I see no reason why the profession of journalism should not measure up as well. What lies in the way of it is simply the profound, maudlin sentimentality of the average American journalist—his ingenuous and almost automatic belief in everything that comes to him in writing. One would think that his daily experience with the written word would make him suspicious of it; he himself, in fact, believes fondly that he is proof against it. But the truth is that he swallows it far more often than he rejects it, and that his most eager swallowing is done in the face of the plainest evidence of its falsity. Let it come in by telegraph, and his mouth flies open. Let it come in by telegraph *from a press association* and down it goes at once. I do not say, of course, that *all* press association news is thus swallowed by news editors. When the means are readily at hand, he often attempts to check it, and sometimes even rejects it. But when such checking presents difficulties—in other words, when deceit is especially easy, and hence should be guarded against most vigilantly —he succumbs nine times out of ten, and without a struggle. It was precisely by this process that the editors of the *Times,* otherwise men of extraordinary professional alertness, were victimized by the Russian "news" that made that paper ridiculous. In the face of great improbabilities, they interpreted their inability to dispose of them as a license to accept them as truth. Journalism will be a sounder and more dignified profession when a directly contrary interpretation of the journalist's duty prevails. There will then be less news in the papers, but it will at least have the merit of being true.

Nor is the typical American journalist's credulity confined to such canards and roorbacks from far places. He is often victimized just as easily at home, despite his lofty belief that he is superior to the wiles of press agents. The plain fact is that most of the stuff he prints now emanates from press agents, and that his machinery for scrutinizing it is lamentably defective. True enough, the bold, gay liars employed by theatrical managers and opera singers no longer fool him as they used to; he has grown so suspicious of them that he often turns them out when they have real news. But what of the press agents of such organizations as the Red Cross, the Prohibition Unit, the Near-East Relief, the Chamber of Commerce of the United States, the Department of Justice, the Y. M. C. A., and the various bands of professional patriots? I do not say that the press agents of such bodies are always or necessarily liars; all I say is that, nine times out of ten, their statements are accepted as true by the newspapers without any attempt to determine accurately whether they are true or not. They may be simple statements of plain fact; they may, on the contrary, conceal highly dubious purposes, of organizations and individuals. In both cases they are set forth in the same way—solemnly and without comment. Who, ordinarily, would believe a Prohibition agent? Perhaps a Federal judge in his robes of office and full of seized evidence; I can think of no one else. Yet the American newspapers are filled every day with the dreadful boasts and threats of such frauds: it is set before the people, not as lies, but as news. What is the purpose of such rubbish? Its purpose, obviously, is to make it appear that the authors are actually enforcing Prohibition—in other words, to make them secure in their jobs. Every newspaper man in America knows that Prohibition is not being enforced—and yet it is rarely that an American newspaper comes out in these days without a gaudy story on its first page, rehearsing all the old lies under new and blacker headlines.

I do not argue here, of course, that only demonstrable facts are news. There are times and occasions when rumor is almost as important as the truth—when a newspaper's duty to its readers requires it to tell them not only what has happened, but also what is reported, what is threatened, what is merely said. What I contend is simply that such quasi-news, such half-baked and still dubious news, should be printed for exactly what it is—that it ought to be clearly differentiated from news that, by an overwhelming probability, is true. That differentiation is made easily and as a matter of course by most European newspapers of any dignity. When they print a dispatch from the Russian border they indicate its source, and not infrequently follow it with a cynical comment. If they had Prohibition agents on their hands, they would print the fulminations of those gentlemen in the same way—with plain warnings to stop, look and listen. In brief, they make every reasonable effort to make up for their own technical limitations as news-gatherers—they do the best they can, and say so frankly when it is not very good. I believe that American newspapers might imitate them profitably. If it were done, then the public's justifiable distrust of all newspapers, now rising, would tend to ebb. They would have to throw off their present affectation of omniscience, but they would gain a new repute for honesty and candor; they would begin to seem more reliable when they failed than they now seem when they succeed. The scheme I propose would cost nothing; on the contrary, it would probably save expense. It would throw no unbearable burden upon the journalistic mind; it would simply make it more cautious and alert. Best of all, it would increase the dignity of journalism without resort to flapdoodlish and unenforceable codes of ethics, by Mush out of Tosh.

3

In their private communions, though seldom in public, the more conscientious and unhappy variety of journalists commonly blame the woes of the craft upon the entrance into newspaper ownership of such opulent vacuums as Cyrus H. K. Curtis and the late Frank A. Munsey. As a result of the application of chain-store methods to journalism by these amiable Vandals there are fewer papers than there used to be, and the individual journalist is less important. All the multitudinous Hearst papers are substantially identical, and so are all the Scripps-Howard papers, and all the Curtis papers, and so were the Munsey papers in the great days of that pathetic man. There is little room, on the papers of such chains, for the young man who aspires to shine. Two-thirds of their contents are produced in great factories, and what remains is chiefly a highly standardized bilge. In the early days of Hearst, when he had only a few widely-scattered papers, his staffs were manned by men of great professional enterprise and cunning, and some of them became celebrated in the craft, and even generally. But now a Hearst paper, however inflammatory, is no more than a single unit in a long row of filling-stations, and so it tends to attract only the duller and less picturesque sort of men. There is scarcely a Hearst managing editor to-day who amounts to anything professionally, or is heard of outside his own dung-hill. The platitudes of Brisbane and Dr. Frank Crane serve as pabulum for all of them. What they think is what the machines at the central factory think; what they do is determined by men they have never seen. So with the Scripps-Howard slaves, and the slaves of Cox, and those of Curtis, and all the rest. Their predecessors of a generation ago were gaudy adventurers, experimenters, artists; they themselves are golf-players, which is to say, blanks. They are well paid, but effectively knee-haltered. The rewards of their trade used to come in freedom, opportunity, the incomparable delights of self-expression; now they come in money.

But the sweet goes with the bitter. The newspapers of to-day, though they may be as rigidly standardized as Uneeda biscuits, are at least solvent: they are no longer the paltry freebooters that they used to be. A Munsey, perhaps, is a jackass, but he is at least honest; no one seriously alleges that his papers are for sale; even the sinister Wall Street powers that Liberals see in the background must get what they want out of him by being polite to him, not by simply sending him orders. The old-timers, contemplating the ghastly spectacle of a New York *Sun* submerged in the Munsey swamp and an *Evening Post* descending from a Villard to a Curtis, forget conveniently how bad most of the papers they once worked for really were. In the town where I began there were five papers, and four of them were cheap, trashy, stupid and corrupt. They all played politics for what there was in it, and leaped obscenely every time an advertiser blew his nose. Every other American city of that era was full of such papers—dreadful little rags, venal, vulnerable and vile. Not a few of them made great pretensions, and were accepted by a naïve public as organs of the enlightenment. To-day, I believe, such journalistic street-walkers are very rare. The consolidations that every old-timer deplores have accomplished at least one good thing: they have got the newspapers, in the main, out of the hands of needy men. When orders come from a Curtis or a Munsey to-day the man who gets them, though he may regard them as ill-advised and even as idiotic, is seldom in any doubt as to their good faith. He may execute them without feeling that he has been made an unwilling party to an ignominious barter. He is not condemned daily to acts whose true purpose he would not dare to put into words, even to himself. His predecessor, I believe, often suffered that dismaying necessity: he seldom had any illusions about the *bona fides* of his boss. It took the whole force of his characteristic sentimentality to make him believe in his paper, and not infrequently even that sentimentality was impotent without the aid of ethyl alcohol.

Thus there is something to be said for the new newspaper Babbitts, as reluctant as every self-respecting journalist must be to say it. And in what is commonly said against them there is not infrequently a certain palpable exaggeration and injustice. Are they responsible for the imbecile editorial policies of their papers, for the grotesque lathering of such mountebanks as Coolidge and Mellon, for the general smugness and lack of intellectual enterprise that pervades American journalism? Perhaps they are. But do they issue orders that their papers shall be printed in blowsy, clumsy English? That they shall stand against every decent thing, and in favor of everything that is meretricious and ignoble? That they shall wallow in trivialities, and manhandle important news? That their view of learning shall be that of a bartender? Has any newspaper proprietor ever issued orders that the funeral orgies of a Harding should be described in the language of a Tennessee revival? Or that helpless men, with the mob against them, should be pursued without fairness, decency or sense? I doubt it. I doubt, even, that the Babbitts turned Greeleys are responsible, in the last analysis, for the political rubbish that fills their papers—the preposterous anointing of Coolidge, the

craven yielding to such sinister forces as the Ku Klux
Klan and the Anti-Saloon League, the incessant, humor-
less, degrading hymning of all sorts of rogues and
charlatans. The average newspaper proprietor, I suspect,
gets nine-tenths of his political ideas from his own men.
In other words, he is such an ass that he believes political
reporters, and especially his own political reporters. They
have, he fancies, wide and confidential sources of information: their wisdom is a function of their prestige as
his agents. What they tell him is, in the long run, what
he believes, with certain inconsiderable corrections by
professionals trying to work him. If only because they
have confidential access to him day in and day out, they
are able to introduce their own notions into his head. He
may have their jobs in his hands, but they have his ears
and eyes, so to speak, in theirs.

Even the political garbage that emanates from Washington, and especially from the typewriters of the more
eminent and puissant correspondents there resident, is
seldom inspired, I am convinced, by orders from the
Curtis or Munsey at home: its sources are rather to be
sought in the professional deficiencies of the correspondents themselves—a class of men of almost incredible
credulity. In other words, they are to be sought, not in
the corruption and enslavement of the press, but in the
incompetence of the press. The average Washington
correspondent, I believe, is honest enough, as honesty
goes in the United States, though his willingness to do
press work for the National Committees in campaign
time and for other highly dubious agencies at other times
is not to be forgotten. What ails him mainly is that he is
a man without sufficient force of character to resist the
blandishments that surround him from the moment he
sets foot in Washington. A few men, true enough, resist,
and their papers, getting the benefit of it, become notable
for their independence and intelligence, but the great
majority succumb almost at once. A few months of
associating with the gaudy magnificoes of the town, and
they pick up its meretricious values, and are unable to

distinguish men of sense and dignity from mountebanks. A few clumsy overtures from the White House, and they are rattled and undone. They come in as newspaper men, trained to get the news and eager to get it; they end as tin-horn statesmen, full of dark secrets and unable to write the truth if they tried. Here I spread no scandal and violate no confidence. The facts are familiar to every newspaper man in the United States. A few of the more intelligent managing editors, cynical of ever counteracting the effects of the Washington miasma, seek to evade them by frequently changing their men. But the average managing editor is too stupid to deal with such difficulties. He prints balderdash because he doesn't know how to get anything better—perhaps, in many cases, because he doesn't know that anything better exists. Drenched with propaganda at home, he is quite content to take more propaganda from Washington. It is not that he is dishonest, but that he is stupid—and, being stupid, a coward. The resourcefulness, enterprise and bellicosity that his job demands are simply not in him. He doesn't wear himself out trying to get the news, as romance has it; he slides supinely into the estate and dignity of a golf-player. American journalism suffers from too many golf-players. They swarm in the Washington Press Gallery. They, and not their bosses, are responsible for most of the imbecilities that now afflict their trade.

4

The journalists of the United States will never get rid of those afflictions by putting the blame on Dives, and never by making speeches at one another in annual conventions, and never by drawing up codes of ethics that most of their brethren will infallibly laugh at, as a Congressman laughs at a gentleman. The job before them—that is, before the civilized minority of them—is to purge their trade before they seek to dignify it—to clean house before they paint the roof and raise a flag. Can the thing be done? It not only can be done; it *has* been done. There are at least a dozen newspapers in the United States that already show a determined effort to get out of the old slough. Any managing editor in the land, if he has the will, can carry his own paper with them. He is under no compulsion, save rarely, to employ this or that hand; it is not often that owners, or even business managers, take any interest in that business, save to watch the payroll. Is his paper trifling, ill-informed, petty and unfair? Is its news full of transparent absurdities? Are its editorials ignorant and without sense? Is it written in English full of *clichés* and vulgarities—English that would disgrace a manager of prize-fighters or a county superintendent of schools? Then the fault belongs plainly, not to some remote man, but to the proximate man—to the man who lets such drivel go by. He could get better if he wanted it, you may be sure. There is in all history no record of a newspaper owner who complained because his paper was well-edited. And I know of no business manager who objected when the complaints pouring in upon him, of misrepresentations, invasions of privacy, gross inaccuracies and other such nuisances, began to lighten.

Not a few managing editors, as I say, are moving in the right direction. There has been an appreciable improvement, during the past dozen years, in the general tone of American newspapers. They are still full of preposterous blather, but they are measurably more accurate, I believe, than they used to be, and some of them are better written. A number of them are less absurdly partisan, particularly in the smaller cities. Save in the South and in the remoter fastnesses of New England the old-time party organ has gone out of fashion. In the big cities the faithful hacks of the New York *Tribune* type have begun to vanish. With them has gone the old-time drunken reporter, and in his place is appearing a young fellow of better education, and generally finer metal. The uplifters of the craft try to make him increase, and to that end encourage schools of journalism. But these seminaries, so far, show two palpable defects. On the one hand, they are seldom manned by men of any genuine professional standing, or of any firm notion of what journalism is about. On the other hand, they are nearly all too easy in their requirements for admission. Probably half of them, indeed, are simply refuges for students too stupid to tackle the other professions. They offer snap courses, and they promise quick jobs. The result is that the graduates coming out of them are mainly second-raters—that young men and women issuing from the general arts courses make better journalistic material.

What ails these schools of journalism is that they are not yet professional schools, but simply trade schools. Their like is to be found, not in the schools of medicine and law, but in the institutions that teach barbering, bookkeeping and scenario-writing. Obviously, the remedy for their general failure is to borrow a leaf from the book of the medical men, and weed out the incompetents, not after they have finished, but before they have begun. Twenty-five years ago any yokel who had got through the three R's was free to study medicine in the United States. In three years, and sometimes in two years, he was turned out to practice upon his fellow hinds, and once he had his license it was a practical impossibility to challenge him. But now there is scarcely a medical school in the United States that does not demand a bachelor's degree or its equivalent as a prerequisite to entrance, and the term of study in all of them is four years, and it must be followed by at least one year of hospital service. This reform was not achieved by passing laws against the old hedge schools: it was achieved simply by setting up the competition of good schools. The latter gradually elbowed the former out. Their graduates had immense advantages. They had professional prestige from the moment of their entrance into practice. The public quickly detected the difference between them and their competitors from the surviving hedge schools. Soon the latter began to disintegrate, and now all save a few of them have disappeared. The medical men improved their profession by making it more difficult to become a medical man. To-day the thing is a practical impossibility to any young man who is not of genuine intelligence.

But at least two-thirds of the so-called schools of journalism still admit any aspirant who can make shift to read and write. The pedagogues who run them cannot be expected to devote much thought or money to improving them; they are in the position of the quacks who used to run the hedge medical schools. The impulse toward improvement, if it ever comes at all, must come from the profession they presume to serve. Here is a chance for the editorial committees and societies of journalists that now spring up on all sides. Let them abandon their vain effort to frame codes of ethics and devote themselves to the nursery. If they can get together a committee on schools of journalism as wise and as bold as the Council on Medical Education of the American Medical Association they will accomplish more in a few years than they can hope to accomplish with academic codes of ethics in half a century.

All the rest will follow. The old fond theory, still surviving in many a newspaper office, that it is somehow discreditable for a reporter to show any sign of education and culture, that he is most competent and laudable when his intellectual baggage most closely approaches that of a bootlegger—this theory will fall before the competition of novices who have been adequately trained, and have more in their heads than their mere training. Journalism, compared to the other trades of literate men, is surely not unattractive, even to-day. It is more amusing than the army or the cloth, and it offers a better living at the start than either medicine or the law. There is a career in it for the young man of original mind and forceful personality—a career leading to power and even to a sort of wealth. In point of fact, it has always attracted such young men, else it would be in an even lower state than it is now. It would attract a great many more of them if its public opinion were more favorable to them—if they were less harassed by the commands of professional superiors of no dignity, and the dislike of fellows of no sense. Every time two of them are drawn in they draw another. The problem is to keep them. That is the central problem of journalism in the United States to-day.

I seem to be in a mood for constructive criticism. Let me add one more pearl of wisdom before I withdraw. I put it in the form of a question. Suppose the shyster lawyers of every town organized a third-rate club, called it the Bar Association, took in any Prohibition agent or precinct politician who could raise the dues, and then announced publicly, from the Courthouse steps, that it represented the whole bar, and that membership in it was an excellent form of insurance—that any member who paid his dues would get very friendly consideration, if he ever got into trouble, from the town's judges and district attorney. And suppose the decent lawyers of the town permitted this preposterous pretension to go unchallenged—and some of them even gave countenance to it by joining the club. How long would the legal profession in that town retain its professional honor and dignity? How many laymen, after two or three years, would have any respect left for *any* lawyer, even a judge?

Yet the journalists of the United States permit that precise thing to go on under their noses. In most every city of the country there is a so-called Press Club, and at least three-fourths of them are exactly like the hypothetical Bar Association that I have described. They are run by newspaper men of the worst type—many of them so incompetent and disreputable that they cannot even get jobs on newspapers. They take the money of all the town grafters and rascals on the pretense that newspaper favors go with its receipt. They are the resorts of idlers and blackmailers. They are nuisances and disgraces. Yet in how many towns have they been put down? In how many towns do the decent newspaper men take any overt action against them? My proposal is very simple. I propose that they be shut up, East, West, North and South, before anything more is said about codes of newspaper ethics.

ON CONTROVERSY

Any man engaged habitually in controversy, as I have been for twenty years past, must enter upon his declining days with a melancholy sense of its hollowness and futility. Especially in this great Republic, where all ideas are suspect, it tends almost inevitably to degenerate into a mere exchange of nonsense. Have you ever examined carefully the speeches made by the candidates in a Presidential campaign? If so, you know that they are of bilge and blather all compact. Now and then, true enough, one of the august aspirants to the Washingtonian breeches is goaded or misled into saying something pungent and even apposite, but not often, not deliberately. His daily stint is simply balderdash.

It is rare, indeed, to encounter a controversialist who states his own case clearly, or who shows any sign of understanding his opponent's. Turn, for example, to the current combat between the Fundamentalists and the Modernists—an academic and puerile duel in our great Sodoms and Ninevehs, but raging like an oil fire in the Bible and Hookworm Belt, where men are he and Hell yawns. Both sides wallow in pishposh. The Fundamentalists, claiming a monopoly of faith, allege that they believe the whole Bible *verbatim et literatim,* which is not true, for at least 99% of them reject Exodus xxii, 18, to say nothing of I Timothy v, 23. And the Modernists argue that there is no conflict between science and Holy Writ, which is even less true. This controversy, in fact, is almost classical in character. Neither side is able to stick to the question at issue. Each tries to dispose of the other by delivering mighty wallops below the belt—the Fundamentalists by passing laws converting the Modernists into criminals (that is, as criminality is now defined by American jurisprudence), and the Modernists by depicting the Fundamentalists as a horde of gibbering baboons, sworn to uproot civilization and not above suspicion of cannibalism.

I have had a hand in this great battle of scattered wits myself, striving in an austere and lofty manner to introduce the sublime principles of Aristotle's "Organon" into it. I have got the traditional reward of one stopping to preach in front of a house afire. The more extreme Modernists—which is to say, the professional atheists—discontented because I haven't advocated hanging the Fundamentalists, denounce me as a Crypto-Calvinist, and hold me up to obloquy in their papers. The Fundamentalists, suspecting me of a partiality for Darwin, accuse me of trying to upset the Ten Commandments, and one of the most eminent of them lately hinted that I have personally had a bout with No. 7, and come to grief in the manner described by the late Dr. Sylvanus Stall, in his well-known work on pathology, "What Every Boy of Fourteen Should Know." This last accusation was novel, but, as they run in such affairs, very mild. The usual charge against an opponent, in the America of to-day, is that he is a Bolshevist, and in receipt of traitor's gold. It has been leveled at me so often that probably a majority of the persons who have heard of me at all believe it, and there are even dismal days when I half believe it myself, though I have been denouncing Socialism publicly for twenty years, and am, in fact, an incurable Tory in politics. A short while ago a Boston critic, becoming aware of the latter fact by some miracle, at once proceeded to denounce me because my radicalism, as he thought he had discovered, was bogus.

During the decade 1910–1920 I was chiefly engaged in literary controversies, and so my politics were aside from the issue. But when the great wave of idealism engulfed the United States in 1917, I was at once bawled out as a German spy, and open demands were made that my purely æsthetic heresies be put down by the *Polizei*. One of my opponents, in those days, was an eminent college professor, now unhappily deceased. He not only attempted to dispose of my literary judgments by arguing that they were inspired by the Kaiser; he even made the same charge against the works of the writers I was currently whooping up. And so did many of his learned colleagues. It was not easy to meet this onslaught by logical devices; logic, in those days, was completely adjourned, along with the Bill of Rights. Moreover, there was a considerable plausibility in the general charge. So I attempted no defense; it is, indeed, against my nature to take the defensive. Instead, I launched into an elaborate effort to prove that all college professors, regardless of their politics, were hollow and preposterous asses, and to this business I brought up all the ancient and horrifying devices of the art of rhetoric.

The issue of the controversy was characteristic: thus all combats in the realm of so-called ideas end. The moment the War to End War was over there came a revulsion against its blather, and so it was no longer damaging to me to be accused of taking the money of the Hohenzollern. Thus the professor I have mentioned suddenly found his principal ammunition gone, and in an effort to unearth more he began reading the books I had been advocating. To his surprise he found that many of them were works of high merit, whereupon he began whooping for them himself, and even going beyond my loudest hurrahs. In the end he was actually searching them for evidences of Teutonic influence, and hailing it with enthusiasm when found! His poor fellow-professors, meanwhile, were the goats. I ceased to revile them, once the war was over, and devoted myself mainly to political and moral concerns, but various other controversialists took up the jehad where I left off, and in a short time it was raging from coast to coast. It got far beyond anything I had myself dreamed of. Indignant publicists, quite unknown to me, began grouping all professors with chiropractors, Congressmen and spiritualists. In dozens of colleges large and small, North, East, South and West, the students began holding meetings and flinging insults at their tutors. Scores of college papers, for flouting them in contumacious terms, had to be suppressed. In several great institutions of learning the thing actually reached the form of physical assault. When the smoke cleared away the professor, once so highly respected by every one, found himself a sort of questionable character, and he remains so to this day. In many cases, I believe, he actually is, but surely not in all. The point is that the virtuous have suffered with the guilty. Many an honest and God-fearing professor, laboriously striving to ram his dismal nonsense into the progeny of Babbitts, is bombarded with ribald spit-balls as a result of a controversy which began quite outside his ken and speedily got far beyond the issue between the original combatants.

Such are the ways of war in the psychic field. Why they should be so I don't know, but so they are. No controversy to my knowledge has ever ended on the ground where it began. Even the historic one between Huxley and Wilberforce, two of the most eminent men of their time in England, ranged all over the landscape before the contestants had enough. It began with Huxley trying to prove that Darwin's "Origin of Species" was a sound book; it ended with Bishop Wilberforce trying to prove that Huxley's grandfather was a gorilla. What was its issue? Did Huxley convert Wilberforce? Did Wilberforce make any dent in the armor of Huxley? I apologize for wasting your time with silly rhetorical questions. Did Luther convert Leo X? Did Grant convert Lee?

THE EMPEROR OF WOWSERS

ANTHONY COMSTOCK: ROUNDSMAN OF THE LORD, by
Heywood Broun and Margaret Leech. New York: *Albert
& Charles Boni*. [Books, March 6, 1927.]

In an appendix to this amusing and instructive
work, Mr. Broun states the case against comstockery in
a neat, realistic and unanswerable manner, but the book
itself is by no means a philippic against old Anthony. On
the contrary, it deals with him in a very humane and
even ingratiating way. And why not? He was, in point
of fact, a man of manifold virtues, and even his faults
showed a rugged, Berserker quality that was sneakingly
charming. It is quite impossible, at this distance, to doubt
his *bona fides,* and almost as difficult, despite his notorious extravagances, to question his essential sanity. Like
all the rest of us in our several ways, he was simply a
damned fool. Starting out in life with an idea lying well
within the bounds of what most men would call the
rational, he gradually pumped it up until it bulged over
all four borders. But he never departed from it altogether; he never let go his hold upon logic; he never
abandoned reason for mere intuition. Once his premises
were granted, the only way to escape his conclusions was
to forsake Aristotle for Epicurus. Such logical impec-
cability, as all connoisseurs must know, is very common
among theologians; they hold, indeed, almost a monopoly of it. The rest of us, finding that our ratiocination is
leading us into uncomfortable waters, give it the slip
and return to dry land. But not the theologians. They
have horribly literal minds; they are less men than intellectual machines. I defy any one to find a logical flaw

in their proofs of the existence of Hell. They demonstrate it magnificently and irrefutably. Do multitudes of wise men nevertheless deny it? Then that is only because very few wise men have any honest belief in the reality of the thing that the theologians and other logicians call truth.

Mr. Broun, in his appendix, tries to find holes in Anthony's logic, but it turns out to be far from easy: what he arrives at, in the end, is mainly only proof that a logician is an immensely unpleasant fellow. Turn, for example, to a typical and very familiar comstockian syllogism. First premiss: the effect of sexual images, upon the young, is to induce auto-erotism. Second premiss: the effects of auto-erotism are idiocy, epilepsy and locomotor ataxia. *Ergo,* now is the time for all good men to put down every book or picture likely to evoke sexual images. What is wrong with all this? Simply that Mr. Broun and you and I belong to a later generation than Anthony's, and are thus skeptical of his premisses. But let us not forget that they were true for him. His first came out of the hard, incontrovertible experience of a Puritan farm-boy, in executive session behind the barn. His second was supported, when he was getting his education, by the almost unanimous medical opinion of Christendom. And so his conclusion was perfect. We have made no progress in logic since his time; we have simply made progress in skepticism. All his grand truths are now dubious, and most of them are laughed at even by sucklings.

I think that he himself had a great deal to do with upsetting them. The service that he performed, in his grandiose way, was no more than a magnification of the service that is performed every day by multitudes of humble Y. M. C. A. secretaries, evangelical clergymen, and other such lowly fauna. It is their function in the world to ruin their ideas by believing in them and living them. Striving sincerely to be patterns to the young, they suffer the ironical fate of becoming horrible examples. I remember very well, how, as a boy of ten, I

was articled to the Y. M. C. A.: the aim was to improve
my taste for respectability, and so curb my apparently
natural flair for the art and mystery of the highwayman.
But a few months of contact with the official representatives of that great organization filled me with a vast
loathing, not only for the men themselves, but also for
all the ideas they stood for. Thus, at the age of eleven,
I abandoned Christian Endeavor forevermore, and have
been an antinomian ever since, contumacious to holy
men and resigned to Hell. Old Anthony, I believe, accomplished much the same thing that the Y. M. C. A.
achieved with me, but on an immeasurably larger scale.
He did more than any other man to ruin Puritanism
in the United States. When he began his long and brilliant career of unwitting sabotage, the essential principles
of comstockery were believed in by practically every
reputable American. Half a century later, when he went
upon the shelf, comstockery enjoyed a degree of public
esteem, at least in the big cities, half way between that
enjoyed by phrenology and that enjoyed by homosexu-
ality. It was, at best, laughable. It was, at worst, revolting.

So much did one consecrated man achieve in the short
span of his life. I believe that it was no mean accomplishment Anthony managed it, not because there was
any unusual ability in him, but simply because he had
a congenital talent for giving shows. The fellow, in his
way, was a sort of Barnum. A band naturally followed
him, playing in time to his yells. He could not undertake
even so banal a business as raiding a dealer in aborti-
facient pills without giving it the melodramatic air of a
battle with a brontosaurus. So a crowd always followed
him, and when he made a colossal ass of himself, which
was very frequently, the fact was bruited about. Years of
such gargantuan endeavor made him one of the national
clowns—and his cause one of the national jokes. In
precisely the same way, I believe, such gaudy zanies as
the Rev. Dr. Billy Sunday and the Rev. John Roach
Straton are ruining the evangelical demonology in the

Bible Belt. They make so much uproar that no one can
fail to notice them. The young peasants, observing them,
are gradually enlightened by them—unintentionally, but
none the less surely. The men themselves are obviously
charlatans; *ergo,* their ideas must be fraudulent too.
What has been the net effect of the Scopes trial, with its
solemn martyrdom of William Jennings Bryan? Its chief
effect seems to be that societies of young atheists are
now flourishing in all the Southern colleges. Has the
study of Darwin been put down? Far from it. Darwin
is now being read below the Potomac, and by the flower
of Christian youth, as assiduously as "Only a Boy" used
to be read in New York in the great days of Anthony's
historic offensive against it.

Comstockery, of course, still lives, but it must be manifest that its glories have greatly faded. There is, anon,
a series of raids and uproars, but they soon pass, and
the work of the Devil goes on. It would be hard to imagine Anthony taking orders from district attorneys, or
going into amicable conference with his enemies (and
God's), or consenting to the appointment of joint committees (mainly made up of obvious anti-Puritans) to
discover and protect the least dirty among the dirty plays
of Broadway; he would have raided them all, singlehanded and alone. His heirs and assigns are far milder
men, and hence, I sometimes fear, more dangerous.
Their sweet reasonableness is disarming; it tends to conceal the fact that they are nevertheless blue-noses at
heart, and quite as eager to harry and harass the rest of
us as Anthony was. Those opponents who now parley
with them had better remember the warning against
making truces with Adam-Zad. They may end by re-
storing to comstockery some of its old respectability, and
so throw us back to where we were during the Grant
administration. I sound the warning and pass on. It
will take, at best, a long time, and I'll be beyond all
hope or caring before it is accomplished. For Anthony's
ghost still stalks the scenes of his old endeavors, to plague
and palsy his successors. His name has given a term of

opprobrium to the common tongue. Dead, and—as Mr. Broun and Miss Leech so beautifully suggest, an angel with harp, wings and muttonchops—he is yet as alive as Pecksniff, Chadband or Elmer Gantry.

Well, here is his story, done fully, competently, and with excellent manners. There is much in it that you will not find in the earlier biography by Charles Gallaudet Trumbull, for Trumbull wrote for the Sunday-schools, and so had to do a lot of pious dodging and snuffling. The additional facts that Mr. Broun and Miss Leech set forth are often very amusing, but I must add at once that they are seldom discreditable. Old Anthony was preposterous, but not dishonest. He believed in his idiotic postulates as devotedly as a Tennessee Baptist believes that a horse-hair put into a bottle of water will turn into a snake. His life, as he saw it, was one of sacrifice for righteousness. Born with a natural gift for the wholesale drygoods trade, he might have wrung a fortune from its practice, and so won an heroic equestrian statue in the Cathedral of St. John the Divine. Perhaps there were blue days when regret crept over him, shaking his Christian resolution. His muttonchop whiskers, the stigma and trademark of the merchant princes of his era, had a pathetic, Freudian smack. But I don't think he wobbled often. The Lord was always back of him, guiding and stimulating his fighting arm. So he was content to live in a drab suburb on the revenues of a second-rate lawyer, with his elderly, terrified wife and his half-witted foster-daughter. There was never any hint, in that humble home, of the gaudy connubial debaucheries that the modern sex hygienists describe so eloquently. Anthony had to go outside for his fun. Comstockery was his corner saloon.

I confess to a great liking for the old imbecile. He is one of my favorite characters in American history, along with Frances E. Willard, Daniel Drew and Brigham Young. He added a great deal to the joys of life in the Federal Republic. More than any other man, he liberated American letters from the blight of Puritanism.

HYMN TO THE TRUTH

On December 28, 1917, in the midst of war's
alarums, I printed in the New York *Evening Mail,* a
journal now happily extinct, an article purporting to
give the history of the bathtub. This article, I may say
at once, was a tissue of somewhat heavy absurdities, all
of them deliberate and most of them obvious. I alleged
that the bathtub was unknown in the world until the
'40's of the last century, and that it was then invented in
Cincinnati by a contemporary of *Stammvater* Long-
worth. I described how the inventor, in the absence of
running water in the town, employed Aframericans to
haul it in buckets from the adjacent Ohio river. I told
how a bathtub was put into the White House in the
'50's, and how the intrepid Millard Fillmore, of Cayuga,
N. Y., took the first presidential bath. I ended by saying
that the medical faculty of the Republic opposed the new
invention as dangerous to health, and that laws against
it were passed by the legislators of Virginia, Pennsylvania and Massachusetts.

This article, plainly enough, was of spoofing all compact. I composed it, in fact, to sublimate and so make
bearable the intolerable libido of the war for democracy,
and I confess that I regarded it, when it came out in
the *Mail,* with a certain professional satisfaction. It was
promptly reprinted by various other great organs of the
enlightenment, sometimes with credit, and after a while
a stream of letters began to reach me from persons who
had read it. Then, of a sudden, all my satisfaction turned
to consternation. For it quickly appeared that at least
nine-tenths of these readers took my idle jocosities with
complete seriousness! Some of them, of antiquarian

tastes, asked for further light upon this or that phase of
the subject. Others offered corrections in detail. Yet
others offered me corroboration! But the worst was to
come. Soon I began to discover my preposterous "facts"
in the writings of other men, some of them immensely
earnest. The chiropractors and other such quacks col-
lared them for use as evidence of the stupidity of medical men. They were cited by medical men as proof of
the progress of public hygiene. They got into learned
journals and the transactions of learned societies. They
were alluded to on the floor of Congress. The editorial
writers of the land, borrowing them in toto and without
mentioning my begetting of them, began to labor them
in their dull, indignant way. They crossed the dreadful
wastes of the North Atlantic, and were discussed horribly by English uplifters and German professors. Finally, they got into the standard works of reference, and
began to be taught to the young.

For a while I was alarmed; then I was amused; then
I began to be alarmed again. In the early part of 1926,
having undergone a spiritual rebirth and put off sin, I
resolved to confess, and so put an end to the imposture.
This I did formally on May 23. I admitted categorically
that I had invented the whole tale, and that there was
not a word of truth in it. I pointed out its obvious and
multitudinous absurdities. I called upon the pedagogues
of the land to cease teaching such appalling nonsense to
the young, and upon the historians to take it out of their
books. This confession and appeal were printed simul-
taneously in thirty great American newspapers, with a
combined circulation, according to their sworn claims,
of more than 250,000,000. One of them, and perhaps the
greatest of them all, was the eminent Boston *Herald,*
organ of the New England illuminati. The *Herald,* on
that bright May Sunday, printed my article on a leading
page of its so-called Editorial Section, under a black
and beetling four-column head, and with a two-column
cartoon labeled satirically "The American Public Will
Swallow Anything." And then, three weeks later, on

June 13, in the same Editorial Section, but promoted to page one, the same *Herald* reprinted my ten-year-old fake—soberly and as a piece of news!

Do not misunderstand me: I am not seeking to cast a stone at the *Herald,* or at its talented and patriotic editors. It is, as every one knows, one of the glories of American journalism, and is awarded Pulitzer prizes almost as often as the Pulitzer papers themselves. It labors unceasingly for public morality, the Andy Mellon idealism, and the flag. If it were suppressed by the Watch and Ward Society to-morrow New England would revert instantly to savagery, wolves and catamounts would roam in Boylston Street, and the Harvard Law School would be engulfed by Bolshevism. Little does the public reck what great sums such journals expend to establish and disseminate the truth. It may cost $10,000 and a reporter's leg to get a full and accurate list of the guests at a Roxbury wake, with their injuries. My point is that, despite all this extravagant frenzy for the truth, there is something in the human mind that turns instinctively to fiction, and that even the most gifted journalists succumb to it. A German philosopher, Dr. Hans Vaihinger, has put the thing into a formal theory, and you will find it expounded at length in his book, "The Philosophy of As If." It is a sheer impossibility, says Dr. Vaihinger, for human beings to think exclusively in terms of the truth. For one thing, the stock of indubitable truths is too scanty. For another thing, there is the instinctive aversion to them that I have mentioned. All of our thinking, according to Vaihinger, is in terms of assumptions, many of them plainly not true. Into our most solemn and serious reflections fictions enter—and three times out of four they quickly crowd out all the facts.

That this truth about the so-called truth is true needs no argument. Every man, thinking of his wife, has to assume that she is beautiful and amiable, else despair will seize him and he will be unable to think at all. Every 100% American, contemplating Dr. Coolidge, is psychically bound to admire him: the alternative is anarchy. Every Christian, viewing the clergy, is forced into a bold theorizing to save himself from Darwinism and Hell. And all of us, taking stock of ourselves, must resort to hypothesis to escape the river. What ails the bald truth is that it is mainly uncomfortable, and never caressing. What the actual history of the bathtub may be I don't know: digging it out would be an endless job, and the result, after all the labor, would probably be only a string of banalities. The fiction I concocted back in 1917 was at least better than that. It lacked sense, but it was certainly not without a certain charm. There were heroes in it, and villains. It revealed a conflict, with virtue winning. So it was embraced by mankind, precisely as the story of George Washington and the cherry-tree was embraced, and it will live, I daresay, until it is displaced by something worse—and hence better.

In other words, it was poetry, which is to say, a mellifluous and caressing statement of the certainly not true. The two elements, of untruth and of beauty, are both important, and perhaps equally. It is not sufficient that the thing said in poetry be untrue: it must also be said with a certain grace—it must soothe the ear while it debauches the mind. And it is not sufficient that it be voluptuous: it must also offer a rock and a refuge from the harsh facts of everyday. Poets, of course, protest against this doctrine. They argue that they actually deal in the truth, and that their brand of truth is of a peculiarly profound and esoteric quality—in other words, that their compositions add to the sum of human wisdom. It is sufficient answer to them to say that the chiropractors make precisely the same claim, and with exactly the same plausibility. Both actually deal in fictions. Those fictions are not truths; they are not even truths in decay. They are simply better-than-truths. They make life more comfortable and happy. They turn and dull the sharp edge of reality.

It is commonly held that the vast majority of men are anæsthetic to the poetry, as they are alleged to be anæsthetic to other forms of beauty, but this is itself a fiction,

devised by poets to dignify their trade, and make it seem
high-toned and mysterious. The fact is that the love of
poetry is one of the most primitive of human traits, and
that it appears in children almost as soon as they learn
to speak and steal. I do not refer here to the love of
verbal jingles, but to the love of poetry properly-so-called
—that is, to the love of the agreeably not-so. A little girl
who nurses a rag-doll is a poet, and so is a boy who plays
at soldiers with a box of clothes-pins. Their ma is another poet when she brags about them to the neighbors,
and their pa when he praises the cooking of their ma.
The more simple-minded the individual, indeed, the
greater his need of poetry, and hence the more steady his
demand for it. No poet approved by the *intelligentsia*
ever had so many customers as Edgar A. Guest. Are
Guest's dithyrambs laughed at by the *intelligentsia?*
Then it is not because the things they say are not so,
but because the fiction in them is of a kind not satisfying to sniffish and snooty men. It is fiction suitable to
persons of a less critical habit. It preaches the joys open
to the humble. It glorifies their dire necessities. It cries
down their lacks. It promises them happiness, and if not
happiness, then at least contentment. No wonder it is
popular! No wonder it is intoned every time Kiwanians
get together, and the reassuring slapping of backs begins.
It is itself a sort of backslapping. And so is all other
poetry. The strophes of Robert Browning elude the
Kiwanian, but they are full of soothing for the young
college professor, for they tell him that it is a marvelous
and exhilarating thing to be as intellectual as he is. This,
of course, is not true—which is the chief reason why it
is pleasant. No normal human being wants to hear the
truth. It is the passion of a small and aberrant minority
of men, most of them pathological. They are hated for
telling it while they live, and when they die they are
swiftly forgotten. What remains to the world, in the
field of wisdom, is a series of long-tested and solidly
agreeable lies. It is out of such lies that most of the so-
called knowledge of humanity flows. What begins as

poetry ends as fact, and is embalmed in the history books. One recalls the gaudy days of 1914–1918.

But I am forgetting the coda to my story. On July 25, six weeks after the *Herald's* astounding *faux pas* and nine weeks after my exposure of the original fraud, I printed another article on the subject, disclosing the complete facts once more, and cackling over the joke at the *Herald's* expense. This second article got a great deal of attention: it was reprinted from end to end of the Republic, and discussed in such remote and barbarous places as Liverpool, Melbourne and Cape Town. And then, early in 1927, the distinguished *Scribner's Magazine* printed a learned article on the history of bathing, and in it all my stale nonsense was once more set forth as fact!

CHIROPRACTIC

This preposterous quackery is now all the rage in the back reaches of the Republic, and even begins to conquer the less civilized of the big cities. As the old-time family doctor dies out in the country towns, with no trained successor willing to take over his dismal business, he is followed by some hearty blacksmith or ice-wagon driver, turned into a chiropractor in six months, often by correspondence. In Los Angeles the damned there are more chiropractors than actual physicians, and they are far more generally esteemed. Proceeding from the Ambassador Hotel to the heart of the town, along Wilshire boulevard, one passes scores of their gaudy signs; there are even many chiropractic "hospitals." The morons who pour in from the prairies and deserts, most of them ailing, patronize these "hospitals" copiously, and give to the chiropractic pathology the same high respect that they accord to the theology of Aimée McPherson and the art of Cecil De Mille. That pathology is grounded upon the doctrine that all human ills are caused by the pressure of misplaced vertebræ upon the nerves which come out of the spinal cord—in other words, that every disease is the result of a pinch. This, plainly enough, is buncombe. The chiropractic therapeutics rest upon the doctrine that the way to get rid of such pinches is to climb upon a table and submit to an heroic pummeling by a retired piano mover. This, obviously, is buncombe doubly damned.

Both doctrines were launched upon the world by an old quack named Andrew T. Still, the father of osteopathy. For years his followers merchanted them, and made a lot of money at the trade. But as they grew opulent they grew ambitious, *i.e.*, they began to study anatomy and physiology. The result was a gradual abandonment of Papa Still's ideas. The high-toned osteopath of to-day is a sort of eclectic. He tries anything that promises to work, from tonsillectomy to the vibrations of the late Dr. Abrams. With four years' training behind him, he probably knows more anatomy than the average graduate of the Johns Hopkins Medical School, or, at all events, more osteology. Thus enlightened, he seldom has much to say about pinched nerves in the back. But as he abandoned the Still revelation it was seized by the chiropractors, led by another quack, one Palmer. This Palmer grabbed the pinched nerve nonsense and began teaching it to ambitious farm-hands and out-at-elbow Baptist preachers in a few easy lessons. To-day the backwoods swarm with chiropractors, and in most States they have been able to exert enough pressure on the rural politicians to get themselves licensed. Any lout with strong hands and arms is perfectly equipped to become a chiropractor. No education beyond the elements is necessary. The whole art and mystery may be imparted in a few months, and the graduate is then free to practise upon God's images. The takings are often high, and so the profession has attracted thousands of recruits—retired baseball players, plumbers, truck-drivers, longshoremen, bogus dentists, dubious preachers, village school superintendents. Now and then a quack doctor of some other school—say homeopathy—plunges into it. Hundreds of promising students come from the intellectual ranks of hospital orderlies.

In certain States efforts have been made, sometimes by the medical fraternity, to make the practice of chiropractic unlawful. I am glad to be able to report that practically all of them have failed. Why should it be prohibited? I believe that every free-born man has a clear right, when he is ill, to seek any sort of treatment that he yearns for. If his mental processes are of such a character that the theory of chiropractic seems plausible to him, then he should be permitted to try chiropractic And if it be granted that he has a right to do so, then it follows clearly that any stevedore privy to the technique of chiropractic has a right to treat him. To preach any contrary doctrine is to advocate despotism and slavery. The arguments for such despotism are all full of holes, and especially those that come from medical men who have been bitten by the public hygiene madness, *i.e.,* by the messianic delusion. Such fanatics infest every health department in the land. They assume glibly that the whole aim of civilization is to cut down the death-rate, and to attain that end they are willing to make a sacrifice of everything else imaginable, including their own sense of humor. There is, as a matter of fact, not the slightest reason to believe that cutting down the death-rate, in itself, is of much benefit to the human race. A people with an annual rate of 40 a thousand might still produce many Huxleys and Darwins, and one with a rate of but 8 or 9 might produce nothing but Coolidges and Billy Sundays. The former probability, in truth, is greater than the latter, for a low rate does not necessarily mean that more superior individuals are surviving; it may mean only that more of the inferior are surviving, and that the next generation will be burdened by their get.

Such quackeries as Christian Science, osteopathy and

chiropractic work against the false humanitarianism of the hygienists and to excellent effect. They suck in the botched, and help them on to bliss eternal. When these botched fall into the hands of competent medical men they are very likely to be patched up and turned loose upon the world, to beget their kind. But massaged along the backbone to cure their lues, they quickly pass into the last stages, and so their pathogenic heritage perishes with them. What is too often forgotten is that nature obviously intends the botched to die, and that every interference with that benign process is full of dangers. Moreover, it is, like birth control, profoundly immoral. The chiropractors are innocent in both departments. That their labors tend to propagate epidemics and so menace the lives of all of us, as is alleged by their medical opponents —this I doubt. The fact is that most infectious diseases of any seriousness throw out such alarming symptoms and so quickly that no sane chiropractor is likely to monkey with them. Seeing his patient breaking out in pustules, or choking, or falling into a stupor, he takes to the woods at once, and leaves the business to the nearest medical man. His trade is mainly with ambulent patients; they must come to his studio for treatment. Most of them have lingering diseases; they tour all the neighborhood doctors before they reach him. His treatment, being entirely nonsensical, is in accord with the divine plan. It is seldom, perhaps, that he actually kills a patient, but at all events he keeps many a worthy soul from getting well.

Thus the multiplication of chiropractors in the Republic gives me a great deal of pleasure. It is agreeable to see so many morons getting slaughtered, and it is equally agreeable to see so many other morons getting rich. The art and mystery of scientific medicine, for a decade or more past, has been closed to all save the sons of wealthy men. It takes a small fortune to go through a Class A medical college, and by the time the graduate is able to make a living for himself he is entering upon middle age, and is commonly so disillusioned that he is unfit for practice. Worse, his fees for looking at tongues and feeling pulses tend to be cruelly high. His predecessors charged fifty cents and threw in the pills; his own charges approach those of divorce lawyers, consulting engineers and the higher hetæræ. Even general practice, in our great Babylons, has become a sort of specialty, with corresponding emolument. But the chiropractor, having no such investment in his training, can afford to work for more humane wages, and so he is getting more and more of the trade. Six weeks after he leaves his job at the filling-station or abandons the steering-wheel of his motor-truck he knows all the anatomy and physiology that he will ever learn in this world. Six weeks more, and he is an adept at all the half-Nelsons and left hooks that constitute the essence of chiropractic therapy. Soon afterward, having taken post-graduate courses in advertising, salesmanship and mental mastery, he is ready for practice. A sufficiency of patients, it appears, is always ready, too. I hear of no complaint from chiropractors of bad business. New ones are being turned out at a dizzy rate, but they all seem to find the pickings easy. Some time ago I heard of a chiropractor who, having once been a cornet-player, had abandoned chiropractic in despair, and gone back to cornet-playing. But investigation showed that he was really not a chiropractor at all, but an osteopath.

The osteopaths, I fear, are finding this new competition serious and unpleasant. As I have said, it was their Hippocrates, the late Dr. Still, who invented all of the thrusts, lunges, yanks, hooks and bounces that the lowly chiropractors now employ with such vast effect, and for years the osteopaths had a monopoly of them. But when they began to grow scientific and ambitious their course of training was lengthened until it took in all sorts of tricks and dodges borrowed from the regular doctors, or resurrection men, including the plucking of tonsils, adenoids and appendices, the use of the stomach-pump, and even some of the legerdemain of psychiatry. They now harry their students furiously, and turn them out ready for anything from growing hair on a bald head to frying a patient with the *x*-rays. All this new striving, of course, quickly brought its inevitable penalties. The osteopathic graduate, having sweated so long, was no longer willing to take a case of sarcoma for $2, and in consequence he lost patients. Worse, very few aspirants could make the long grade. The essence of osteopathy itself could be grasped by any lively farm-hand or night watchman in a few weeks, but the borrowed magic baffled him. Confronted by the phenomenon of gastrulation, or by the curious behavior of heart muscle, or by any of the current theories of immunity, he commonly took refuge, like his brother of the orthodox faculty, in a gulp of laboratory alcohol, or fled the premises altogether. Thus he was lost to osteopathic science, and the chiropractors took him in; nay, they welcomed him. He was their meat. Borrowing that primitive part of osteopathy which was comprehensible to the meanest understanding, they threw the rest overboard, at the same time denouncing it as a sorcery invented by the Medical Trust. Thus they gathered in the garage mechanics, ash-men and decayed welter-weights, and the land began to fill with their graduates. Now there is a chiropractor at every cross-roads, and in such sinks of imbecility as Los Angeles they are as thick as bootleggers.

I repeat that it eases and soothes me to see them so prosperous, for they counteract the evil work of the so-called science of public hygiene, which now seeks to make morons immortal. If a man, being ill of a pus appendix, resorts to a shaved and fumigated longshoreman to have it disposed of, and submits willingly to a treatment that involves balancing him on McBurney's spot and playing on his vertebræ as on a concertina, then I am willing, for one, to believe that he is badly wanted in Heaven. And if that same man, having achieved lawfully a lovely babe, hires a blacksmith to cure its diphtheria by pulling its neck, then I do not resist the divine will that there shall be one less radio fan in 1967. In such matters, I am convinced, the laws of nature are far better guides than the fiats and machinations of the medical

busybodies who now try to run us. If the latter gentlemen had their way, death, save at the hands of hangmen,
Prohibition agents and other such legalized assassins,
would be abolished altogether, and so the present differ-
ential in favor of the enlightened would disappear. I
can't convince myself that that would work any good
to the world. On the contrary, it seems to me that the
current coddling of the half-witted should be stopped
before it goes too far—if, indeed, it has not gone too far
already. To that end nothing operates more cheaply and
effectively than the prosperity of quacks. Every time a
bottle of cancer specific goes through the mails *Homo
americanus* is improved to that extent. And every time
a chiropractor spits on his hands and proceeds to treat
a gastric ulcer by stretching the backbone the same high
end is achieved.

But chiropractic, of course, is not perfect. It has superb
potentialities, but only too often they are not converted
into concrete cadavers. The hygienists rescue many of its
foreordained customers, and, turning them over to agents
of the Medical Trust, maintained at the public expense,
get them cured. Moreover, chiropractic itself is not certainly fatal: even an Iowan with diabetes may survive
its embraces. Yet worse, I have a suspicion that it sometimes actually cures. For all I know (or any orthodox
pathologist seems to know) it *may* be true that certain
malaises are caused by the pressure of vagrom vertebræ
upon the spinal nerves. And it *may* be true that a hearty
ex-boilermaker, by a vigorous yanking and kneading,
may be able to relieve that pressure. What is needed is
a scientific inquiry into the matter, under rigid test conditions, by a committee of men learned in the architecture and plumbing of the body, and of a high and
incorruptible sagacity. Let a thousand patients be selected, let a gang of selected chiropractors examine their
backbones and determine what is the matter with them,
and then let these diagnoses be checked up by the exact
methods of scientific medicine. Then let the same chiropractors essay to cure the patients whose maladies have

been determined. My guess is that the chiropractors' errors in diagnosis will run to at least 95% and that their failures in treatment will push 99%. But I am willing to be convinced.

Where is such a committee to be found? I undertake to nominate it at ten minutes' notice. The land swarms with men competent in anatomy and pathology, and yet not engaged as doctors. There are hundreds of roomy and well-heated hospitals, with endless clinical material. I offer to supply the committee with cigars and music during the test. I offer, further, to supply both the committee and the chiropractors with sound pre-war wet goods. I offer, finally, to give a bawdy banquet to the whole Medical Trust at the conclusion of the proceedings.

THE EXECUTIVE SECRETARY

Some time ago, encountering an eminent bishop of my acquaintance, I found him suffering from a bad cold and what used to be called a fit of the vapors. The cause of his dual disorder soon became manifest. He was smarting under the slings and arrows of executive secretaries. By virtue of his lofty and transcendental office, he was naturally a man of wide influence in the land, and so they tried to enlist his interest in their multitudinous and often nefarious schemes. Every morning at 8 o'clock, just as he was rolling over for a last brief dream of Heaven, he was dragged to the telephone to hear their eloquent and lascivious night-letters, and there, on unlucky days, he stood for as much as half an hour, with his episcopal feet bare, and rage gradually mounting in his episcopal heart. Thus, on a cold morning, he had caught his cold, and thus he had acquired his bad humor.

This holy man, normally a most amiable fellow, told me that he believed the number of executive secretaries in the United States was increasing at the rate of at least a thousand a week. He said that he knew of 30,000 in the field of Christian and moral endeavor alone. There were, he told me, 8000 more engaged in running various pacifist societies, and more than 10,000 operating organizations for the detection and scotching of Bolsheviki. He estimated that the average number of dues-paying members behind each one did not run beyond half a dozen. Nine-tenths of them, he said, were supported by two or three well-heeled fanatics. These fanatics, mainly retired Babbitts and their wives, longed to make a noise in the world, and so escape oblivion. It was the essence of the executive secretary's art and mystery to show them how to do it. Chiefly it was done by discovering bugaboos and giving chase to them. But secondarily it was done by hauling poor ecclesiastics out of bed on frosty mornings, and making them listen to endless night-letters about the woes of the Armenians, the need of intensive missionary effort in Siam, the plot of Moscow to set up soviets in Lowell, Mass., the high ideals of the Woodrow Wilson Foundation, and the absolute necessity of deeper waterways from the Lakes to the Atlantic.

The executive secretary is relatively new in the world. Like his colleague in well-paid good works, the Y. M. C. A. secretary, he has come into being since the Civil War. Compared to him, his predecessor of ante-bellum days was an amateur and an idiot. That predecessor had no comfortable office in a gaudy skyscraper, he got no lavish salary, and he had no juicy expense-account. On the contrary, he paid his own way, and, especially when he worked for Abolition, which was usually, he sometimes had to take a beating into the bargain. The executive secretary of to-day, as Perlmutter would say, is something else again. He belongs to the order of live wires. He speaks the language of up-and-coming men, and is not sparing with it at the sessions of Rotary and Kiwanis. In origin, not uncommonly, a shady and unsuccessful newspaper reporter or a press-agent out of a job, he quickly becomes, by virtue of his craft, a Man of Vision. The cause that he represents for cash in hand is not merely virtuous; it is, nine times out of ten, divinely inspired. If it fails, then civilization will also fail, and the heroic doings at Chateau Thierry and Hog Island will have been in vain.

It is a good job that he has—far better than legging it on the street for some gorilla of a city editor—far, far better than traversing the sticks ahead of a No. 4 company. There is no need to get up at 7 A.M. and there is no need to fume and strain after getting up. Once three or four—or maybe even only one or two—easy marks with sound bank accounts have been snared, the new "national"—or perhaps it is "international"—association is on its legs, and all that remains is to have brilliant stationery printed, put in an amiable and sightly stenographer, and begin deluging bishops, editors and the gullible generally with literature. The excutive secretary, if he has any literary passion in him, may prepare this literature himself, but more often he employs experts to do it. Once a year he launches a drive. But it is only for publicity. The original suckers pay the freight. When they wear out the executive secretary starts a new "international" association.

Such sharks now swarm in every American city. The office-buildings are full of them. Their prosperity depends very largely upon the singular complaisance of the newspapers. The average American managing editor went through so dreadful a bath of propaganda during the late war, and was so thoroughly convinced that resisting it was a form of treason, that he is now almost unable to detect it from genuine news. Some time ago Mr. Stanley Walker, a New York journalist of sense and experience, examined a typical copy of one of the great New York dailies. He found that there were sixty-four items of local news in it—and that forty-two of them could be plainly traced to executive secretaries, and other such space-grabbers. The executive secretary, of course,

does not have at his editors crudely. He seldom accompanies his item of "news" with any intimation that he is paid a good salary for planting it, and he discourages all inquiries into the actual size, aims and personnel of his organization. Instead he commonly postures as the mere agent of men and women known to be earnest and altruistic philanthropists. These philanthropists are the suckers upon whom he feeds. They pay his salary, maintain his office, and keep up his respectability in newspaper offices. What do they get out of it themselves? In part, no doubt, an honest feeling that they are doing good: the executive secretary, in fact, has to convince them of it before he is in a position to tackle the newspapers at all. But in part, also, they enjoy the publicity— and maybe other usufructs too. In the United States, indeed, doing good has come to be, like patriotism, a favorite device of persons with something to sell. More than one great national organization for lifting up the fallen, especially in foreign lands, might be investigated to advantage. In such cases charity not infrequently gets its reward in the form of concessions.

Some time ago, sweating under this assault of executive secretaries, the editors of a great American newspaper hit upon a scheme of relief. It took the form of a questionnaire—something not seldom used, and to vast effect, by executive secretaries themselves. This questionnaire had a blank in which the executive secretary was asked to write his full name and address, and the amount of his annual salary. In other blanks there was room for putting down the total income and outgo of his association, with details of every item amounting to more than one per cent. of the whole, and for a full list of its contributors and employees, with the amount given by every one of the former contributing more than one per cent. and the salary received by every one of the latter getting more than one per cent. This simple questionnaire cut down the mail received from executive secretaries by at least one half. Many of them did not answer at all. Many others, answering, revealed the not surprising fact that their high-sounding national and international organizations were actually small clubs of a few men and women, and that they themselves consumed most of the revenues. It is a device that might be employed effectively by other American newspapers. When the executive secretaries return their answers by mail, which is usually the case, they are under pressure to answer truthfully, for answering otherwise is using the mails to obtain money by fraud, and many worthy men are jugged at Atlanta and Leavenworth for that offense.

I suggest this plan as a means of cutting down the present baleful activity of executive secretaries, but I am not so optimistic as to believe that it could conceivably dispose of them altogether. In the higher ranks of the profession are gentlemen so skillful that they no longer send out press-matter: they make actual news. To that aristocracy belong the adept executive secretaries who run such organizations as the Anti-Saloon League. These masters of the art do not beg for good-will in newspaper offices: they thrive upon ill-will quite as well as upon good-will. How are they to be got rid of? I am sure I don't know. In all probability the American people are doomed to suffer them forever, as they seem to be doomed to suffer Prohibition agents, revivalists, the radio and Congress.

HENRY LOUIS MENCKEN was born in Baltimore in 1880 and died there in 1956. Educated at Baltimore Polytechnic, he began his long career as a journalist, critic, and philologist on the Baltimore Morning Herald *in 1899. In 1906 he joined the staff of the Baltimore* Sun *and thus began an association with the distinguished* Sun *papers that lasted until a few years before his death. He was co-editor of* The Smart Set *with George Jean Nathan from 1908 to 1923, and with Nathan he founded in 1924* The American Mercury, *of which he was editor until 1933. He edited* A New Dictionary of Quotations. *Among his many other books are* The Philosophy of Friedrich Nietzsche *(1908),* A Book of Burlesque *(1916),* Damn *(1917),* A Book of Prefaces *(1918), the three-volume* The American Language *(1919, 1945, 1948), and* Minority Report: H. L. Mencken's Notebooks *(1956). In addition there are three autobiographical books,* Happy Days, Heathen Days, *and* Newspaper Days.

Also available in the Series:

The Amiable Baltimoreans, by Francis F. Beirne
The Oyster, by William K. Brooks
Run to the Lee, by Kenneth F. Brooks, Jr.
The Lord's Oysters, by Gilbert Byron
The Mistress of Riversdale, edited by Margaret Law Callcott
The Potomac, by Frederick Gutheim
Spring in Washington, by Louis J. Halle
Mencken: A Life, by Fred Hobson
Bay Country, by Tom Horton
The Bay, by Gilbert C. Klingel
Home on the Canal, by Elizabeth Kytle
The Dawn's Early Light, by Walter Lord
Happy Days: 1880-1892, by H. L. Mencken
Thirty-five Years of Newspaper Work, by H. L. Mencken,
    edited by Fred Hobson, Vincent Fitzpatrick, and
    Bradford Jacobs
The Tuesday Club, edited by Robert Micklus
Tobacco Coast, by Arthur Pierce Middleton
Watermen, by Randall S. Peffer
Young Frederick Douglass: The Maryland Years, by
    Dickson J. Preston
Maryland's Vanishing Lives, by John Sherwood
The Premier See, by Thomas W. Spalding
Miss Susie Slagle's by Augusta Tucker

Library of Congress Cataloging-in-Publication Data

Mencken, H. L. (Henry Louis), 1880–1956.

Prejudices : a selection / H. L. Mencken ; made by James T. Farrell
and with an introduction by him.

    p.   cm. — (Maryland paperback bookshelf)

Originally published : New York : Knopf, 1919.

ISBN 0-8018-5341-9 (pbk. : alk. paper)

    1. American essays—20th century.   I. Title. II. Series.

PS3525.E43P912   1996

814'.52—dc20   95-42524